Understanding Music

Antony Hopkins

Understanding Music

J. M. Dent & Sons Ltd

London, Toronto and Melbourne

First published 1979
© Text, Antony Hopkins, 1979
All rights reserved. No part of this publication
may be reproduced, stored in a retrieval system,
or transmitted, in any form or by any means,
electronic, mechanical, photocopying, recording or
otherwise, without the prior permission of
J. M. Dent & Sons Ltd.

Phototypeset in V.I.P. Times by
Western Printing Services Ltd, Bristol
Printed in Great Britain by
Billings Ltd, London, Guildford & Worcester for
J. M. Dent & Sons Ltd
Aldine House, Welbeck Street, London

British Library Cataloguing in Publication Data

Hopkins, Antony
  Understanding music.
  1. Music – Analysis, appreciation
  I. Title
  780′.15   MT6

  ISBN 0-460-04376-5

Contents

Author's Note

In a book of this kind, directed towards the general music-lover rather than the qualified musician, it is hard to judge how much one should assume is already known. It is insulting to tell an experienced and dedicated amateur how many quavers there are in a minim, or even whether an oboe has a single or double reed. On the other hand, I do not want to discourage the inexperienced. I have therefore compiled an Appendix and a Glossary which contain the rudiments of musical terminology, notation – all those aspects of music which make up a basic literacy in the art. If you feel the same alarm on seeing a number of music examples that I sense on opening a book containing mathematical or algebraic formulae, the Appendix should quell your fears. It will not teach you to read music fluently, but it should enable you to read it adequately for full comprehension of the main text. As a further aid, technical words which are defined in the Appendix are marked throughout with an asterisk. The order of entries in the Appendix corresponds with the order in which the terms referred to appear in the text, page references being included to help the casual reader.

My thanks are due to David Epps who kindly read the manuscript and led me into the paths of righteousness and truth where necessary.

August 1978

Dedicated to all those who have said to me,
'I enjoyed your talk very much,
but why didn't you tell us . . .?'

1   Beginnings

IN THE BEGINNING . . . Curiously enough, sound is taken for granted in the magnificent opening chapter of *Genesis* which describes with such poetic simplicity the creation of the world. The recurring phrase 'And God said' fails to take into account one of the most intriguing phenomena associated with sound; even God would speak in vain if there were no one to hear Him. Surprisingly, sound does not exist unless it has a receiver; to produce sound, three things are needed—an initiator (be it the human voice, bird-song, a thunder-clap, a violin, an engine), molecules of air that are set in vibration by the initiator and which act as transmitters or carriers and, lastly, a receiver, that miraculous organ the ear, whether human or animal. Without the ear there is no sound. We cannot know for certain which form of life emerging from the primeval sludge first had a voice of sorts; but whatever grunt, squeak, cry or rattle it emitted, its vocal effort would have been impotent unless a fellow-creature had been equipped with ears. Indeed, if it did not have ears itself it would not know it had even created what we call a sound. Before life there was silence; all the chaotic turbulence of the earth's birth-pangs, the gaseous vortices, the clash of rocks in rivers of lava, the volcanic upheavals as mountain-peaks emerged, split and reformed, all the vast convulsions that ultimately assumed the global shape now so familiar took place as silently as if we were to watch a film of an earthquake with the sound switched off. Of course immense vibrations were set up in the air, but with no receiver to translate them into what we term sound, they were dissipated in space.

This concept is hard to believe at first, yet when I drive past that skeletal metallic forest of radio masts at Daventry I know that it is emitting beams in all directions; I cannot see them, feel them nor hear them. Yet I have only to flick a switch on my car-radio for those beams instantly to be translated into sound. The radio is an 'ear' equipped to convert wireless-waves into sound; *we* are equipped to convert sound-waves into music, speech, gun-shots or whatever their initiating source may dictate. The unfortunate who is totally deaf is like a defunct radio which is no longer capable of carrying out its

9

proper purpose. His ears, by failing to respond to the stimulus of the sound-waves, help to prove the contention that without the 'receiver', there is no sound. At the end of the first performance of his Ninth Symphony, Beethoven remained facing the orchestra, still continuing to beat time even though the music had finished. Kindly, the contralto soloist took his arm and turned him round so that he could *see* the applause which he was unable to hear. For him, applause had become a visual not an aural experience.

So refined is the ear as a receiving sensor, it is amazing that it does not fail more frequently than statistics of deafness would indicate. The softest audible sound produces an intensity equal to the light and heat given off by a fifty-watt light-bulb at a distance of 3,000 miles. This minute movement of air which we call a sound-wave is received by the ear-drum (which is roughly one square centimetre in size); as the atmospheric pressure in the outer ear changes, the drum responds with a reciprocal movement no larger than one four-millionth part of the diameter of a fine silk thread. But since the pressure is entering the ear in the form of a recurring wave, the drum must be sufficiently sensitive to accept 3,500 separate stimuli in a single second.[1] To put it another way, if an insect weighing one ten-thousandth part of the weight of a mosquito were to dance a tattoo of 3,500 steps upon your ear-drum in the course of a second, you would hear a sound.[2] This truly amazing organ can take in a range of sounds from the extreme depths of some twenty cycles per second to an approximate 25,000 at the very top, roughly ten octaves. With age, deterioration sets in, especially with the higher frequencies; but there is always an area of sound-waves which the human ear cannot cope with, as the 'silent' dog-whistle proves. Blow on such a whistle and you will hear nothing, since the vibrations it sets up are too rapid for the human ear to assimilate; the dog, which might be said to have 'short-wave' ears as opposed to our 'long-to-medium-wave' equipment, will be able to hear what we cannot.

While on the subject of the nature of sound, it is worth mentioning that sound-waves do not only travel by air. Used as we are to the concept that water or solids have a greater resistance than air, it comes as a surprise to learn that sound travels more than four times as fast through water, and roughly ten times as fast through (or 'along') a solid. In one second, sound-waves will travel a mere 340 metres through the air, 1,420 metres through water and, depending on its substance (metal, wood, glass, etc.) between 3,000 and 4,000 metres through a solid. When back in 1946 I wrote a substantial score for a radio version of *Moby Dick*, it was generally thought that whales were mute. On the principle of Art improving on Nature, I invented the sound that I felt whales *would* make if they could—four horns in unison making great whoops up to the top of their compass. Well, Art did

[1] 3,500 cycles per second being the period of optimum receptivity.
[2] For these and other scientific facts I am indebted to Alexander Wood's *The Physics of Music* (London, 1975).

10

improve on Nature, for we now know the sounds that whales make; coming from the world's largest mammal their assorted clicks, squeaks and hoots are a considerable disappointment. However, since they communicate through water, presumably a large volume of sound is not needed.

Before deserting the animal kingdom and coming to music, let us return briefly to the earliest period in which it is likely that living creatures actually made sounds. It is generally argued that of the three components of music, rhythm, melody and harmony, rhythm is the prime. One thinks of primitive drums, of the pulse or heartbeat, even the rhythm of the seasons. I would maintain that the first *consciously* created sounds would come, however tenuously, into the category of melody, since they would involve a change of pitch. The screech of the pterodactyl, the roar of tyrannosaurus rex were undoubtedly sounds of varying pitch and intensity; furthermore the function of such sounds was expressive—of rage, of pain, of fear, of the desire to intimidate, or of companionship in the sense of the tribal community that still causes starlings to chatter or crickets to sustain their monotonous fiddling.

RHYTHM

Having established a few facts about the basic relationships between sound and hearing, let us now move on to those fundamental components I have just mentioned; rhythm, melody and harmony. I suppose that another argument for placing rhythm first is that it is the only one of the three able to lead a satisfactory existence on its own. It *is* possible for HARMONY to exist as a single static entity; the very first chord of the Emperor Concerto or the Eroica Symphony is undeniably a harmony but not a very satisfying musical experience. As soon as one plays a second chord, whether by repetition or alteration, one has established a rhythm of sorts, however ill-defined. MELODY is paralysed without rhythm, literally transfixed upon its first note; it cannot move without rhythm since rhythm is the motor force that enables music to move forward. RHYTHM however can manage on its own for a surprisingly long period, whether it is actually marking time with the measured precision of the pendulum in a grandfather clock, the hectic ticking of a watch, or the more sophisticated drumming of soldiers marching and countermarching on a parade-ground. If we make an analogy with speech, melody conveys the expressive content of the thought ('I love you', 'Isn't it peaceful', 'The sky is threatening' . . .), harmony underlines the expressive content as adjectives and adverbs do ('I love you tenderly/passionately/hopelessly', 'It's peaceful but cold and bleak', 'The sky is black and threatening' . . .). Rhythm simply represents the sequence of syllables with which the thought is expressed; accents correspond to verbal stress or hard consonants; the organization of rhythm into units may be rigidly metrical, as it is in strict verse forms, or free as in blank verse or prose.

11

Since this is not a book written by a musicologist for musicologists but one written by a lover of music for music-lovers, I do not intend to become ensnared in a semantic tangle about the differences between rhythm and time. I have already used terms such as 'motor force' and 'pulse' to describe rhythmic function; one of the first ways of detecting if a person is still alive is to take his pulse, and by this analogy, rhythm is indeed the pulse of music, the means by which its vitality is assured. But rhythm is not necessarily equal in its disposition of accents, though an overriding grouping similar to the scansion of poetry can usually be sensed.

In ordinary speech we would never dream of enunciating words in exactly regular syllables; we use, just as musicians do, a flexibility of accent and even tempo. If we want to soothe someone, we instinctively slow our speech down, if we are excited words tumble out rapidly at a higher pitch. Any group of words has a natural rhythm that can be translated into musical notation. Say those last seven words aloud and you are virtually certain to produce a musical rhythm on these lines:

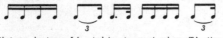

that can be trans-LA - ted in - to mu-si-cal no - TA - tion.

By starting on the word 'that' we will inevitably tend to give it a first-beat stress; unimportant syllables are shovelled onto the shortest 'notes', the more musical vowels, 'trans-*LA*-ted, no-*TA*-tion' are slightly extended. Add one more word to the beginning of the phrase and the accentuation will be changed:

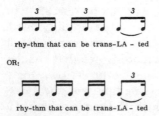

rhy-thm that can be trans-LA - ted

OR:

rhy-thm that can be trans-LA - ted

Either way the stress has been taken away from the word 'that' which has now become subsidiary to the much more important 'Rhythm'.

If we try to imagine the way in which the concept of rhythm evolved in the consciousness of man we would presumably be compelled to begin with what is known as Simple Duple Time, 1–2 1–2 1–2, as in a relaxed version of the Left, Right, Left, Right that is drilled into soldiers. If we had been born with three legs we would presumably think in Triple Time, but since we only have two it would be sheer perversity to proceed on a Left, Left, Right, Left, Left, Right, basis. Duple Time it is then, and the heart oblingly conforms to the same pattern. A great number of primitive work activities also reveal a bias towards Duple Time, the In-Out of the canoeist's paddle, the rise and fall of the axe, the rocking of a heavy stone back and forth to shift it. It is no coincidence that the best-known work-song in the Western world, 'The Volga Boat-song', is in Duple Time. The repetition of its simply shaped phrases is another universal characteristic of work-songs, be they African, Asiatic, European or American. Listen to a young child humming to itself as it plays with a toy. The chances are that the 'tune' it unconsciously composes will rock to and fro across a more or less fixed interval in a constant repetition of the same rhythmic pattern.

If the child monotonously repeats 'See-saw See-saw', the listener will hear it as Simple Duple Time. (Incidentally, the melodic interval will almost certainly be a falling 3rd*; try singing it with the *higher* note on '-saw' and see how unnatural it feels.) However, the moment the child embellishes the pattern by introducing a more complex word-structure, 'Margery Daw', he has introduced Compound Time, in which the main pulse is sub-divided into three, as the word 'Margery' dictates. Here then, in the simplest terms, we have two basic rhythmic families, the prime beat being divided into two (or multiples thereof) or into three, also with its multiples.

Now no academic mind would be content to leave things in this simple state; more complex categories must be properly labelled, rhythmic caprice must be tidied up into neat arithmetical tables. Time-signatures and bar-lines were invented in the early seventeenth century as a way of packaging music that previously had wandered free of such constraints. As we shall increasingly find in the course of this voyage of discovery, a great deal of musical terminology is based on illogicality; such is the case with time-signatures, which are expressed as fractions of a time unit which itself is already a fraction. The longest written note we now use is a *breve*, written either as ⊨ or ◫. Bearing in mind my earlier remarks it comes as no surprise that the name of this longest note is derived from the Latin, 'brevis', or 'short'. In terms of a normal pulse-rate a breve would last 8 'beats'. Half a breve is understandably called a *semibreve*, 4 beats, and it is from the semibreve, itself already a fraction, that further fractions are derived to make up time-signatures in Simple Duple Time. The upper figure (numerator) tells us how many of a particular unit of time we will find in a bar, the lower figure (denominator) specifies the time-unit; thus 2/4 indicates 2 crotchet 'beats' to the bar, a crotchet being 1/4 of a semibreve; 2/2 indicates 2 minim beats, a minim being 1/2 of a semibreve. 2/8 (very rare) would mean 2 quavers to the bar, a quaver being 1/8 of a semibreve.

American nomenclature is at least more sensible since a minim is called a half-note, a crotchet a quarter-note, a quaver an eighth and so on. Once we move on to notes of shorter duration both systems begin to have a manic look and I am equally as disenchanted with a semiquaver dividing into two demi-semiquavers or four hemi-demi-semiquavers as I am with 16th notes,

32nds and 64ths. It seems to me a great deal simpler to learn what the notation actually looks like rather than to be bogged down in a morass of names. (A fuller explanation will be found in the Appendix.)

Having discovered how rhythms may be written down, we have to realize that we are still only at a very rudimentary stage, since in a large-scale piece of music many rhythms may occur simultaneously. While we are still dealing with fundamentals, though, it would be opportune to return to my small child singing 'See-saw Margery Daw'. You will remember that it was the word Margery that elicited the Compound rhythm, and it was almost certainly *words* that decided the course of rhythmic evolution.

I have already mentioned work-songs. Such songs often have a leader, whether they are sea-shanties or African tribal chants. The leader will exhort, goad or cajole the workers with his chant, they will respond with a simple repetitive refrain, their energies being more occupied with their heavy task than in remembering a number of verses or a complex tune. Their refrain will often be wordless, a simple expression of physical effort such as 'A-eee-yah!' For them both melody and rhythm remain essentially primitive. The leader has a different responsibility; his chant will grow more elaborate as he wills them to greater effort, yet the rhythm of the work must not be disturbed. In packing more words into a given space of time he produces more complex, often irregular rhythms; these in turn have an exciting (or do I mean *in*-citing) effect. It is not too far-fetched to suggest that listening to tribal chanting of this type we are witnessing the first step in the evolution of the concerto, the soloist dominating a group.

Still with the thought of words and their effect on rhythm in mind, let us turn to the inevitable companion to work-songs, worship-songs. As soon as man turned his thoughts to a god or gods, ritual of a sort invariably emerged. Ritual means stylization of behaviour, of movement, of speech. Stylized speech moves very soon to chanting; religion and music have moved hand in hand since the dawn of civilization. It is not within the scope of this book to speculate about the music of earlier civilizations than our own, but it is more or less certain that the rather surprising dominance of Compound Time in mediaeval music came about through the Margery Daw principle. A great part of the more enduring performed music in the thirteenth and fourteenth centuries would have been Church music. The language (a language of ritual) was Latin, and the normal metre of the Latin verse was a triple metre known as *tempus perfectum*, consisting of trochees (long-short) and iambs (short-long). In musical notation today this rhythm would be written o ♩ or ♩ o, both of which are in 3/2. However, such a concept as 3/2 was not even thought of, the natural metre of the verse making so rigid a constraint unnecessary. What *was* taken into consideration was a form of musical symbolism by which the religious concept of the Trinity came to be associated with a Triple metre; the time-signature for such a rhythm was shown not as 3/2 but as a perfect circle, itself a symbol of perfection.

Co-existing with this rhythmic song, in which Compound Time was so important a factor, was an infinitely more flexible style of singing known as plainsong or Gregorian chant. Here the rhythm was continually bent to accommodate the words. An expressive melodic line was formed from a relatively limited number of notes so that voices would not be unduly strained. Frequent pauses served a two-fold function: spiritually to allow time to dwell upon the religious significance of the words and materially to enable the excessive echo to disperse. Such is the freedom of plainsong when it is properly performed that it virtually defies any attempt to parcel it up into bar-lengths or time-signatures. Even Holst, who was not one to shrink from complex or unorthodox time-signatures, gave up when, at the start of the 'Hymn of Jesus', he decided to use an extensive plainsong passage. Since it was to be played by the brass of the orchestra, not sung, one would expect him to have measured it into bars with some comprehensible time-signatures to simplify the problems of co-ordination. With the quite proper excuse of authenticity he left the music unfettered, assuming that any conductor competent enough to tackle the work could be trusted to find a solution to the problem.

In its early stages European vocal music was mostly sung in unison or in two parallel lines that kept a 4th or a 5th apart. This latter style of singing, known as *organum*, was almost certainly dictated by pure practicality; on the principle of 'You take the high notes and I'll take the low notes', the monastic choir would divide into higher and lower voices while pursuing a more or less identical melodic line. Since the words were still exactly synchronized there was no need for bar-lines nor for any great exactitude in rhythmic notation. However, once the vocal parts began to assume a genuine independence, experience showed that some sort of communal landmark would be useful. Bar-lines first appeared in instrumental music of the latter part of the sixteenth century and in due course were adopted in all forms of western music for some 300 years or more. Some recent composers have begun to dispense with them again.

For a long period, during mediaeval and renaissance times, instrumental music had tended to play a subsidiary role to vocal music, either literally duplicating the voice-parts, or being used to play dances, where the need for a consistent and positive rhythmic pulse had a restricting effect on the development of rhythm as an independent force. With the gradual emergence of solo performers of brilliance, especially keyboard performers, music took off into flights of fantasy undreamed of in earlier years; that the name given to such improvised extravagances was often Fantasia[3] is proof of the sense of new-found freedom such music brought to the composer. While

---

[3] Composers in Elizabethan England used the word 'Fancy'.

dance-forms still predominated right up to J. S. Bach's day, Toccatas, Fantasias and Preludes allowed an escape from metric constraint, enabling instrumental music to develop a true independence, no longer subservient to words nor to the steps of dancers, whether rustic or aristocratic.

The history of music tends to show a gradual but continuous increase in resources coupled with an ever-growing complexity of texture. But after the sheer exuberance of the early keyboard fantasias of Frescobaldi (1583–1643), Buxtehude (1637–1707) or Bach (1685–1750) which un-doubtedly began as spontaneous improvisations that were written down only as recollections of the original performance, a reaction set in, almost as though composers felt it improper thus to preserve the ephemera of impro-visation without subjecting them to some discipline.[4] A Fantasia by Bach is not the same either to the eye or to the ear as a Fantasia by Mozart. Both will be powerfully expressive and encourage the performer to introduce varia-tions of tempo that would not be acceptable in a more formally contrived piece; but Mozart, even in a Fantasia, will show a certain constraint, a tendency to prefer understatement; the music will be more symmetrical in construction, its emotional content achieved by the subtle use of dissonances placed with the utmost delicacy against surprisingly simple accompanying figures. A comparison of two very well-known pieces, the organ Toccata in D minor of Bach (BWV 565) and the piano Fantasia in D minor (K.397) by Mozart will illustrate the point to perfection.

Ex. 1

---

[4] It is interesting that for a time the outstanding moment for improvization in a concerto, the cadenza, was *not* written out.

Bach: Toccata and Fugue in D minor

Ex. 2

Mozart: Fantasia in D minor (K. 397)

It is hard to demonstrate precisely how the rhythmic element in music has evolved over the centuries. We have seen how its first liberation came through its association with words, followed by what might be called a true Independence Movement once instrumental music began to develop on its own. But however forceful an element it may be in the percussive sense, rhythm tends in the nature of things to be a background, an incidental factor. It may be profitable, then, to pursue some typical accompanying figures in order to see how the simple options were used initially. If we analyse the components of an instrumental piece by Mozart or Haydn, whether Sonata, Concerto or Symphony, the melodic line, however elaborately decorated, will essentially be vocal in conception. Mozart slow movements in particular tend to be sublimated soprano arias, but the natural stress and accentuation of even quicker themes will correspond to the syllables of language. The *instrumental* concept is to be found in the display passages, the swift running scales, brilliant arpeggios,* chains of 3rds or 6ths and so on which would be beyond the capabilities of even the most gifted singer. Meanwhile, wherever it is needed, the pulse beats, usually in the form of repeated chords:

repeated chords over a sustained bass:

or the rocking to and fro of the component parts of a chord which is known as an Alberti bass:

19

Each one of these simple devices is a way of overcoming an inherent defect in the piano (or harpsichord) which is that if you play a chord  it will inevitably begin to die away. No amount of pressure will save it, and so the methods shown above were devised to give artificial respiration to sounds that were in danger of extinction. However, since these patterns also frequently appear in orchestral and chamber music where the problem of sustaining sound is easily solved, it seems that their function is also very much involved with rhythmic vitality, though some performances would seem to take little account of this.

It is a cliché that has survived amazingly successfully for some three centuries or more; we find it in innumerable instances in Beethoven, we find throbbing repeated chords in the most passionate outbursts of Schumann, Tchaikovsky or Wagner, we find 'stretched' versions of an Alberti bass in Chopin,

we find Stravinsky pounding the earth with stamping chords in *The Rite of Spring*, or pop singers thumping out endless repetitions of the three-chord trick on their electric guitars. But while the cliché has essentially continued, its rhythm has grown more complex. Initially designed as a way of giving life to Harmony, it has increasingly demanded to be given a life of its own. The first step in this direction was to break the regularity of the pattern by introducing either silences or syncopations. ♫ ♪ ♫ ♪ is more interesting than ♫♫ ♫♫; stressing the second note of each group adds pathos: ♫ ♫ But syncopation can also introduce a sense of unease, of emotional intensity. Music example 3 is a passage from the central section of the Nocturne in B, Op. 62 No. 1 as Chopin did NOT write it.

Ex. 3

If we compare this to the real thing (Ex. 4), we see how wonderfully Chopin increases the emotional content of what could easily be a fairly innocent-sounding theme. The core of the emotion is to be found in the rhythmic disturbances in the left hand which prevent the melody from merely sounding bland.

Ex. 4

Although Berlioz and Liszt both use the throbbing repeated chord technique at moments of high passion, they were perhaps the most inventive of nineteenth-century composers when it came to the use of irregular rhythms. In the *Symphonie Fantastique* Berlioz uses repeated chords in a quite astonishing way when the theme associated with the hero's beloved, the *idée fixe*, first appears (see Ex. 5).

Ex. 5

If this truly occurred in the original version (1830) it must count as one of the most revolutionary concepts in music; it is possible, though, that it represents one of many revisions Berlioz made to the work over some twenty years. Even so it would be remarkable. If its accompanying figures could be said to anticipate the sort of dynamic rhythms we find in Stravinsky, example 6 may legitimately be said to anticipate Bartók. It comes from a Liszt piano-piece called *Pensée des Morts*, No. 4 of the *Harmonies poétiques et religieuses*.

Ex. 6

The alternations of 7/4 and 5/4 would be unusual enough in the mid-nineteenth century, but the irregularity of the rhythms set up between the two hands is something that one would scarcely expect to find before 1920.

Tracing the lines of descent from the repeated chords in the Berlioz example we arrive at the famous passage in *The Rite of Spring* where Stravinsky takes the single chord—

and repeats it 32 times.

Although written out as a straightforward 2/4, the sound is of irregular patterns, as shown numerically below, the accents being reinforced by angry barks from eight horns. Rhythm here has taken over to the exclusion of all else, the harmony being a scrunch rather than a chord, deliberately planned to be ambiguous.

From the Liszt example I would travel to Bartók, perhaps the tune from the finale of the *Music for Strings, Percussion and Celeste* in which, though the content is very different, asymmetry is as notable a factor.

The left-hand chords here may seem a long way away from my hypothetical Mozart-Haydn examples given on p. 19 yet their function is identical. The fact is that rhythm has become a far more obtrusive element in the twentieth century than it ever was in earlier times. The 5/4 movement in Tchaikovsky's Sixth Symphony (even though anticipated by Chopin in his first piano sonata) caused something of a furore. Nowadays some music seems to be more concerned with higher mathematics than anything so elementary as mere rhythm. Cross-fertilization between Eastern and Western cultures has produced some fascinating results; even computers have been brought into play. On one hand we have a figure such as Messiaen (born 1908) experimenting with the logical reduction or extension of note values—

♩　♩♪ ♩. ♩ ♪♩ ♪. ♪♪ (each unit reduced by a ♪)

on the other we have aleatoric* composers playing with the random effects that arrive when a section of violins is asked to play in their own time but as fast as practical some such pattern as

It could be argued that this is a denial of rhythm, yet, looked at without prejudice, one can see it as a logical, if distant, descendant of the Alberti bass. If rhythm has taken a far more important place in the musical landscape than it held in earlier times, melody has gone into a relative decline. The reasons for that will emerge during the exploration of the melodic aspects of music which we should now undertake.

MELODY

Melody by definition must involve changes of pitch; if I simply chant words on the same note I may be singing but I am not singing a melody. An alternation of only two notes is enough to start a reasonably successful tune:

If I now repeat this pattern a 3rd higher and vary it slightly, I can exploit one of the subtler aspects of music.

The first phrase of my tune started with a rise of a tone; but if I also begin my second phrase with the same interval I will have to use a C sharp instead of the C natural, since the interval B-C is a semitone.[5] C sharp though is not part of the scale or key of G major in which I began, and the intrusion of this foreign element has immediate repercussions in that the phrase is no longer (by implication) in a *major* key. The final twist to the second phrase confirms this: the new tonality is B minor.* The similarity of shape has produced a satisfying symmetry, but the different *feeling* introduced by the brief suggestion of a minor key provides an emotional contrast. However it is unlikely in a tune as basically unadventurous as this that I will want to stray far from the 'home' base of G major; in my next phrase, then, I will cancel the alien note C sharp, and introduce a different sort of variant by widening the initial interval from a tone to a third.

I am now ready to return home by recalling the initial phrase, perhaps modifying it slightly as a result of the experience acquired on the journey:

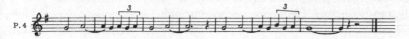

[5] As an experiment, try playing it with C naturals and 'taste' the difference.

—and that last little twist was pinched from the ending of the second phrase.

Now while I make no great claims for this singularly trite melody, it serves to show several fundamental attributes we are likely to find in a very large proportion of Western music. First there is the matter of form. Form in the larger sense is applied to the structure of the large-scale movements we find in Symphonies, Concertos, Sonatas and the like; but even a simple tune like this has a clearly defined form. Phrase 1 is copied or balanced by Phrase 2; the central section, Phrase 3 introduces an element of contrast; Phrase 4 recalls Phrase 1. In classic text-book terms it is summed up as

$$A^1 - A^2 - B - A^1$$

Each phrase is conceived as a four-bar unit so as to give a comforting feeling of predictability. As written out there is actually one bar missing, at the point marked with a cross at the end of Phrase 1. If you play Phrases 1 and 2 consecutively, exactly as marked, you will feel disturbingly hurried where they join; the reason for this is that the bars fall naturally into groups of four.

One therefore needs a note to be tied over into that blank space. It is *not* needed at the end of Phrase 2 since the third phrase begins with three preliminary notes which fill the space. You will see, though, that it has duly been provided at the end of Phrases 3 and 4.

If we look closer we will see a few small but significant attempts to avoid total banality. The triplet rhythm $\overset{3}{\sqcap}$ (the bracket and figure 3 indicate that 3 crotchets are to be played in the time normally taken by 2) gives a lazy swing to the rhythm, while the tie across the bar-line prevents every first beat from striking us with an audible thump. The three notes that lead into Phrase 3 might easily have been echoed at the point marked with two crosses (*BAG* instead of *BAB*), but to have done so would have been too predictable even by these lowly standards of craftsmanship. Phrase 4 could also have been identical to Phrase 1, whereas the fusion of even a tiny fragment from Phrase 2 makes a notable difference.

Now my reason for constructing such a banality as this (I refuse to dignify it with the term 'composing') was that I wanted to put off the unavoidable issue of the relationship that exists between Melody and Harmony. It is virtually impossible to discuss one without bringing in the other. As we have seen, Rhythm can have an existence of its own, so much so that if you tap out the rhythm of a well-known tune on a table it can usually be recognized fairly easily, whereas if you play a melodic line with its rhythm completely altered,

26

it is much harder to identify. Melodics however are full of harmonic implications; by starting with just two notes I thought I could avoid these, but by the second phrase we found ourselves faced with an implied modulation to B minor and the need to cancel it. Given a tune of even this basic simplicity, a musician would instantly see the implications of the final note of Phrase 3; he would put the notes D sharp and B underneath it, a chord that in isolation could be named as B major but which, in this context, would be a way of opening the door marked E minor. This would mean that the final reprise of Phrase 1 could be presented in quite a different light, the first note of the melody becoming the third degree of the scale of E minor instead of the first degree of the scale of G. You see now why I wanted to postpone the discussion of harmony in relation to melody, even though the two are inseparable. I shall try to clarify things in the section on Harmony.

Meanwhile let us return to basics, even as far as my pterodactyl's cry and the roar of tyrannosaurus rex. When I mentioned them earlier I drew attention to the fact that animal noises are expressive. We are all familiar with the plaintive bleat of the lost lamb, the indignant squawk of a cat accidentally trodden on, the forlorn howl of the dog deserted or the rich vocabulary of bird-song. At moments of high emotion or when we wish to project sound over a distance, the human voice 'aspires to the condition' of song. If you say the words 'I hate you!' with vehemence and passion you will raise the pitch of your voice substantially on the word 'hate' and drop it again on 'you'. One could represent the shape of the phrase diagrammatically in some such way as this:

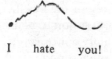

I   hate   you!

It is a very small step from this to musical notation and the world of Grand Opera.

Children unwittingly go very near to song when they call to each other from quite small distances, while anyone who cries 'Coo-ee' to attract attention literally sings. These sounds then, involving variation of pitch and the prolongation of vowels, are the source from which song, and therefore melody, springs—there being surely no question that vocal music, however primitive, came before instrumental.

The deliberate and conscious combination of sounds we call harmony must have been quite a late development in the evolution of music, yet

27

harmonic implications are to be found in every sequence of tones. The earliest tune which I have been able to trace (Ex. 7) is an Entrance Hymn for the Chinese Emperor, estimated to date from *c*. 1000 B.C.

Ex. 7

(Davison & Apel: *Historical Anthology of Music*, O.U.P.)

Based on a pentatonic (five-note) scale, it would be quite incorrect to harmonize it with conventional Western harmonic progressions. Nevertheless, intervals such as rising 5ths and 6ths, the recurring pattern

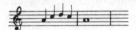

and even the last five notes all contain clear suggestions of chords that are very familiar to us, and the form of the tune falls naturally into four-bar phrases so long as I add a final tied semibreve. The overall shape could be described as $A^1 - B - B - A^2$, or more pedantically as $A - B - B - C$; I would have thought, though, that the final phrase could legitimately be regarded as a variant of the first.

I realize that to jump from China in 1000 B.C. to Italy in the twelfth century leaves something of a gulf, but this book has no pretension to being historically comprehensive. Plainsong, though, was certainly conceived as pure melody, never being intended to have any harmonic support; yet listening to it in a resonant cathedral, one soon hears suggestions of harmony, ghost-like chords which hang in the air in surprisingly modern clusters of sound. Here is a setting of Benedicamus Domino, one of the great liturgical melodies.

Be - ne - dicamus Do -   -   -   -   -   -   mi - no _____

(Notice the huge extension of the first syllable of Domino, a musical equivalent to the illumination of a capital letter.)

If one presents this as a series of harmonies it is something of a revelation, though not one readily acceptable to the musical historian; yet this in essence is what, after a couple of repetitions, the ear will hear.

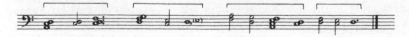

I have put this forward only in order to demonstrate that try as one can, it is impossible to separate a melodic line from harmonic implications unless one proceeds purely stepwise, as in a scale. Move by any other interval, a 3rd, a 4th, a 5th, a 6th or a 7th, and one inevitably suggests a harmony of sorts. Now while scales may seem dull when we practise them, they are indeed the foundation of a large proportion of melodies, whether as hallowed by tradition as 'The First Nowell':

or as truly inspired as the second subject of Beethoven's Violin Concerto.

Here the scale is broken up by the occasional intrusion of intervals such as a falling 4th or 5th but composers frequently disguise the scale-like origin of a theme in this way. One of the most magnificently disguised scales occurs at the start of Bach's St. Matthew Passion whose immense opening phrase rises with an almost relentless consistency, like a huge curtain opening to reveal the drama that is to be unfolded before us.

Throughout this ascent and the two subsequent bars the bass remains rooted to the spot; but once released, it too rises in an unashamed scale of one-and-a-half octaves, to memorable effect.

It would be absurd to attempt to compile a sort of catalogue of themes consisting of scale elements; the sole point I want to make is that the step-by-step progress of such themes is a way of avoiding positive harmonic implications. The fact is that the vast bulk of thematic material used by composers in what (for want of a better term) is known as classical music is specifically designed to *create* harmonic implications. In due course we shall be taking a much closer look at the immeasurably important aspect of music known as Key or Tonality. For the moment let us just accept that the establishment of the key of a work is of prime importance to the composer, certainly between about 1650 and 1830. The best way to establish such a key—is it to be A major, C minor, B flat major etc?—is to spell out the notes of the so-called Tonic chord, the chord built upon the first Tone of the scale. Here are some examples:

Bach: Prelude in D Bk.II

implied chord:

Mozart: Pf.Sonata in C minor K 457

implied chord:

Beethoven: Eroica Symphony

implied chord:

Brahms: Violin Concerto

implied chord:

Stravinsky: Dumbarton Oaks Concerto (Schott)

implied chord:

Britten: Serenade (Boosey & Hawkes)

implied chord:

A fairly wide range of music that could be multiplied literally a thousand-fold.

The components of melody, then, can be described either as intervals, with their inevitable harmonic implications, or scale-fragments that tend to stimulate if they rise and bring a sense of release or even repose when they fall. Wide intervals are more rhetorical than narrow ones; chromatic intervals, introducing notes foreign to the key, are the most expressive. Nationalist elements can be traced to the different accentuation of languages, remembering, as we discovered earlier, that rhythm tends to be closely associated with words, even in instrumentally conceived music. A tune by Bartók, Janáček, Dvořák, Borodin or Falla will be easily recognized as having national characteristics both rhythmically and melodically. Different scale-formations give a curiously angular character to music that still carries traces left behind from the East, whether Turkish or Moorish. To Hungarian ears, English music presumably sounds as exotic as Kodály or Bartók may sound to us; but with a rapidly shrinking world such national differences are being eroded. Folk music as an influence on serious composers has virtually had its day, and a possible criticism of contemporary methods of composition is that they have led to the severing of the roots of native culture.

When the ordinary uninitiated listener of today complains in forlorn tones that composers no longer write memorable tunes, he is, though he may not realize it, acknowledging the power of the relationship between melody and harmony. Since there is no denying the fact that harmony has grown increasingly dissonant (for reasons we shall discover) there is also no denying that melody has grown harder to assimilate. The reason for this is logical enough; each of the examples quoted on p. 30 is based upon what is called the common chord. If one starts to use very *un*common chords they will inevitably have a distorting effect on any hypothetical melodic line that one superimposes above them. Operatic composers such as Rossini, Donizetti or Bellini thought primarily in melodic terms; harmonically and rhythmically the support given to the vocal line tended to be unadventurous. Such dissonance as there was consisted for the most part of clichés whose function was as easily comprehended by the audience as was the pianist's accompaniment to a silent film. Once composers felt the need to elaborate their harmonic resources, there arose an inevitable conflict between the *simple* harmonic implications of 'easy' melody and the *complex* harmonic actuality with which it had to compete. You cannot superimpose Bellini-type melodies on to an orchestral accompaniment as extreme as that of *Wozzeck*. One can see the process very clearly in the vocal music of Benjamin Britten; his earlier works,—*Les Illuminations*, the Serenade, the Sonnets of Michelangelo—show an unashamed though brilliantly inventive use of very orthodox harmonies. For instance the opening fanfare of *Les Illuminations* consists almost entirely of alternations between the common chords of B flat major and E major.

31

(Boosey & Hawkes)

Having once established a tonal idiom such as this, having as it were laid down the ground rules for this particular game, it was easy enough for him to write a vocal line that had an instant appeal, since it could conform to my suggested formula of intervals-with-clear-harmonic-implications plus scale-fragments. Once he was driven by the relentless march of musical evolution to forsake tonal harmony for something more abstruse, it was inevitable that his voice parts should become more tortuous. *Death in Venice* is less 'singable' than *Peter Grimes*, an objective statement that is not intended to be pejorative. If you ask why did his harmonic style have to change, you raise one of the most significant issues in music, one that I shall now attempt to tackle.

HARMONY

The last thing I would want to do is to make this next section look like a harmony text-book, filled as they so often are with dreary dirges to be sung by lethargic village choirs. In my first definition of harmony I stressed that its function is to underline emotion, and it is a source of sadness to me that this magical and mysterious element in music is habitually taught on a Ten Commandments basis of 'Thou shalt not' commit consecutive 5ths, doubled leading notes and the like. One can search the pages of most harmony text-books in vain for any mention of emotional effect, just as one can read a handbook on car maintenance without being given an inkling of the thrill of speed.

Harmony consists of the combination of two or more sounds of identifiable pitch. The whole concept of Western harmony is founded on an instinctive awareness of what might be termed the Tonal Spectrum. Just as 'white' light can be shown by analysis to consist of violet, indigo, blue, green, yellow, orange and red, so individual sounds are formed by a composite known as the harmonic series. The intervals between each of the components decrease by mathematical ratios as they rise. Taking the C below the bass stave as a fundamental or principal note, the series would read:

The notes marked with a cross, 7, 11, 13 and 14, are not in tune with the 'tempered' scale we have grown accustomed to, but these 'overtones' or 'upper partials' must obey the laws of mathematics rather than the requirements of tuning. Although the sound of the individual overtones seems so faint as to be inaudible to any but a highly trained ear, it is their presence that gives quality to sound. A scientist named Seashore once analysed the sound of the open G string on a violin (its lowest note); the result, published in his book *The Psychology of Music*, is amazing since the fundamental tone which one would expect to be the predominating one (in terms of energy emitted) turns out to generate only 0·1% of the energy. The 2nd partial produces 26%, the 3rd 45·2%, the 4th 8·8%, the 5th 8·5%, the 6th 4·5%, the 8th 4·8%, and all others with the exception of the 17th (1·1%) 0·2% or less. It appears, then, that the quality of the particular sound so analysed is due mostly to the 2nd, 3rd, 4th, 5th, 6th, 8th and 17th upper partials; it is these that give the note its lustre. If the dominance of these partials were to be altered, then the tone-quality or timbre would change.

Before I get lured away from music into acoustical science, let us return to the harmonic series shown above and think of its musical considerations. The first six notes of the sequence comprise the chord commonly known as C major.

The partials 5, 6 and 8 also produce a variant of the same chord:

as do 6, 8 and 10, 8, 10 and 12, and 10, 12 and 16. Three-note chords such as these are called triads, although strictly speaking the external boundaries of a triad should not exceed a 5th. Thus this chord is the triad of E major

in what is called its 'root' position; if I shift the root to the top of the chord it is known as an 'inverted' triad, the first inversion; correspondingly the other alternative spacing

is called the second inversion.

Such chords are the absolute fundamentals of Western harmony, and it is because between them they carry so much of the 'C-ness' that comprises the note C or the 'E-ness' that comprises the note E that our feeling of Tonality is so well founded. Notice though that of the sixteen notes specified in the series only six are not duplicated at some point (Nos. 7, 9, 11, 13, 14 and 15). These are elements which are more alien to the principal note than the others, introducing a touch of dissonance which might be compared to salt and seasoning. Even so, there are other notes that do not appear in the series at all, and their dissonance may be judged according to the degree that they clash with the 'majority' in the series. Assuming our fundamental note to be C, and the harmonic series to be represented by the massive cluster of notes at the beginning of this next example, the remaining notes will be seen to be 4 in number.

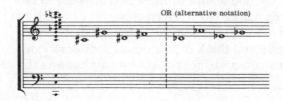

These are the notes which might be described as most hostile to the concept of C major since they contradict its most essential elements. E flat cancels the vital major 3rd and turns the triad of C major into C minor. C sharp cancels the very foundation of C major, while G sharp eliminates the next most important note in the scale, the 5th or dominant, G. At first glance the alternative notations (C sharp = D flat, F sharp = G flat, etc.) may seem to be no more than an academic diversion; in fact they lead to some fascinating paradoxes. Suppose we take this interval, known as an augmented 5th:

Logically it is regarded as a dissonance—which it is, the G sharp contradicting the harmonic series generated by the note C. But if we present it with a different notation, it ceases to be a dissonance, since it now comfortably fits into the harmonic series generated by the note A flat. If we put an A flat into the bass, the notes C–A flat will be part of the 'majority' in the A flat harmonic series.

Now though we can *see* the difference in notation we cannot *hear* a difference in sound with the system of tuning known as equal temperament. (see pp. 98–101) A string-player or a wind-player *can* convey the difference between G sharp and A flat but a pianist cannot. (Surprisingly, by true intonation G sharp is a fraction flatter than A flat.) In terms of keyboard harmony one needs a third note, a 'casting vote' to tilt the harmony in one direction or another. Let us explore some possibilities with this very interval. We have seen an element of ambiguity already; the addition of a third note can have a startling effect. If we put an E natural in the middle

we will hear it quite positively as what is called an 'augmented' triad, i.e. this chord

with its top note sharpened. Even if we write A flat at the top it's still an augmented triad since harmonically

is simply a redistribution of these notes:

Now before identifying any other possibilities we need to pursue one of music's enigmas as propounded by that great musical scholar, the late Donald Tovey. 'When is a key not a key?' he asked; and the answer, meaningless to the uninitiated, is 'When it's a dominant.' Does this riddle signify anything of importance or is it an exercise in academic wit? If we return to the harmonic series once more, you will see that I grouped together the first six notes into a chord which I said was 'commonly known' as C major. In fact, if I play this chord a number of times, it will develop a strong desire to drift to the chord of F.

It therefore has just as much right to be called the Dominant harmony of F as the Tonic chord of C. The reason for this phenomenon presumably lies with the 7th partial, the slightly out of tune B flat which makes its irritating presence increasingly felt, compelling this resolution.

The only way we can really establish a chord as C major is by positively exterminating this suggestion of an alien B flat; this means that you cannot really assert a tonality unless it is preceded by its dominant.

The B natural marked with a cross is strong enough to kill the ghostly suggestion of a B flat which otherwise taints the second of the two chords. If we select the 5th, 6th and 8th upper partials from a low C,

the 7th partial will exert a powerful if secret influence, causing the harmony to want to move towards F.

If we select the 6th, 8th and 10th upper partials,

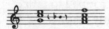

they too will be affected by the suggested 7th and will respond accordingly.

Here then is the substance of Tovey's riddle since each chord I have derived from the upper partials 2, 3, 4, 5, 6, 8, 10 has the appearance of C major and yet proves to have a distinct leaning towards F. In other words harmonies need to be considered in context before they can be correctly identified. Armed with this information let us return to the two-note interval

Remembering the principle of the 'casting vote', if we put an E flat in the middle

we produce a chord which traditionally would be called the first inversion of A flat major but which is more likely to be the dominant of D flat major—a foot in the door as one might call it.

Put an F in as casting vote and we find (in academic terminology) the second inversion of F minor

which can be more intelligently regarded as a chord demanding a release of tension by this progression.

The insertion of G flat clearly creates a different situation:

the G flat 'wants' to fall to F, the C 'wants' to rise to D flat; the chord is therefore the dominant seventh of D flat major (or minor!)

Now so far we have made three discoveries about harmony; *a* that the foundation of harmony is derived from the components of sound itself, *b* that while two notes may be said to be harmony they cannot be committed to a key or tonality without the casting vote of a third note, and *c* that certain notes and chords seem to be subject to a force comparable to the pull of gravity. I have just mentioned the chord which perhaps more than any other illustrates this last basic truth. The so-called dominant 7th

contains a number of inner tensions; the C (the *seventh* note up from the bass from which it derives its name) 'wants' to fall to B, the A 'wants' to fall to G, the F sharp has an almost irresistible urge to go to the G above. Of the three 'wants' this is the strongest, so powerful that it will drag the two lower notes in its wake.

37

As we have seen, dominant 7ths are the same in major or minor keys so that this resolution works equally well.

The point to grasp is that while consonances are content to rest where they are, not being subject to gravitation, dissonances always create a sense of 'wanting' to go on to another chord. Music moves in two ways then, by the motive power of rhythm and the tension created by dissonance. If I put down two notes next door to each other

in the words of the popular song, 'Something's gotta give'. If the upper note gives way by rising to E flat, I'll be 'in' C minor; if it goes to E natural, I'll be 'in' C major; if the lower note yields and falls to B, I will be either in G or further on the way to C; if it drops to a B flat, I shall have arrived fairly conclusively at B flat major.[6] The dissonance has generated an impulse to move.

It is the differing qualities of consonance and dissonance that are the basis of the subtler aspects of emotion in music. Obviously loud quick music is exciting, slow quiet music is soothing; but if that was all there was to it, what a paltry art it would be. A melodic line can be inherently expressive, as we have seen. Take a neutral tune, though, that has no clearly emotional character.

The phrase is so simple that we could compare it in language to a basic sentence such as 'The cat sat on the mat'. Put harmonies underneath it and I can conjure up two entirely different pictures; if I choose rich, widely-spaced chords—

col 8va

I now have a 'silky black cat sitting on a deep crimson carpet'. Change the harmonization—

[6] The 3rd-note rule would still apply to confirm these identifications of key, but they indicate the most likely interpretation.

and the *adjectives* change; a 'thin wet cat sits on a sack'. Truly, harmonies can transform the emotional content of a phrase. While the material function of harmony may be to confirm, deny or postpone arrival at a tonality or key, its spiritual function is intimately concerned with the creation of emotion, a fact sadly neglected by those who teach it by rule alone. Composers do not use harmony to pass examinations but to convey constantly varying degrees of tension; as the tension lessens or increases so does the emotion. As a supreme example of the subtlety with which it can be done take Ex. 8, a deceptively simple looking phrase of Mozart's from the Fantasia in D minor, K.397.

Ex. 8

The cliché accompaniment in the left hand leads us to believe that very little is happening here. Mozart's language is so subtle that he will frequently suggest dissonance rather than state it outright. For instance, in bar 1 there are three pressure points in the harmony of which the first is almost concealed, the second understated, and only the third actually allowed to sound positive. Play the bar this way, emphasizing the implied tensions, and you will hear how truly poignant the harmonies are.

As to the next bar, it has a violent dissonance on the third beat, D sharp against E natural. Treat bar 3 in the same way as bar 1 and you will arrive at a harmony such as this:

If you feel that this is cheating, I would reply that our ears have grown insensitive to dissonance, but that in Mozartian terms this phrase is heavy-laden with grief. The depth of feeling is none the less for being expressed with so little rhetoric.

In the course of a book such as this I cannot attempt to explore harmony comprehensively, though it will be cropping up all the time; obviously it is an area in which immense changes have been wrought, some of which I shall try to deal with when we come to the consideration of Idiom. One last aspect must be mentioned, however, Spacing—the way in which a chord is distributed across the keyboard or the orchestra. Even the simplest chord can be radically affected by the way it is spaced; here are several versions of G major, the first calculated to bring an English audience to its feet, the others more imaginative.

As with so many aspects of music, the more obvious spacings were used first, forcing later composers to deliberate about the precise disposition of every note. To quote this same G major chord, when Beethoven began his Fourth Piano Concerto with this unforgettable version—

he made it so much his own that thereafter nobody else could ever put down the chord in precisely that way. Similarly, no poet or dramatist could ever begin a soliloquy with the words 'To be . . .' or 'Tomorrow and tomorrow . . .' once Shakespeare had penned them.

2 The Key Question

The title of this chapter is more than just a pun, for the whole question of 'key' or tonality is vital to the understanding of music. Inevitably I have already referred to it a number of times, but while even the musical tyro is aware that classical works are often described as being 'in' A major, C minor or whatever, it takes a practical musician to develop a feeling for the true and significant functions of tonality. In our brief exploration of the harmonic series we have seen how the note C in isolation will generate a tonal 'spectrum' that carries strong implications of the chord known as C major; needless to say, A will generate the overtones that imply A major, E flat will produce an E flat major spectrum and so on. This much is easy enough to comprehend; the concept that we call C major is what one might term the family of sounds derived from the scale of C major, whether approached through the medium of melody (horizontally) or harmony (vertically). But since, as we have seen, no two notes in conjunction are sufficient to establish a positive tonality, there is room for a considerable amount of ambiguity in even quite simple music. A casual glance would lead one to identify this chord as essentially C major

but, as we have seen, the addition of a B flat above it will give it an overwhelming urge to drift towards F major

while putting an A beneath it will confirm it as quite content to be reconsidered as A minor.

Since these changes of identity are so easily achieved, they are regarded as shifts to closely 'related' keys, and it is key-relationships that are integral to

41

the construction of music, whether as smooth and satisfying transitions or abrupt and dramatic changes of course.

If for a moment we visualize a piano keyboard, the scale of C is all on the white notes. The scale of G is all white save one (F sharp), the scale of F is also all white save one (B flat). The shift from the concept of C major as a tonality to the concept of G major involves changing only one note; therefore the keys are regarded as closely related. The same applies to the C major–F major shift. If however we play the scale of D, we will have to use two black notes, thus cancelling out two essential features of C major; the relationship C–D is therefore more distant. (Notice that the terms 'close' and 'distant' here have nothing to do with proximity on the keyboard itself. The most distant key from C major in musical terms is C sharp major, which has not a single note in common, yet it is based on the note immediately adjacent to C.) As we increase the number of black notes so we obliterate more and more of the identity of C major; a key with four sharps (or four flats) contradicts the essential features of C major four times. Logically, though, it will be seen to be closely related to keys having three or five sharps (or flats) since here again the difference will only be one note. The whole scheme of key relationships is normally shown as a circle:

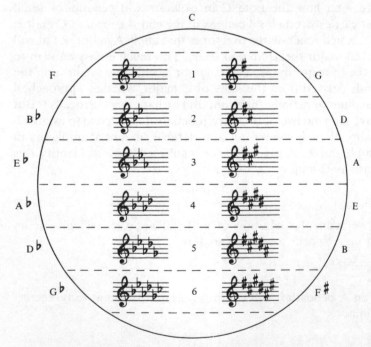

The figures down the centre show the number of 'accidentals' (sharps or flats) or, as I have put it, the degrees of difference from C major. The keys to the right of the circle are called 'sharp' keys and will be notated in sharps;

conversely the keys to the left are 'flat'. The actual scales of G flat and F sharp are identical on the piano since 6 out of a possible 7 notes are different from C major. D flat major is a marginal case since it *can* be written as C sharp major with a key-signature of 7 sharps (every note being different from C major). The area at the bottom of the circle where sharps and flats converge is susceptible to ambiguity in notation.

What one might term the 'family' principle that needs to be borne in mind here is that relationships are always close between keys that are next door to each other in the diagram. If a composer in the period between approximately 1650 and 1830 writes a piece in D major, we would expect him in the natural course of events to pay frequent visits to the immediate neighbours G and A. If, however, he crosses over to the other side of the globe by entering the territory of A flat, D flat, or G flat, then that must be regarded as a dramatic excursion into a virtually forbidden land.

Now so far I have dealt only with major keys. Minor keys raise a host of new issues. The key signature of C minor is three flats, the same as E flat major—indeed E flat is known as the relative major of C minor. If an eighteenth-century composer writes a piece in C *major*, he will spend most of the time in the upper segment of the circle,

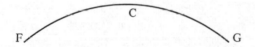

these keys being mutually easy of access. A piece in C *minor* will open up a much wider segment, not only making E flat easy to get at, but also (on the good neighbour principle) B flat and A flat.

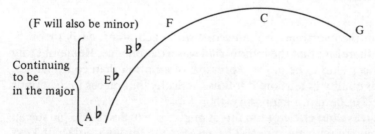

The continued presence of G within this drift to the left is explained by the fact (already shown on p. 37) that chords of the 'dominant' are the same whether the tonality is major or minor; G can therefore co-exist equally happily with C major or minor. The rule by which we find the key signature for a minor key is to look three places round the circle in an anti-clockwise direction, with the proviso that G flat and F sharp count as one. Thus the key signature of F minor is the same as A flat major; B flat minor–D flat major; A flat minor is a difficult one. Counting G flat and F sharp as a single step, we find that the progression A flat → D flat → G flat/F sharp leads us to B major. How can A flat minor have a *sharp* key signature? The answer is that it is more convenient to think of it as G sharp minor which involves fewer accidentals. One might ask then whether there is any justification for preserving A flat minor as other than a purely theoretical concept; the reason for its continuing existence is that if one is writing a piece that is basically in a flat key, such as F minor or D flat major, it would be bewildering to the eye suddenly to jump into sharps at the first brush with A flat minor, a key which could easily be 'visited' from such a starting point. For the same reason D flat minor is almost invariably written as C sharp minor, unless the surrounding context compels the retention of flats.

Theoretical considerations apart, the much more significant consequence of the larger segment of the tonal sphere opened up by writing in a minor key is that it not only gives wider scope for modulation but also has a less positive commitment to the Tonic or 'home'-note. This was one reason why composers of Bach's era and earlier disliked ending a piece with a minor chord, feeling it had a quality of insecurity. The other reason was based on sound acoustic theory; if one mingles the harmonic series that stems from the fundamental C with the series rooted on E flat it will produce a number of unacceptably conflicting clashes, as can be seen by putting these two clusters side by side.

Very few of the overtones are in accord with each other; early theoreticians argued therefore that the minor triad was a dissonance. Remembering that dissonances tend to be more expressive of emotion than consonances, owing to their quality of tension, it follows logically that pieces in the minor keys will tend to be more expressive than those in the major.

Before we leave our circle of tonality it might be worthwhile to pursue an intriguing analogy with the tides. The movement through adjacent keys (modulation) could be compared to the waves of the sea; but waves are borne on a tide. A piece in a major key will tend to drift to the right (clockwise) since the principal modulation will almost invariably be to the dominant—one degree 'sharper'; even the modulation D flat–A flat or A flat–E flat can be said to be 'sharper' since it means cancelling out one flat in the key. On the other hand, a piece in a minor key will have a strong tidal flow in the opposite (anti-clockwise) direction. Shown diagrammatically, the small 'waves' represent the standard modulations into closely related keys, a back-and-forth motion, while the large encircling arrows represent what I would term the 'current of modulation'.

Needless to say this is a generalization, not a universal plan; all the same it represents a trend that was followed fairly consistently until the start of the nineteenth century. If a piece is in G major, a modulation to areas such as E flat, A flat or D flat will be 'against the tide'; similarly, for a piece in G *minor* to go to E or B would be against the natural current. However, just as the tides cause an erosion of the land, so the increasing flexibility of modulation brought about by nineteenth-century composers eroded the demarcation lines between keys until, in the period from 1860 to 1900, tonality became

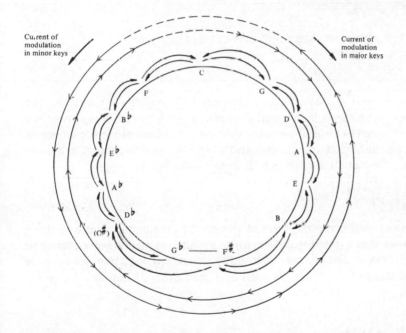

increasingly ill-defined, so that for considerable periods of time the music seems to hang in a limbo between tonalities. One of the principal factors in bringing this about was the increasing use of the chord known as the diminished 7th. Once referred to by Samuel Butler as the Clapham Junction of music, the diminished 7th is the primary tool in a 'do-it-yourself' modulation kit. It enables one, by shifting each of its notes in turn to modulate into almost any key, its singular advantage being that it itself is in *no* key, existing in a perpetual limbo. Simply pile up three minor 3rds and a diminished 7th appears:

drop the bottom note a semitone and you open the door to F major:

drop the next note a semitone and you open the door to A flat major:

drop the third note a semitone and you slide effortlessly to B major:

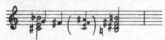

drop the top note a semitone and you are in D major:

Since each one of these transitions goes equally smoothly to the respective minor keys, we already have eight different keys that can be approached with ease through this one chord. Another option is to explode the harmony outwards by raising the upper note and dropping the lower; this, with one intervening chord will lead us into E (major or minor)

Small wonder that composers found the chord invaluable. It is one thing though to use it as a pivoting device, quite another to prolong a sequence of diminished 7ths so that all sense of tonality is lost. Passages like this became a standard climax for composers such as Tchaikovsky, Liszt and Wagner:

Ex. 9

Wagner: *Siegfried*, Act I, sc. iii.

Although essentially a chromatic scale, the consistent harmony (marked by crosses) is the diminished 7th throughout.

The twentieth century has seen a virtual collapse of tonality. The expressive resources of the language used by the late Romantic composers became exhausted; a number of new concepts were developed. One, which proved to be something of a *cul-de-sac*, was the so-called 'whole-tone scale'; its invention is normally ascribed to Debussy, quite incorrectly since it was used by Liszt and, to a lesser degree, by Wagner. It is true to say that Debussy exploited it more extensively than anyone else, but it proved to have built-in limitations for it exists in only two forms. Like any other scale it is basically a ladder, its rungs being spaced a tone apart.

Its alternative formation would start a semitone higher:

Wherever you begin the sequence you will always arrive at one of these two alternatives since, there being only twelve semitones available, all have now been disposed of. In comparison to the rich possibilities contained in the varied formations of previous scales, major, harmonic minor, melodic minor and chromatic, its potential is relatively restricted. Having no semitones, it lacks a 'sense of direction'. It did open a whole new world of evocative and sensuous harmony, but it was a world that took a comparatively short time to explore. Its appeal for Debussy lay partly in the fact that it dispenses with the concept of a Tonic or 'home'-note. Everything can be left vague and nebulous, hauntingly beautiful since it never puts its foot upon the solid foundation of tonality (see p. 142).

Meanwhile the restless search for new approaches to tonality went on with some urgency. Some composers, our own Vaughan Williams and Holst among them, looked back to much earlier scale-formations known as modes. We have found that if we start off on C on the piano and continue (either upwards or downwards) on the white notes we will produce the scale of C major. However if we do the same thing starting on D, we will discover a 'scale' that is neither D major nor D minor since the disposition of tones and semitones has now been altered.

If we do the same thing starting on E we will find yet another arrangement of tones and semitones; all scales arrived at in this way are known as modes and have been duly catalogued with charmingly antique names such as Dorian, Phrygian, Lydian, Mixolydian, etc. As is so often the case the nomenclature is unimportant; the different flavour given to music by the employment of modal melodies or harmonies is what concerns us as listeners. The haunting quality of Ravel's *Pavane pour une Infante Défunte* comes from the modal character of its melody, although Ravel does not attempt to harmonize the tune according to any rigid precepts. In such works as the *Benedicite* of Vaughan Williams we find a perfectly satisfying mixture of conventionally tonal music and phrases based upon earlier modes. These two phrases, for instance, were obviously not conceived as being 'in' C major or G major but rather as two different modes, both based on E.

(O.U.P.)

Other passages are clearly in normal tonalities such as D major or E minor.

Composers who felt no radical wish to turn their backs entirely on conventional tonality often toyed with the simultaneous mixture of conflicting keys. The blend of two keys is called Bi-tonality; more than two, Polytonality. Perhaps the most famous example is Petrushka's plaintive cry in Stravinsky's justly celebrated ballet where two clarinets combine two perfectly familiar harmonies (C major and G flat major) to memorable effect.

The absolute departure from all previous concepts of tonality came with the emergence of twelve-note music organized on 'serial' lines. As a theory of composition developed by Schoenberg (1874–1951) it has proved to be the most significant change in the musical language of our times, although even its revolutionary impact has now been superceded by the developments brought about by electronics.

As briefly and simply as possible, serialism might be described as the ultimate extension of democratic principles in musical terms. Within the confines of normal tonality, the Tonic of any key might be looked on as the 'father' of the particular family represented by that key. The 5th note of the scale, the Dominant, would then be the 'mother', the 3rd note (Mediant) the eldest son, the 7th note (Leading note)—being very close to but subsidiary to the Tonic—would perhaps be the father's younger brother. The other notes of the scale would be the junior members of the family, while chromatic notes not included in the scale or key would be acquaintances to whom the family as a whole would feel sympathy or hostility according to the degree of harmonic compatability that conventional behaviour made acceptable.

Schoenberg questioned the validity of this entire hierarchal structure; why, he argued, should the 'outsiders' not have an equal say? Why should not all twelve semitones be regarded as potentially similar in importance? Instead of using the rather limited major, minor, or modal scales as the basis for a composition, why not use the much richer resources of the whole chromatic scale; the greatly increased chromaticism to be found in the harmony of late nineteenth-century composers seemed to be pointing clearly in this direction.

One immediate problem had to be faced. A chromatic scale is not 'in' a key unless it is supported by some definitive harmony; by itself this chromatic scale is just a shape, a sequence of semitones:

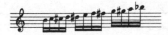

but if I put a particular chord underneath it and run it on a couple of notes, I can make it seem to be a chromatic scale not 'in' but *within* C.

However, Schoenberg was not thinking of the chromatic scale as a scale but as a resource. Suppose, he argued, a way could be discovered of organizing the twelve semitones available so that some inner logic *comparable to but wholly different from* conventional tonality could be provided. It was thus, after some fifteen years of intellectual struggle, that he arrived at the theory known as 'serialism' which was to have such immense repercussions.

The method of organization he hit upon was four-fold. First, take a sequence of notes in which all twelve semitones appear, for example,

No note should reappear at a later point in the series since for it to do so would give an 'anchor' effect that might reassert the very 'father'-type dominance he wanted to escape from.[1] Now it should be made absolutely clear that this is no more to be regarded as a *theme* than the scale of D should be thought of as the theme of a piece in D. Elements of it might appear as a thematic unit, just as elements of the chord of E flat major appear as the main theme of the Eroica symphony. The serial composer regards the series or 'tone-row' as a complete entity, and any possible thematic concept is dispelled when we realize that C sharp means any or all C sharps, D any or all Ds and so on. Pitch is irrelevant and this 'row' would be considered identical with the one above.

Notice that the notation of notes 5 and 9 has changed; since conventional harmonic usage has become obsolete, notation no longer has the same functional significance. As a first step let us breathe a little rhythmic life into this rather meaningless sequence.

You will see that after note 12 the series begins again, though the two versions of notes 1–5 look completely different. Suppose now that we try writing in two parts with the lower line starting at note 8 in the series; we could arrive at something like this:

---

[1] Repetition at the proper numerical appearance is permitted, e.g. notes 5-6-7 could appear rhythmically as

Notice how the 8–9–10–11 group in the lower line anticipates the 5–6–7–8 in the upper part and how the rhythm of the lower line in bars 2–3 prepares the way for the rhythmic change (bar 3) which in the original version may have seemed a little abrupt and unjustified.

Having seen how the tone-row may be manipulated in the most elementary manner it is time to move on to the next step. I said that the serial composer sees the whole row as a single entity; it is therefore logical to look at it vertically as well as horizontally. In other words its notes can be used to form chords:

In terms of serial composition this is about as elementary as 'Three Blind Mice' but it is at least a start on the road to understanding the METHOD. Were it to have stopped here it would have little potential for development. Schoenberg therefore evolved three basic alternative treatments of the initial row; it could be Inverted (rising intervals become falling and vice versa), turned back to front (Retrograde), or Inverted *and* turned back to front (Retrograde Inversion).

The Inversion of the original row would read:

the Retrograde would be:

while the Retrograde Inversion is

Any one of these versions of the original row may be used vertically or horizontally in conjunction with any other, the range of possibilities thus becoming very large. Schoenberg still felt however that the system was too rigid and that tonal implications of intervals such as 6ths and 3rds would gradually reassert implications of the traditional harmonic concepts he wanted so much to replace. He therefore decided that the entire row could be transposed so as to start on any note of the chromatic scale in any of its four versions. This gives 48 alternative 'readings' of the original series, any section of which may be combined in a virtually infinite number of ways with any other section. If serial technique seems at first glance to be an intellectual straitjacket it is truly built to extremely liberal dimensions. . . .[2]

Once the agonizing break with tonality had been accomplished the system could be relaxed so as to allow tonal elements to creep back in. The tone-row in the Alban Berg Violin Concerto (1935) consists of a sequence of triads plus three extra notes:

(Universal Edition)

The main theme of Frank Martin's *Petite Symphonie Concertante* (1945) one of the most beautiful twentieth-century works I know, consists of a twelve-note series:

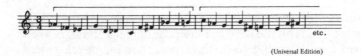

(Universal Edition)

Martin, however, does not treat his material according to the strict precepts of serialism, and other composers too have embraced the tonally democratic vistas of twelve-note music without allowing themselves to be imprisoned within the confines of theory.

Now we have seen on p. 30 how closely inter-related melody and harmony have been over the centuries; the general tendency of tone-rows used by serial composers is to avoid intervals which suggest traditionally tonal harmony since the whole purpose of the operation is to escape from the sense of period such harmonies inevitably bring in their wake. The tone-row I have proposed in my brief exploration of the method might be frowned on by the more ruthless practitioners of the art as having too many implications of 'normal' harmony. It is possible to fit it onto a fairly traditional framework:

[2] It has been calculated that there are 479,001,600 possible series of notes in all.

Such a treatment has little or nothing to do with serial technique since it contradicts the inherent fusion of the vertical and horizontal aspects of the tone-row just as perversely as if I were to harmonize the opening of the Eroica symphony like this.

The second is perverse because it disguises the essentially *pro*-harmonic nature of the top line, the first is equally destructive in that it denies the essentially *anti*-harmonic quality implicit in the tone-row. Wait a minute though; have I not said all along that the tone-row should be regarded as a vertical (harmonic) and horizontal (linear) concept? Certainly; but not in such a way as to convey a feeling of conventionally tonal harmonic progressions.

In other words the dissonance in serial music that so offends the traditionally-minded listener is arrived at by perfectly logical and theoretically justifiable means. Such an argument is scarcely new since dissonance has been regarded as legitimate for centuries providing that it derives logically from the direction of the counterpoint.* Example 10 is an extract from a Bach three-part invention in F minor which has a positively Schoenbergian look about it, so chromatic is the texture, so angular are the intervals.

Ex. 10

53

The essential difference between the dissonance of earlier periods and that of the twentieth century is that composers no longer feel the need to 'resolve' it, that is to allow the tension to give way by sliding to a more acceptable note. Thus a chord as markedly dissonant as this can appear in early Beethoven (op. 22)

but only on condition that it is followed by a logical resolution.

Even by Liszt's time attitudes had changed, and in a remarkable late piano piece called 'Unstern' we find a violent and unresolved dissonance which predates *The Rite of Spring* by over thirty years.

There is, like it or not, an historical inevitability about the increasing emergence of dissonance. It could be argued that any age gets the music it deserves and our times have been made so hideous by the scream of jet engines, the roar of traffic, the pounding of pneumatic drills, the thunder of underground railways, the howl of vacuum cleaners or the metallic clatter of lawn-mowers that it's small wonder that composers need ever more strident voices to make themselves heard. To coin an Irishism, 'if the aeroplane didn't exist, we'd have had to invent it'; even if dissonance didn't have a long and perfectly respectable ancestry, it would surely have arrived as a reflection of our age.

3   Form and Its Function

When one looks at a painting or a piece of sculpture one sees it as a whole;
one can take in details and appreciate them at leisure. Painters and sculptors
are very aware of Form, by which in classical terms they mean an innate
almost geometric design that gives what might be termed a bone structure to
a picture(see p. 56). Form of this sort exists in music, but there is an added
complication in music and spoken language. If we look at a poem on the page
we can see its structure; if we listen to the same poem we can readily
appreciate that structure providing that it has a clear rhyming scheme or a
regular metre. Suppose though that we were to listen to a recitation of free
verse, would we be able to transcribe it accurately onto paper? I doubt it,
since the quality that makes it poetry rather than prose lies simply in the
choice and juxtaposition of words rather than a metric scheme. In music
there is a comparable problem; whether we listen to words or music, we hear
only one sound at a time. The ear learns to store these sounds and group
them so that, providing a sentence is reasonably coherent, we remember
how it began and link up subjects, verbs, objects, subsidiary clauses and the
like into a composite whole. Even if we *look* at a sentence of some twenty or
more words it does not have the direct impact of a picture; our eyes are
trained to scan words line-by-line, and only someone with a photographic
memory can see a page as a single unit, as lesser mortals look at a picture.

   Listening to music is very comparable to listening to language; we hear it
sound-by-sound but automatically learn to link certain familiar groups of
notes together. Look at these two passages—and notice I say 'look' rather
than listen.

Reconstruction of 'The Sistine Madonna' by Raphael (Dresden Gallery).

Our ears instinctively recognize the first 'shape' as a scale just as our eyes see it as a diagonal descent. If we have a musically perceptive ear we will spot that it isn't a pure scale, for there is a slight chromatic blur in the second beat. No matter; the shape is readily apparent. The second pattern is more complex both to the eye and the ear; we need some degree of musical training to be able to identify it as 'an arpeggio in A flat major' simply by

56

looking at it. Yet the ear will easily recognize it as an athletic version of this harmony, spread over a fairly wide range.

On the piano, this harmonic aspect can be emphasized by using the sustaining (right-foot) pedal which enables us to hear all the tones simultaneously. Play the same two passages on a violin or clarinet or harpsichord and however rapidly the performer's fingers fly across the instrument, we still only 'hear' one note at a time, though our mind comprehends the shapes as scale or arpeggio respectively. Suppose however that this sequence of notes is played with corresponding rapidity:

(Not as totally fanciful as it looks; comparable passages *do* exist!)

The 'patterns' can now only be vaguely understood as high-and-low, up-and-down. The ear, having no consistent guide-line, such as the linear conception of a scale or the chordal concept of an arpeggio, can identify this only as aural chaos. Now this is NOT to say that the ear need necessarily reject it out of hand; the sound might be intrinsically fascinating in its own right, just as the apparent visual chaos of a Jackson Pollock painting can exert a fascination of its own, providing the viewer doesn't ask 'What's it supposed to *be*?' If order exists in the world, then logically disorder must also exist, and it seems perfectly legitimate to say that if scales and arpeggios represent order, then the example above represents disorder. (The fact that such passages usually occur in the most intellectually constructed forms of music in which every note is serially predetermined is just one of life's little paradoxes.)

Now the musical units we have looked at so far have been brief and consistent, a descending scale, a mainly rising arpeggio. Quite a number of compositions have been written exploiting the repetition of similar shapes; such 'pattern' pieces could be said to correspond to the repetitive patterns one finds in Nature, the recurring shape of waves in the sea, the delicate tracery of veins upon a leaf, the geometric symmetry of snow-crystals. Such compositions are usually called Prelude or Study (also a painter's term, though not used in the same sense). The most famous of such Preludes is probably the one in C major that begins Bach's First Book of Preludes and Fugues—the so-called '48' since there are 24 in each volume, one for each of the 12 major and 12 minor keys. The C major Prelude is an archetypal 'pattern' piece, using this figure almost throughout.

Apart from the final three bars, Bach sticks to this pattern consistently; even they continue a 'wave' pattern, slightly extended, except for the final bar which is a single chord of C major.

Such a composition is pure abstract art and its 'meaning' is entirely concerned with the relationships between the harmonies which it spells out so elegantly. The bone structure is absolutely clear:

indeed such preludes were often written out using a shorthand such as this, leaving the performer to devise his own figuration. When Gounod superimposed his famous *Ave Maria* above this prelude he completely distorted Bach's intentions; at no point would Bach have conceived this as a *melodic* piece; it is pure harmony, and its substance, as with all harmony, lies in its roots and not its branches. (Hence his insistence on sustaining the first two notes of each group.)

If we turn to the first of the Chopin Studies, Op. 10 No. 1, its basic musical conception could be said to be identical. Like Bach's prelude it can be reduced to a clear harmonic sequence.

Needless to say, Chopin's figuration is much more elaborate than Bach's.

The fundamental difference lies in the essentially athletic challenge of Chopin's writing which makes it a Study rather than a Prelude. Notice that Chopin indicates a tempo, volume, and accents, all of which Bach happily omits, since tempo is immaterial (the abstract quality of the music ensuring that it makes sense at any speed), volume was an irrelevance and accents a virtual impossibility.

When Chopin does write a Prelude in C, as opposed to a Study, we find an intriguing difference of approach. The left-hand part is still a sequence of harmonies:

and one can easily imagine Bach making a Prelude for unaccompanied cello out of such a sequence apart from the problem presented by the low B in bar 2 or the bottom G in bar 8 which are outside the cello's compass. Disregarding this purely physical limitation one can fabricate a pseudo-Bach prelude without difficulty.

There is enough here to show the ancestry of the Chopin Prelude; but while Chopin is content to regard a Study as pure pattern music, his essentially lyric gift tends to make him veer towards a more melodic approach. The C major Prelude symbolizes the aspirations of harmony to flower into melody. The right-hand part begins as pure pattern:

(Chopin, Op. 28 no. 1)

but gradually, as the music gains in intensity, the melodic implications become more apparent until at the climax we sense an overwhelming need for it to 'burst into song', only to disintegrate again into fragmented patterns in the closing bars. The simplified version given in Ex. 11 should make the process clear.

Ex. 11

N.B. Chopin uses $\frac{2}{8}$ as a time-signature, but to simplify I have used the more practical $\frac{6}{16}$.

Clearly the first sixteen bars are nothing but patterns; from bar 17 the line becomes sustained, and therefore melodic, building to a climax in bar 21 and then descending, instantly beginning to break up as it does so. Bars 25–6 represent a last attempt by the melodic element to re-assert itself, only to lose its grip in bars 27–8. This little musical drama takes some forty seconds to play and yet contains within its brief span a powerful symbol of the emergence of the spirit of Romanticism out of a Classical heritage. As the Romantic approach became increasingly dominant, so the emotional and melodic aspects of music displaced the abstract concept largely favoured by

Bach and his contemporaries; a Prelude by Rakhmaninov or Skryabin will be primarily an emotional conception, evoking despair, joy, turbulence, stillness, albeit usually being limited to one basic figuration. Of course, there are Preludes by Bach—such as the one in E flat minor Book I—which are clearly melodic and expressive; but there is a fairly well defined distinction between the neutral emotion we find in most Bach Preludes and the positive emotion of the Romantics.

FUGUE

Since Preludes and Fugues are so often coupled together it seems logical that we should now explore the Fugue as a form. Few of the uninitiated listeners who dismiss fugues scornfully as mathematical abstractions realize that many of the choruses of their beloved *Messiah* are masterly fugues. The form may be subject to intellectual disciplines, but there is no reason why a fugue should not be as emotionally rewarding as any other type of music. It is obviously as futile to expect Bach fugues to sound *like* Tchaikovsky as it is to expect the Tchaikovsky Violin Concerto to sound like a fugue; different listening processes are required for different types of music. We understand this well enough in literature and do not embark upon a paperback thriller, a contemporary love-story, a classic novel or a philosophical treatise with similar anticipations. By calling a piece a Fugue or a Sonata or a Rondo, a composer is simply warning us how to listen to it, pre-supposing that we will understand the significance of the title.

Now it may be no more than a coincidence, but it seems entirely proper that if the patterns of the typical Bach prelude are primarily conceived as harmonies, they should be balanced by fugues, which are essentially linear in concept. (I avoid the word 'melody' as an antithesis to harmony since in this context it would be misleading; nevertheless, every fugue must begin with a melodic idea.) In the simplest possible diagrammatic form a 'pattern' prelude and its accompanying fugue could be shown as blocks and lines, verticals and horizontals.

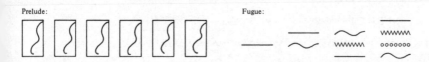

But since Fugues can exist without Preludes and Preludes without Fugues, I would hesitate to make too much of this felicitous contrast. However, given the eighteenth-century's delight in symmetry, such a juxtaposition of two fundamental aspects of music may have been unconsciously assumed.

The initial strand of material from which a fugue is constructed is called the Subject. To begin with it will appear as a single line, usually referred to as a 'voice', presumably since the form first appeared in vocal rather than instrumental music. A second 'voice' will then take up the Subject, usually a 5th higher or a 4th lower than the original pitch, thus underlining the essentially vocal origins since altos sing at a different pitch from basses, and sopranos from tenors. While this second voice spells out the Subject, Voice I will be given a contrasting idea which, since it fits against the Subject, is reasonably labelled Countersubject. (Since Voice II's version of the Subject is rather charmingly called the Answer, it might be more logical to call Voice I's continuation the Counter-answer, but logic is not the most notable aspect of musical terminology.) Depending on the number of parts or 'voices', the entries will continue in an orderly manner, though it is quite acceptable to delay one or the other by spinning the music out a little with a section called a Codetta—a maddeningly confusing term since it appears in quite a different guise in a Sonata-form movement. (q.v.) Here is a plan of the Exposition (the initial entries of the 'voices').

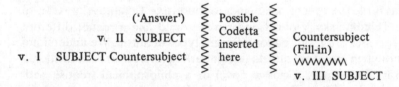

Such would be the Exposition of a three-part fugue; what happens next depends on the skill and imagination of the composer. A number of possibilities are open to him, so many that one could properly argue that Fugue is more a matter of texture than a specific form. If he wishes to modulate to a new key he may use an excursion into a new (or related) idea called an Episode; he may exploit Invertible Counterpoint, switching material from upper to lower voices and vice versa, or use a Stretto, a device whereby the Subject overlaps itself, entries crowding in before one voice can reach the end of the Subject.

v. I   SUBJECT ᴟᴟᴟᴟᴟᴟᴟᴟ SUBJECT ᴟᴟᴟᴟ

v. II   SUBJECT ᴟᴟᴟᴟᴟᴟᴟᴟᴟᴟ SUBJECT ᴟᴟᴟ

v. III   SUBJEC ᴟᴟᴟᴟᴟᴟᴟᴟᴟ SUBJ ᴟᴟ

The slightly truncated versions in voice III signify the small adjustments that may have to be made to make a Stretto fit.

Another possibility of great effectiveness is Augmentation (doubling the length of the notes) or its opposite, Diminution (halving the length). As in serial music the Subject may also be Inverted (turned upside down) or, though this is rare, turned back-to-front (Retrograde).

It is natural enough that fugues should give an impression of accumulating, beginning as they do with a single line and then gradually increasing in density. In an age when keyboard instruments in general were incapable of making a crescendo by varying the touch, fugues had an especial appeal since one experienced an *impression* of a crescendo through the simple addition of 'voices'. For this reason it is likely to be stylistically misguided to end a fugue with a diminuendo, much though such an approach may have appealed to earlier generations of performers.

As with most enduring forms, fugues have been subject to change over the centuries; Bach was the greatest master of the form, his manipulation of the Subject invariably seeming effortless in craftsmanship and often inspired in invention; Beethoven was fascinated by fugue as a texture, but would become involved in Homeric struggles as he wrestled with somewhat recalcitrant material. On the whole, Romantic composers turned against fugal writing, though Schumann often uses 'fugato' (an incompletely worked-out fugue) while Mendelssohn's precocious technical mastery enabled him to write well-oiled fugues from his boyhood years onwards. César Franck produced a remarkable *Prelude, Chorale and Fugue* in which all three musical elements are fused in a final prodigious *tour de force*. Twentieth-century composers as different as Stravinsky, Britten, Shostakovich, Walton, Hindemith and Bartók have all used fugues in major works; there is even an effective one in Bernstein's *West Side Story*, not, one would have thought, a likely setting for an intellectual form. To listen to a fugue is demanding not because of some innately forbidding quality, but because one needs to hear several lines of music at once. When the knack has been acquired, there is a deep satisfaction to be found in following the way in which the composer knits the various strands together, bringing them at last to a glorious final cadence.

VARIATIONS

If Fugues are solid meaty fare, Variations can too readily be dismissed as decorative frivolities; it is true that great numbers of sets of variations have been composed to a simple formula of adding an increasing number of inessential notes to a simple melodic-cum-harmonic framework. Such variations, of which even the greatest composers such as Mozart and Beethoven have not been entirely guiltless, were usually based on popular operatic ditties of the day and were designed to dazzle the audience with a nicely calculated increase in technical virtuosity. The formula was so pat that at one time it was known as 'Doubles', since in each variation the performer would double the number of notes in the bar. Handel's well-known so-called 'Harmonious Blacksmith' variations is a good example, the plan consisting of a theme mostly in quavers:

which in Variation I become semiquavers in the right hand:

in Variation II, semiquavers in the left hand:

in Variation III, triplets[1] in the right hand:

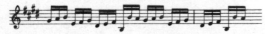

in Variation IV, triplets in the left hand:

culminating in Variation V with demisemiquavers in both hands, alternating.

Storms of applause would inevitably greet such musical circus-acts, but this facile composition-by-numbers held a limited appeal for composers of substance and the form only survived in Victorian parlour pieces of dubious value.

The appeal of variations from the composer's viewpoint is that it is one of the few forms in which even the relatively uninitiated listener can comprehend what is actually happening in a piece of music instead of hearing it as a sequence of random sounds, pleasing or disturbing. Craftsmanship matters to composers and they like to be appreciated; variations, being primarily decorative rather than monumental art, are one area in which craftsmanship can be openly displayed; as the form developed it became more and more a challenge to the composer's ingenuity. What could be done

---

[1] Not strictly speaking a Double, but one cannot expect a blacksmith to be all that good at maths . . .

with a seemingly artless theme, what greater depths could be found in something that at first hearing might sound superficial?

There is a world of difference between the well-known variations in A major which form the first movement of Mozart's Piano Sonata, K.331 and the equally well-known Enigma Variations by Elgar; any attempt to explore the ground between comprehensively would demand a book on its own—variations for solo instruments, in concertos, for orchestra, for chamber combinations, massive variations by Beethoven and Brahms or fragile elusive wisps by Webern. From such an overwhelming choice let me try to pin down a few essentials. A good theme for variations needs two fundamentals; a sound and easily recognizable harmonic structure (literally the 'root' of the matter) and a tune with one or two identifiable characteristics. The most used theme of all time is the A minor Caprice for solo violin by Paganini, a tune of such frightening banality that it is almost impossible to believe how fruitful it has proved to be.

Ex. 12

Its outstanding features are so obvious as to be scarcely worth listing; first an almost totally repetitive rhythmic pattern—so repetitive that it might prove to be a handicap in that it offers so few alternatives to develop; second, a very clear harmonic structure initially based on those fundamental harmonies the Tonic and Dominant,

Third is the instantly memorable sequence that begins the second half of the theme, with its subtle contrast between the first descending phrase (D minor) and the second (C major). Reduce the theme to its bare bones and you would get this: not all that promising at a first glance.

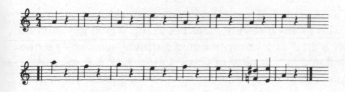

What has been omitted, of course, are the two spinning shapes that prevail throughout, the one rotating

 and the other turning back on itself

These patterns, plus the peremptory rhythm will prove invaluable to anyone attempting to write variations on such a theme.

The basic tonic-dominant harmony switch has often been exploited, a notable example being found in the last movement of Beethoven's Eroica Symphony which, for purposes of comparison, I will transpose from its original key of E flat to A.

It takes little ingenuity to marry off Beethoven and Paganini and produce a convincing variant combining features of both.

It is precisely because both frameworks are so simple that they can so readily be adapted to different circumstances. Here, for instance, is a somewhat less likely marriage, a Royal Consummation that is only made feasible if the monarch is prepared to suffer the loss of one beat in each bar, a reduction from a stately 3/4 to a more nimble 2/4.

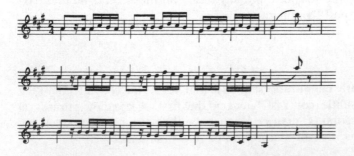

Needless to say, a composer of variations does not normally set out to combine his theme with totally different melodies in this way; I have simply aimed to show how, with a little adjustment, a formula such as Paganini offers can be manipulated in a variety of ways. Let us take a brief look at some of the ingenious things composers have developed from this unpro-

66

pitious material. First Brahms, in two entire books of prodigiously difficult
variations.

Ex. 13

Here, bar 1 in the left hand gives the basic outline of the theme, the
tonic-dominant alternation; bar 2 in the left hand reminds us of the initial
rhythm, albeit on a refreshingly unexpected note; bar 3 puts the basic
pattern of bar 1 into new perspective by beginning on D instead of A. As to
the right hand, it has inverted the spinning shape and changed its stress so
that the second note gains in importance.

 becomes

It was this idea of inverting the initial pattern that Rakhmaninov took over
in his famous Paganini Rhapsody. For convenience I will again transpose
everything into A; suppose we take just this much of the theme:

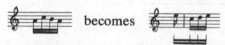

sharpening the third of the scale will put it into the major:

which, turned upside-down, produces the memorable eighteenth variation:

not to mention variation fourteen:

or fifteen:

Incidentally, reverting to the ever-popular eighteenth variation, Rakhmaninov also subtly exploits the idea of inverting another fragment of

Paganini, this part:

which he transforms into the start of his third phrase

His ingenuity in combining the great mediaeval chant *Dies irae* with fragments of Paganini's theme seems highly suitable, having regard to the somewhat Satanic image that the legendary violinist presented to his awe-struck public. However, it can only be sheer coincidence that the opening phrases of Rakhmaninov's Third Concerto also turn out to be a perfectly respectable variation on the Paganini theme.

etc.

The German composer Boris Blacher (1903–75) also wrote an extensive set of variations on the same theme, this time for orchestra. Dating from 1947, they depart a little further from the original than those of Brahms or Rakhmaninov; nevertheless, the derivation is usually quite easy to perceive. Here, for instance, we find the spinning element from bar 1 being exploited at three different speeds simultaneously.

Strings

Trombones

Wind and
Double
Basses

(Bote & Bock; A M P , New York)

(Notice that the second line is an exact 'augmentation' of the first, the third line an augmentation of the second.)

More recently Paganini has been dragged even more sharply into the twentieth century by Andrew Lloyd Webber (composer of *Jesus Christ, Superstar*) in an intriguing set of variations for solo cello and rock group. The spinning motive can easily be spotted in this treatment:

(Chappell)

Once such a pattern has been established, fancy can begin to roam free, as indeed it does in each of the major works I have cited. By now the principles of variation writing should at least be coming clear.

Offshoots of the Variation concept are the Chaconne, the Ground-bass and the Passacaglia. The Chaconne, originally a stately dance in triple time, is essentially a set of variations on a sequence of harmonies as opposed to a melodic line. One doesn't think of Bach's magnificent Chaconne for solo violin as variations on this *tune*:

but as variations on this harmonic framework.

Since, as we have seen, harmonies are founded on roots in the bass rather than suspended from flowers in the treble, it is not surprising that a harmonic conception such as the Chaconne should be closely related to a ground-bass, a form in which the same pattern is repeated over and over again in the bass-line. The wonderful lament 'When I am laid in earth' from the closing scene of Purcell's *Dido and Aeneas* is a classic example of a ground-bass. However, since it is also conceived in terms of a deeply expressive vocal line combined with ever-shifting harmonies, it could not be mistaken for a Chaconne. As for a Passacaglia, it accepts the discipline of a ground-bass insofar as it is built on a recurring phrase; the essential difference lies in the more liberal convention that the 'bass' may rise into other parts, change its rhythm and be altogether less constrained by intellectual rigours. Like the Chaconne, it began as a dance-form, though such noble examples as Bach's C minor Passacaglia for organ, or the final section of the Brahms St. Anthony Variations can scarcely be looked on as dance-music. As for the finale of Brahms's Fourth Symphony, it is a supreme instance of the strict discipline of Passacaglia being used in an inspiringly uninhibited way.

SONATA FORM

Here we have far and away the most significant and varied form in music. Initially the word simply indicated a 'Sounding' piece (*Sonata*) as opposed to a 'Singing' piece (*Cantata*), in other words instrumental music for one or several instruments. During the first half of the eighteenth century the musical structure that we now know as Sonata Form gradually emerged; although it was to become complex and elaborate it has always seemed to me that it reflects the basic format of many simple melodies, though on a very much larger and more dramatic scale. It may seem a far-fetched over-simplification, but the structural basis of a sonata-form movement (which of course is not the same as a whole sonata) seems to have some of its essential features shyly concealed amongst 'The Bluebells of Scotland'.

Here we have a first section which is repeated, a central section developing or extending the initial idea, and lastly a reprise of the opening. As sonata movements go, it is on the short side, but it does show the fundamentals. Now much though I detest analytical jargon, we need a label or two at this point; in sonata-form terms, bars 1 to 2 (plus their repetition 3 to 4) would be called the Exposition, bars 5 to 6 the Development, and bars 7 to 8 the Recapitulation. Needless to say, the scheme of a full sonata-form movement involves considerably more than a simple folk-song, but if we ask ourselves *why* the song is this shape it will give us an initial clue as to the function of the form—which surely is much more important than the mere identification of its component parts. The first phrase sets a mood (gentle, aggressive, melancholy, pensive, brooding, tragic, expansive, compact, etc.); its repetition not only confirms that mood but helps to imprint the details on our memory. The central section extends (and by implication therefore changes) the mood; it modulates into another key. All the same, my analogy is at its weakest here since not enough new material is introduced nor change of mood accomplished for it to be a true Development. However, the final two bars are a valid Recapitulation since they re-establish the opening tonality and bring back the original material.

Starting from this simple plan, let us make it more interesting by elaborating it somewhat, introducing more variety and coupling it to what we now know about keys and tonality (see chapter 2). Instead of the *one* mood we find in bars 1–2 of 'The Bluebells of Scotland', suppose that we aim to provide *two* moods in notable contrast to each other. To point that contrast, let us put them in different keys; but, so as to keep them at least tolerably compatible, let those keys be closely related, either Tonic and Dominant (only one note different in the scale if a major key is chosen) or in the Minor and Relative Major (sharing identical key signatures, but with a different emotional 'feel'). In order to ease the transition from one key to the other, and perhaps more important, from the first 'mood' to the second, let's have a sort of bridge; after all, we don't want to disturb the listeners too much . . . Now, that remark is not so frivolous as it may seem. Sonata form emerged during an age of great superficial elegance, even if the sewage-disposal was less than adequate. Good manners were much valued amongst those members of society likely to listen to pure instrumental music. Symmetry, the balance of one shape against another, was a hallmark of good taste, as we can judge from both the architecture and the elaborate formal gardens that delighted the genteel eye. Thus the design of most sonata-form movements by Haydn or Mozart is as pleasingly symmetrical as 'The Bluebells of Scotland', albeit infinitely more complex in structure.

Before that brief diversion into eighteenth-century *mores* we had in effect constructed an exposition; it could be summed up as

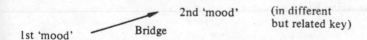

1st 'mood'   Bridge   2nd 'mood'   (in different but related key)

Notice that I have avoided the word Subject which is the term normally used; I have done this because all too often it misleads people into believing that the First and Second Subjects in a sonata movement are clearly defined tunes, as it might be 'What shall we do with the drunken sailor?' and 'Shenandoah'. I hope that this *reductio ad absurdum* finally banishes this particular misconception, since both First and Second Subjects (or Subject 'groups') may often have several notably contrasting elements contained within them. Though I have never used it before in this context, the word 'mood' has a certain appeal since its corresponding adjective 'moody' suggests fluctuating emotions, something we find in the majority of both first and second subjects. Once they have been established, suitably linked by the perfectly aptly named Bridge Passage, good manners dictate that we should round off this presentation of the essential material in a suitably tidy fashion; this rounding-off section, which may be a mere formality but may also contain a tactful reminder of Mood I, is known as a Codetta ('a little tail-piece'). It may even be yet another theme.

By tradition the whole of the Exposition was repeated, not just to make the piece seem longer but because it was highly important to the composer that you should be able to remember the themes and their relationship to each other. Even the two-page exposition of a Haydn sonata may contain half-a-dozen ideas of importance and it is vital to him that you should not only be able to recognize them again but also be aware of their relative dispositions. Unless you do this, what chance do you have of appreciating the drama to come, for it is the Development that will contain the core of the plot. The Exposition is like the first chapters of a novel in which we meet the characters and learn of their background; the Development reveals hidden aspects, changes their relationships, introduces surprise twists and turns, journeys to unexpected places and so on.

The development of a theme is quite a different concept from writing variations on it; it is the art of extension rather than decoration. In particular it is the emphasis upon one or the other 'moods' that is likely to change; thus an aggressive idea may become more aggressive by emphatic repetition or less aggressive by having its rhythms smoothed out; a gentle tune may reveal hidden strengths or become downcast by turning towards a minor key. Totally new ideas may emerge just as new characters can appear in the central chapters of a novel or the second act of a play. In purely musical terms, though, the most significant thing that is likely to happen is modulation into more remote keys. One fragment of a theme may be tossed about through a series of keys, giving an impression of almost chaotic turbulence. Even an innocent little tune such as 'The Bluebells of Scotland' is capable of dramatic change (Ex. 14).

Ex. 14

O where indeed is my Highland laddie gone? Apart from the obvious change of character (loud instead of gentle) bar 1 sees the first significant change of direction, the C sharp instead of C natural on the third beat switching the music to D *minor* (the 'related' minor key to F major since it shares the same key signature). The bass enters in canon* and for two bars the two hands are in conflict. In bar 3, the right hand exploits the rhythm of the initial three notes of the tune as well as taking us into a much more remote key, A minor, remote in that it not only cancels out the B flat essential to F major but cancels the F as well by making it into F sharp; meanwhile the bass thunders away with an extension of the rhythm of the third and fourth beats of the original bar 1. Bar 4 is a dramatic outburst all based on the scale-like shape of the tune;

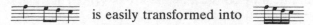 is easily transformed into

but what is more important is the fact that we are now in a minor key alien to the original tonality. Bar 5 attempts to rectify this by re-introducing B flat into the harmony and by smoothing things down with an augmentation of the opening phrase:

However, the lure of a new tonality is too strong to resist and the music heads for the exotic new key of E major, a total contradiction of everything essential to the 'proper' tonality of the piece, F major. Since this is indeed a journey into unexplored territory, the transition is drawn out through bars

6–9 with a nice extension of the opening idea appearing in the left hand in bars 8–9. Notice that while the tonality is in a state of change one keeps the original key signature; only when it settles finally into E major as a new 'home' key does the signature change from one flat to four sharps.

Now so far all this development has stemmed from bar 1 of the tune. In bar 10 we find an interesting treatment of part of the *second* bar of the original. This fragment,

is elongated into notes of twice the length and transposed into E major,

while underneath it, in counterpoint, we find the original bar 1 split up between what might be called 'alto' and 'tenor' parts.

This 'tenor' part, the upper line of the left hand, continues to weave its way using free but fairly obvious references to shapes derived from the original melody while the right hand extends the new lyrical version of the original bar 2 into a sequence. In bar 13 the texture changes from rich harmony to two-part counterpoint, a new twist being given to the tune which is echoed by the left hand. We are moving even further away from our proper tonality of F by venturing into C sharp minor.[2]

Everything that has happened during this surprisingly eventful trip through the Bluebells comes under the heading of Development, the possibilities being literally infinite if we consider all the works written in sonata form.

Once the composer has done as much as he thinks proper with the material he will lead us back to the reprise or Recapitulation. It is easy enough to dismiss this as a boring convention but to do so is to misunderstand the whole dramatic function of the form. If in the Exposition we met the essential characters in this particular plot, in the Development we learned a great deal about them and their inter-relationships that we did not know before; in the Recapitulation we will look at them in quite a different light since not only do we know more about them but we ourselves have had our emotions played upon. If we have been properly involved in the drama

[2] C sharp minor has the same key signature as E major. A glance at the chart on p. 42 will show how truly 'remote' this key is from the starting-point, F major.

(which may be a comedy—not all sonatas being serious), whatever emotional condition we were in at the start of the work will have become subtly changed. To regard Recapitulations as the same as Expositions is a commonly held fallacy but one that negates the whole concept of sonata form.

Musically the Recapitulation has an additional function; during any worthwhile development the music is bound to have modulated into alien keys. In the Recapitulation, normality is restored and the original tonality re-established; it is doubly confirmed by changing the Bridge Passage in such a way that it does *not* modulate. The second 'mood' or Subject will now be in the same key as the first, while the Codetta may also be elaborated in some way, making it into a full Coda. (Codetta is a diminutive of Coda.)

The basic three-part structure, Exposition—Development—Recapitulation, with the various sub-divisions I have mentioned, proved to be so rich in potential that it has served composers from approximately 1750 to the present day. It is the standard form for most of the first movements of sonatas, symphonies, concertos, string quartets, trios, duo-sonatas; although the solo piano sonata may have seemed obsolescent in the latter part of the nineteenth century, giving way to more descriptive or literary forms such as the Ballade, Rhapsody, Intermezzo or Caprice, it made a spectacular come-back in the twentieth century in the hands of composers such as Prokofiev and Skryabin. Inevitably, though, with the erosion of tonality the pre-occupation with key-relationships that was so potent a force in music became less significant; sonata form lost some of its appeal for composers as soon as the demarcations of tonality ceased to be well defined.

RONDO

Although the Rondo began independently as a form on its own, it appears frequently as the finale of a sonata, even at times being fused with sonata form in an ingenious variant of both. It seems logical, therefore, to follow our exploration of sonata form with this, its frequent companion. Let us again take a song as a starting-point.

We are all familiar with the song that has an 'everybody-join-in' chorus; the solo singer tells the story as it were, and at the end of each verse his audience joins in with a recurring refrain that shows they are still with him in every sense of the phrase. The element of participation enhances enjoyment, keeping people involved. Imagine a song in which the solo verses differ, expressing not only a variety of moods but even introducing totally new melodies; the chorus entries remain the same however, and though they might be a little tentative, not sure of where to come in, the singers will still feel a sense of enjoyment once they are confident that the familiar refrain has been safely regained. Here we have the psychological satisfaction of the rondo as a musical form, the main difference from my hypothetical song being that the chorus begins, rather than following on after a soloist.

Repetition of a theme so as to imprint it on the listener's mind is a need so fundamental that composers disregard it at their peril. Many of the problems of contemporary music are caused by the lack of clearly defined themes which audiences can identify at salient points; a rondo is one of the most charming ways of providing such repetition. The composer will begin with a theme, usually of a fairly relaxed nature, and then allow the music to wander off into what is called an episode. Having toyed with this diversion to his satisfaction, he comes back to the original theme, possibly putting it into a different key, decorating it in some way; at any rate it will be clearly recognizable. In due course another diversion will follow, as though one were taking a series of strolls through the adjacent countryside, returning home for refreshment from time to time. The number of such journeys or episodes is entirely up to the composer, the one essential being the recognizable returns to the initial theme. In some rondos a greater sense of unity is imposed by causing the first episode to appear twice, first in the dominant and then in the tonic key; but a second episode, say in the relative minor, will probably appear between these two occurrences. A 'sonata-rondo' will have three sections, corresponding to the Exposition—Development— Recapitulation plan. Within this familiar scheme one is likely to find two episodes, one appearing in both tonic and dominant keys, the other being part of the development and striking out on its own.

There are numerous examples of rondos, ranging from the heart-touching beauty of Mozart's Rondo in A minor, K.511, to the finale of Schubert's great posthumous sonata in B flat. Perhaps the two best-known are the Rondo alla Turca from Mozart's sonata in A, K.331, and the finale of Beethoven's Pathétique Sonata in C minor, op. 13.

THE SONATA

Having explored sonata form, normally used in first movements and rondos, and frequently used in last movements, it remains to survey the sonata as a whole; is it just a piece of music consisting of three or four contrasting movements, or is there more to it than that? Although its origins can be traced to the Suite,* which *was* a group of contrasting pieces in dance-forms, having little in common except the same key (Suite *in* G minor, *in* A major etc.), the Sonata soon acquired more substance than was expected from dance music. The one concession to its past origin was the retention of the minuet, a movement which Beethoven was to relegate in favour of the more exhilarating scherzo. I suppose it could be argued that the slow movement of a sonata comes from the sarabande habitually found in dance suites, but to do so is to stretch the evidence; it would be safer to say that both the sarabande in a suite and the slow movement of a sonata acknowledge the need at some point for a substantial relaxation of tempo and a more openly expressive style. The slow introduction to the opening movement sometimes incorporated (as in Beethoven's Pathétique Sonata or—in truncated form—in the B flat minor sonata of Chopin) may also be a descendant from the earlier Suite, but again I prefer to look on it as a rhetorical gesture rather than as any conscious homage to a past era.

The function of the different movements in a sonata is essentially to explore varying aspects of musical experience. First movements tend to be intellectually the most challenging, slow movements the most lyrical or profound, minuets or scherzos* (Italian: *scherzi*) are designed to be a diversion, finales may be triumphant apotheoses, opportunities for athletic display, charming rondos, sets of variations, or additional sonata-form movements. It is misguided to attempt to be too dogmatic about such matters; composers use all forms to their own ends and sonatas can be in one movement (Liszt, Alban Berg), two movements (Beethoven op. 90 and op. 111) three or four (innumerable examples) or even five (Brahms op. 5). I shall never forget the occasion at a music festival when a young pianist handed me her copy of Beethoven's so-called 'Moonlight' sonata. It was covered with neatly written analytical notes in which she, or presumably her teacher, had discovered a First Subject, a Bridge Passage, a Second Subject, a Development and a Recapitulation regardless of the fact that Beethoven specifically calls the movement a Fantasia and that none of the standard components of a sonata-form movement are actually to be found in it. Presumably they argued that since Beethoven had called it a sonata, a sonata it should be; willy-nilly they forced it into the corset of sonata form, regardless of the musical content. What satisfaction this Procrustean exercise brought, I do not know, though it revealed the idiocy of indiscriminate labelling of music with the stock tags of musical analysis.

SYMPHONY

The simplest definition of a symphony is to say that it is a sonata for orchestra. Just as the meaning of the word sonata changed during the first half of the eighteenth century, so the earliest use of the term 'symphony' or 'sinfonia' implied little more than an instrumental composition, often including voices, but essentially involving a number of performers greater than one would expect to find in a private household. However, the term was even used by composers such as Purcell or Bach as an alternative to Overture, either as an introductory piece to a cantata or in the theatre as a prelude to an act. It was in Italy that a more elaborate three-movement overture developed and it was from that model that the symphony as we think of it today emerged.

Since Haydn (1732–1809) was fortunate enough to have a resident orchestra of good quality at his disposal for much of his creative life, it is not surprising that he exploited this resource to the full. The 104 symphonies that he wrote in his incredibly productive career developed the form so extensively that he effectively bridged the enormous gap in style between J. C. Bach (1732–95) and Beethoven (1770–1827).

Beethoven with a mere nine symphonies accomplished as significant a change, the first one accepting the Haydn model without qualification, the third breaking through to a new concept of symphonic scale, while numbers five to nine increasingly freed the structure from classical restraints and moved towards the more Romantic and subjective approach that became acceptable in the mid-nineteenth century. Even so, despite the huge ego-trip that Berlioz indulged in in his *Symphonie Fantastique*, despite the Romantic rhetoric of Tchaikovsky, the term Symphony tends to have a sobering effect on most composers, representing an intellectual challenge not to be taken on lightly. It is worth saying that this should hold true for audiences as well, and that to listen to and fully appreciate a symphony demands a considerable feat of concentration. Once one learns to follow the composer's line of thought, to comprehend the way material is developed, to be aware of carefully planned surprises that evade predictable solutions, to respond to the changes of tone-colour brought about by use of the orchestra, to *share* the creative process rather than to be a passive witness, the rewards are great; but that reward might be said to be proportionate to the amount of attention the listener is willing to bring.

CONCERTO

Egalitarianism may be the basis of many a popular political slogan, but it is totally unrealistic to assume that given equal facilities and equal training all music students would achieve the same standard of performance. To paraphrase Keats's enigmatic line, 'Heard melodies are sweet, but those unheard are sweeter', it is generally accepted amongst musicians that skills taught are valuable but those untaught are priceless. The true artist in music is the fortunate possessor of some intangible but also unteachable quality that is inbred; providing that he combines this literal gift with those skills that can be acquired by study, he will emerge as a soloist in his own right. In any substantial group of musicians certain individuals will stand out as being more gifted than their fellows; composers, by nature having a comparable individuality, naturally responded to this and devised the concerto as a vehicle for the exceptional performer. Frequently, as in the case of the violin concertos of Corelli, Vivaldi and Vieuxtemps (1820–81), or the piano concertos of Mozart, Beethoven, Chopin, Rakhmaninov, Bartók or Pro-kofiev, the composer had himself in mind as the soloist; but there are many other instances of performers inspiring composers to write for them—Leon Goossens, Rostropovich, Julian Bream or Larry Adler being just a few contemporary examples.

In its earliest form the concerto was designed to pick out a small group of players rather than a single performer; such a work would be called a *concerto grosso*. The understandable human desire to identify with a hero figure soon led to a strong preference for one soloist rather than a group, and since Haydn's day multiple concertos of any kind have been very much the exception.[3]

In essence the concerto is simply another elaboration of the sonata; however, the presence of a soloist gives scope for greater variety. The normal form is to begin with an orchestral Exposition (known as a 'tutti' from the Italian word for 'everybody') in which, as in a sonata, the main themes will be deployed. Instead of the conventional repeat found in a normal sonata, we will now find a second Exposition in which the soloist takes over the leading role, usually accepting the material proffered by the orchestra but adding considerable embellishments to it. However, in some of the finest piano concertos of Mozart the soloist embarks on a completely independent path, making an entry with themes not even suggested by the orchestra. It was a typically brilliant solution to the fundamental problem of balance created by the small-toned fortepiano for which he was writing. By giving the soloist themes that were reserved exclusively for the piano, it was easier to avoid a situation where, if the orchestra were to share the same material, the stature of the solo instrument might seem to be diminished. Thus in his great concerto in C minor (K.491) the pianist never actually plays the theme which the orchestra presents in stark angular unisons at the beginning of the work, since inevitably by comparison it would have seemed ineffectual. Instead, the soloist is given a phrase of poignant understatement that establishes a feeling of isolation from the throng, a Hamlet rather than a Henry V.

The development of the piano as an instrument enormously affected the growth of the piano concerto. As the instrument developed more power, so the hero-figure could take on his adversaries with ever greater confidence; the last truly classical concerto in which the soloist's ascendancy had to be established without recourse to sheer volume was Beethoven's Fourth Piano Concerto in G, op. 58. The slow movement, in which the initial aggressive-ness of the orchestra is gradually tamed by a soloist who consistently refuses to be provoked, is a supreme example of the soft answer turning away wrath

---

[3] Concertos for orchestra such as those by Bartók or Tippett are designed to exploit the virtuosity of modern orchestral players; they are a derivation of sorts from the concerto grosso of old.

(see pp. 135–40). In the Fifth Concerto, the 'Emperor', Beethoven was clearly writing for a substantially different instrument; even in his deafness he was able to estimate how the relationship between piano and orchestra would inevitably change; from then on the absolute dominance of the soloist remained unchallenged.

One aspect of the concerto that does not usually appear in sonatas or symphonies is the Cadenza. During the period when composers tended to write concertos exclusively for their own use, they would often resort to a sort of shorthand when it came to writing out the solo part. It saved time and trouble just to sketch in the outline, to say nothing of using less paper. Towards the end of the first movement there would be a dramatic pause, at which point the orchestra would break off and the soloist would embark on a spectacular improvisation, incorporating some of the themes if he wished, but also indulging in pure display passages, scales, arpeggios and the like, which frankly were boring to write out in full even though they could be exciting to listen to. Why put it down on paper when you could just as well make it up on the spur of the moment? It was an age when improvisation was a widely admired accomplishment amongst all musicians, an age when spontaneous decoration of a melodic line was expected of singers and instrumentalists alike. As tastes changed, and as the publication of music enabled it to be performed in different places outside the supervision of the composer, it was felt advisable to write cadenzas out in full, lest the musical quality of the work should be depreciated by the introduction of inappropriate and shallow inanities. However, since virtuoso display forms an essential part of a cadenza, composers have sometimes been shy of writing cadenzas for instruments which they do not themselves play with adequate skill. Even Beethoven and Brahms, giants both, baulked at the prospect of writing cadenzas for their violin concertos, Brahms leaving it to his friend Joachim, Beethoven leaving it to Providence.

Unlike symphonies, concertos are normally in three movements; again, though, it is a matter of observing custom not law, and there is no reason why there should not be four (as in Brahms's Second Piano Concerto) nor why the cadenza should not be in the last movement, as in Elgar's Violin Concerto. As orchestras have grown larger, the problem of balance has increased, particularly for instruments like the violin, the cello, the flute or oboe, which lack the sheer volume of the modern grand piano. Composers have to pay heed to such practicalities, and, as we listen to a concerto for such an instrument, we must expect a considerable drop-out of orchestral sound whenever the soloist has anything of importance to do. Inevitably some passages get lost in the orchestral wash, but part of the excitement of being present at a concert preformance is to watch the soloist struggling against odds. Perhaps it is this element of drama that has made it the most popular of all symphonic forms.

Before we leave sonata-form works, which include not only sonatas, sym-phonies and concertos, but also virtually all the major examples of chamber music, it is worth pointing out that the function of form is all too often misunderstood. The inventive composer uses form not as a meek com-pliance with convention but as a way of creating surprises. You cannot have a surprise unless you expect something predictable to happen. An estab-lished form nourishes expectation; genius denies or frustrates it. As an example, let me quote a magnificent moment in Brahms's First Piano Concerto, op. 15. Despite the dramatic turbulence of the first movement, it complies with the conventions of sonata form as applied to concertos although the entry of the solo piano is as curiously arresting as the Mozart example I quoted (p. 79) in the way that it rejects the orchestral First Subject. Nevertheless, within its great span the proprieties are mostly observed and such landmarks as Bridge Passage and Second Subject can be clearly identified. Comes the Recapitulation, though, and with one hammer-blow Brahms smashes through the conventions, thereby providing us with one of the best-plotted surprises in all music. The orchestra settles onto a great rumbling D (the Tonic), and by all the laws of expectation, the soloist, if he is to come in at all at this point, *ought* to play these notes, duplicating the very opening bars of the work.

But as I said, genius frustrates expectation; instead of the predictable, Brahms gives us an inspired surprise.

The shock is two-fold; in terms of form the entry of the *soloist* at this point and with this theme does not comply with the original Exposition; in terms of tonality the pianist is literally in the 'wrong' key, not merely denying expec-tation but positively contradicting the very foundation of D minor on which we had assumed the music to be securely reinstated. Neither surprise has any significance for a listener who lives by the moment, experiencing music as a sequence of vaguely related sounds; it is form that creates the situation which Brahms can then exploit by a stroke of genius; it is the denial of conventional form that gives proof of that genius.

SYMPHONIC POEM

Although the terms Classical and Romantic can cause confusion since they are sometimes applied to styles and sometimes to periods, it is generally understood that a major change of direction took place in all the arts from roughly 1830 onwards, a move to a greater freedom of *self*-expression on the part of the artist. There is a clearly recognizable difference between emotion in the abstract and emotion personalized. In the eighteenth century, that era which I have already described as being dominated by Good Manners, composers probably felt that it was in bad taste to express too much of their own selves in music, an attitude that was possibly a remote hangover from the much earlier period when virtually all music had been written in the service of the Church. Needless to say, there are a number of deeply expressive pieces, by Mozart in particular which give us great insight into his personal agonies; but just as he would have spoken about such private despair only to his closest friends, I always feel that such compositions were not really designed for public performance.

Such reticence became increasingly outmoded and would indeed have seemed incomprehensible to the truly Romantic composers, who unhesitatingly used music as a form of emotional self-projection. It could well be that the isolation brought about by Beethoven's deafness drove him increasingly to use music as a means of direct communication; at any rate his later works certainly opened the door, preparing the way for the totally different approach of composers such as Berlioz, Schumann or Tchaikovsky. The most significant milestone is probably the *Symphonie Fantastique* of Berlioz (1830), written a mere three years after Beethoven's death. It is openly autobiographical, the composer seeing himself as a hero-figure, racked by intense emotions brought on by a hopeless love, and even indulging in self-destructive fantasies of death on the scaffold. Now, it is interesting that in Beethoven's Pastoral Symphony, which is a descriptive work, the composer specifically warns us not to read too much into the music; it is, he said, 'more an expression of feeling than a painting'. During preliminary work on the symphony he made a number of notes from which two remarks in particular stand out. 'All painting in instrumental music, if pushed too far, is a failure.' 'People will not require titles to recognize the general intention.' Despite this, Beethoven did give titles to four of the movements—'By the brook', 'A happy peasants' get-together', 'The storm', and 'Shepherd's Hymn of Gratitude and Thankfulness after the Storm'. He was perfectly right in saying that we do not need these titles to recognize the general intention; the structure of the symphony is perfectly 'classical' apart from the extreme expansiveness of the slow movement and the interpolation of the storm—which is not strictly speaking a movement on its own but a dramatic link between the conventional concepts of scherzo and finale. The programme of the work remains subservient to musical considerations, allowing an element of freedom to enter the structure, but not in such a way as to endanger the edifice.

Berlioz's approach is completely different. He supplies a lengthy and detailed programme note to the *Symphonie Fantastique* and would have been devastated if an audience had failed to identify with the hero-figure or to appreciate the significance of every descriptive passage. Not for him vague generalizations about the countryside; we need to know not only when his hero is at a ball, but the precise moment when he sees his beloved gliding aloof across the ballroom floor in the arms of another. Not satisfied with the crash of the falling blade of the guillotine he supplies a graphic bounce as the head rolls off.

Now these two works are landmarks of differing significance; Beethoven's Pastoral dallies with the idea of using music descriptively but still casts its thoughts back to what might be described as a Classical attitude. Berlioz is so fired by the possibilities of the dramatic description of extra-musical events that he barely accepts the symphonic frame as a suitable medium. His work is a powerful symbol of the true spirit of Romanticism, not only self-projecting, but doing so on a scale larger than life.

Composers soon realized that the symphony was quite unsuitable a form for music of this nature; their solution was to borrow a word from literature and to call a work a 'symphonic poem'. Words are a form of communication common to all humanity except the unfortunate dumb, and even they learn to convey words by sign language. Part of the great Romantic wave of the nineteenth century was manifested in a sort of explosion of literature, and in particular the literature of fantasy, whether E. T. A. Hoffmann or Edgar Allen Poe. (Schubert's favourite reading was Fenimore Cooper.) Whereas Bach probably read little except the Bible and theology, and Mozart mostly looked ·for suitable libretti for operas, nineteenth-century composers became absorbed in literature. Liszt kept copies of Goethe's *Faust* and Dante's *Inferno* in every room of his house so that he could put his hand on them at any moment. (The choice of works seems significant.) Schumann was almost as involved in writing as in composition for some time, even embarking on a novel, *Die Davidsbündler*. Chopin's mistress, as we all know, was George Sand (Armandine Dudevant), one of the most acclaimed novelists of the day. Throughout Europe there was a sudden fusion of the arts, especially those of words and music, symbolized perhaps in the flood of songs that poured from the pens of Schubert and Schumann.

Now descriptive music in itself was nothing new. The French composer Jannequin (*c*. 1474–*c*. 1560) wrote a number of delightfully pictorial vocal pieces about subjects as varied as the Battle of Marignan or the chatter of women; birdsong was frequently used by composers as a basis for vocal or instrumental music, and one piece by an obscure Italian called Banchieri (1568–1634) represented a dog, a cuckoo and an owl. What was new about the descriptive element that entered into symphonic music of the nineteenth century was its scale, not only in terms of sheer length but in its dimension—a full symphony orchestra rather than voices or a few instruments. While it would be misleading to suggest that symphonic poems are opera without the singers, it cannot be denied that the ever-growing popularity of opera was another example of the fusion of words and music, even though few operatic libretti could be classified as literature. Operas have plots and so too, to a lesser degree, do symphonic poems. What makes them symphonic as opposed to purely descriptive is that the composer will not necessarily follow a plot-line with a story-teller's exactitude. In the long run musical considerations will govern, and if he feels the need to repeat a theme for symphonic reasons he will do so, even if it denies the 'poetic' logic.

Concert-overtures are an offshoot of the opera-house and the symphonic poem, usually being somewhat more compact than a fully developed symphonic poem. But the term may be used as a simple acknowledgment of a theatrical heritage; Tchaikovsky coined the sub-title Fantasy Overture for *Romeo and Juliet* and *Francesca da Rimini*, but however vivid the descriptive content, both works are organized according to musical disciplines rather than dramatic ones. There are many passages in *Romeo and Juliet* that would perfectly well transplant into a Tchaikovsky symphony; the essential difference is that the title gives us a licence to identify themes as being specific to characters such as Friar Laurence, the Nurse, the ill-fated lovers. It involves a totally different approach to listening, albeit a less demanding one, from that imposed by 'pure' musical forms.

While a title such as 'Romeo and Juliet', 'Night on a Bare Mountain' or 'The Hebrides' gives us a clear idea of the sort of images we should encourage to enter our minds as we listen, there are a number of other names for compositions that are less specific. Ballade, Impromptu, Rhapsody, Capriccio, Intermezzo, Scherzo (in Chopin's meaning) and Phantasie were all words that were increasingly used by composers to describe what might be termed free-form compositions. Like the symphonic poem, they reflect the intrusion of literary concepts into the world of music; unlike the symphonic poem, they do not depend upon narrative or characters. Single-movement works, they might be described as somewhat remote descendants from the Prelude insofar as they tend to be restricted to one figuration, or the development of a single melodic idea. Descriptive elements often creep in, sometimes openly admitted (as when Brahms had an entire poem in Scots dialect printed as a preface to 'Edward', the Ballade from the op. 10 set), or sometimes referred to more enigmatically, as in Schumann's *Papillons* or *Kreisleriana*. Whatever apparent freedom such titles give, the fact is that composers who use them still regard some sort of a formal structure as essential to the presentation of their thoughts. The Ballade in G minor of Chopin may sound like a marvellously spontaneous improvisation, though on closer examination it can be seen to pay a genuine homage to sonata form.

It would be wearisome to attempt to categorize every single form which emerged in the nineteenth century and then to go on to their twentieth-century equivalents. Chopin had as much right to call a piece Fantasie-Impromptu as Stockhausen has to invent a word like Mikrophonie. As I suggested earlier, titles, whether abstract (Symphony) or particular ('The flight of the bumble-bee'), are only a warning to the listener as to *how* he should listen. Every composer has the right to lay down his own rules; apart from convenience, there is no reason why a piece should have a title at all and there are innumerable *Klavierstücken* (piano pieces) to prove it. It is worth mentioning that some of the most vividly descriptive piano pieces in the repertoire, Debussy's Preludes, have their extremely evocative titles printed *at the end*, it being Debussy's intention that we should judge the composition on its merits as a piece of music first and as a 'picture' afterwards. If we go to an art gallery we look at the pictures first and only when we have been attracted to a particular canvas do we peer at the little label that gives us the startling information that it is a seated nude, a still life, the Hon. Mrs. Thynnge or Collation III. Since Debussy's Preludes might aptly be termed 'tone-pictures', it seems logical that he should accept the conventions of the art gallery and relegate the title to the bottom of the page. Let us leave the topic of Form and move on to the more elusive subject of Idiom.

4 Idiom

There are those who claim that they can infallibly tell Mozart from Haydn and others who admit to finding them indistinguishable; that the question should be raised at all is proof of the existence of what I shall refer to as idiom. If I avoid the more commonly used word 'style', it is to save confusion between style of composition and style in performances, two different even if related concepts. To turn again to speech for an analogy, we accept that the characters in plays by Shakespeare, Sheridan and Shaw speak differently even though they all unquestionably speak English. 'Ods Bodikins' has fallen out of favour as an expletive, which is not to say that it wasn't perfectly adequate in its time. Now although we no longer feel the need for quite a number of words that Shakespeare used, and though there is a corresponding (largely technological) vocabulary of twentieth-century words that he wotted not of, a Shakespearean man miraculously reincarnated would not have too much difficulty in communicating with an Englishman of our times, assuming a fair education on both sides. An Elizabethan aristocrat would find it perplexing to speak to an inarticulate Geordie, since he would be accustomed to using a rich vocabulary with elaborate circumlocutions. This elaboration was part of his 'style', whereas the Geordie's accent (a different type of barrier) would be more aptly described as a 'style of performance'; the words themselves might make sense, but the manner of their delivery could well obscure their meaning—a problem not exclusive to a hypothetical Elizabethan.

Without political motivation or prejudice I have already brought class into the arena, something that is unavoidable, since the contention that 'music is for everybody' is patently false. Virtually all music is either popular or elitist, the distinction being inbred (e.g. folk-music, church anthems or ceremonial fanfares) or cultivated, as when Mozart adopts contrary attitudes when writing a Divertimento to entertain an inattentive aristocracy or an Adagio in B minor (K.540) to purge a desperate and private melancholy. Because of the greatly increased availability of music today our horizons are likely to have enlarged enormously in comparison with those of a music-lover of even fifty years ago. In 1934 a music critic of distinction, W. J. Turner, wrote a book on Berlioz in which he said of the *Grande Symphonie Funèbre et Triomphale*, '. . . the only reason I can give for its total and undeserved neglect is that hardly anybody nowadays knows of its existence. Instead of appraising it myself I will quote Wagner's opinion of it'—which he proceeds to do at length. I don't want to seem nasty but it sounds to me as though Turner himself had never heard it. Cecil Forsyth in his classic book on Orchestration (1914) admits to never having heard the Berlioz Requiem, yet these are both works that you or I can buy on disc and play in our living-rooms to our hearts' content.

While this may seem a roundabout way to approach Idiom, it is necessary because in a period when no other music was available except what was being composed at the time, its idiom would have been taken for granted. Just as an adolescent today whose sole musical experience is limited to undiluted 'pop' would think Beethoven boring, unapproachable or just weird, so a listener in Haydn's day would have regarded the music of a previous century as only of antiquarian interest. For the contemporary child 'pop' is the 'natural' idiom, transient though it may be; for an eighteenth-century audience (more cultured by implication since otherwise they wouldn't be listening to music) the language of Alberti basses, decorative slow movements, clearly established tonalities, improvised cadenzas and the like was equally the 'natural' idiom, and any departure from it was well understood, as when ladies in the audience could not restrain themselves from joining in the communal shouts of 'Encore! Encore!' which greeted even the *middle* movement of Haydn's 'Military' Symphony (No. 100) at its first performance in London (1794). The originality and enterprise of his orchestration was fully appreciated because it stretched the idiom of the day without devastating it. Other more adventurous souls, whether their name was Beethoven, Wagner, Stravinsky, Schoenberg or Webern, had less happy experiences, since they chose to *change* the current idiom.

Now the difference between extension of an idiom or radical change may seem difficult to define; examples nearer to our own day may help to clarify what I mean. If we look in general terms at the life-work of several twentieth-century composers, Shostakovich, Britten, Stravinsky and Stockhausen, we can detect not only obvious differences of musical language but also very different attitudes towards change. Shostakovich, enclosed within a conservative and reactionary society, changed his style the least. In his final years his music became more introverted (not surprisingly) but his essential manner of expression remained constant. Even he, though, made a clear distinction between popular and elitist, the openly propagandist works he was required to write being naive and blatant when placed alongside the brooding but powerful intimacy of the string quartets. (How ironic it is that only communist composers today experience that subservience to a master's whim that the eighteenth-century composer knew at the hands of his aristocratic master. The commissars who decide whether a work is acceptable or not are the contemporary equivalent to the notorious Archbishop Colloredo who had Mozart kicked downstairs.)

If we turn to Britten we find a composer whose idiom changed substantially more than Shostakovich's, even toying briefly with serial techniques in *The Turn of the Screw* and, in a very indirect way, in the *Cantata Academicca*. Essentially, however, he accepted the language he was born with (to coin a phrase), writing music that acknowledged traditional tonality but increasingly stretching his harmonic resources. In this respect he can be directly compared to Haydn, who startled his audiences by his virtuosity in handling the orchestra, whose technique showed not only facility but humour, and who, in passages like the closing section of the Representation of Chaos (*The Creation*), pushed the boundaries of harmony to their outer edges. Although audiences might feel that Britten became less 'tuneful', more complex in his closing years, they always sensed a line of continuity in his work since the process of change was gradual. His love for the human voice and his feeling for language was an additional bridge that helped to ease the link between hearing and understanding.

Gradual change is the last phrase one would use about Stravinsky. Suppose that by some miraculous means one were able to find someone of reasonable musical intelligence who by a strange process of insulation had never heard a note of Stravinsky. Expose this phenomenon in rapid succession to the closing scene of *The Firebird*, the closing scene of *The Rite of Spring*, the overture to *The Rake's Progress*, the end of the *Symphony of Psalms*, a passage from *Threni*, and any twenty bars from the Septet. The likelihood of his assuming them all to have come from the same hand would be extremely remote. Stravinsky's restless mind would explore and discard, explore and discard. Realizing that this was indeed the century of change, a century in which material objects often became obsolete in a decade, a century in which entire areas of scientific knowledge were substantially re-thought, he responded in a way that was unique. Having initially inherited the mantle of Russian Nationalism from his teacher Rimsky-Korsakov, as *The Firebird* and *Petrushka* clearly reveal, he decided abruptly that it was time to sever what remnants were left of his cultural umbilical cord. *The Rite of Spring* proved to be a musical equivalent to the atom bomb, smashing every concept of what music 'ought' to sound like. Yet here the Stravinskyan paradox begins, for in the *Rite* what is most 'modern' is most primitive. The emphasis is on obstinately reiterated patterns (*ostinati*), on rough-hewn blocks of harmony, on stark unblended colours; these are primitive devices, as dramatically striking as it would be to transplant Stonehenge into Parliament Square. Often the most complex passages are formed from a mosaic of patterns—each one consisting of a few notes repeated like a child's finger exercise. The act of breaking through every convention that good manners and refinement of taste had ever imposed upon music, seemingly a 'forward' explosion of radical innovation, turned out surprisingly to be a retrogressive move beyond which he could not go. The dragon had swallowed its own tail.

Stravinsky's solution to the impasse was typically original; since the combination of extreme sophistication with the basically primitive contained the seeds of its own destruction, being incapable of going any further in either direction, the thing to do was to narrow the gap between these conflicting extremes. If the twentieth century could not be reconciled with a sort of pre-history, perhaps a marriage of convenience might be arranged between it and the eighteenth. A single work, *Pulcinella*, seems to have sparked off this idea in Stravinsky's mind. Diaghilev had suggested a pastiche ballet to him, to be based on some fragments of music supposedly by Pergolesi. As Stravinsky worked on the score, brilliantly updating the music by seasoning it with touches of dissonance, sharpening the definition of its colour with deft orchestration, he became fascinated by the rhythmic patterns and elegant decorations of the original material. It was as though having demolished a world he had to set about rebuilding it; here was the precision and order needed for such a restoration.

There followed a number of 'neo-classical' works in which he re-established an attitude of mind that had not held sway since the pre-Romantic era, the objective detachment from his work which was the hallmark of the true Classicist. It has been described as an Apollonian phase, and it cannot be coincidence that one of its most elegant examples was the ballet *Apollon Musagètes*. But there was a fourth idiom still to come. For years the contemporary scene had been dominated by two opposed kings, Stravinsky and Schoenberg; each had led a revolution; each had realized the profound need to escape from the nineteenth-century hangover. Just as nineteenth-century composers had had to reject the ethos of the eighteenth, so twentieth-century composers had to reject that of the nineteenth. One could not out-Wagner Wagner, though Richard Strauss tried to for a long time before relinquishing the struggle. Schoenberg, as we have seen, endeavoured to shake off the past by devising a totally new approach, Serialism. Stravinsky had made the break more dramatically with *The Rite of Spring*. But whereas Stravinsky was a restless experimenter, Schoenberg with dedicated persistence kept going along the hard road he had chosen. Unlike Stravinsky, who had the company of eighteenth-century ghosts to support him, Schoenberg went on completely alone. He had followers, of whom Alban Berg was the most notable, but essentially it was a journey into an unknown world of which he had made a map based on purely intellectual speculation. Poles apart, these two kings ruled their different worlds.

And then, just as great political alliances are made between kingdoms, Stravinsky felt that he too must try his hand at serial technique. Although in past years he had openly opposed it, he saw how powerful an influence it had become. His exploration of the possibilities of neo-classicism was exhausted; he needed new ground to work on. The works of his closing years were all built on serial principles, though needless to say he had to make some new rules of his own.

The disproportionate amount of space Stravinsky seems to have occupied in this chapter is due entirely to the fact that unlike my earlier examples, Shostakovich and Britten, he was someone who consciously assumed four completely different idioms. Once, when filling in a form, he gave his profession as 'Inventor'; he prided himself on being able to invent sounds, to rethink the familiar. One can symbolize this with a single chord, the one that comes at the beginning of the *Symphony of Psalms*.

Here are the familiar components of the triad of E minor reassembled in such a way that we feel we have never heard it before. This ability to rethink fundamental concepts was a hallmark of Stravinsky's genius.

My fourth representative figure, Stockhausen, unlike the other three cannot be said to emerge from the past; he starts from the present, beginning with the assumption that we now have the materials to build a totally new concept of music. Conventions of harmony, phrase-lengths, metre and rhythm have all (he argues) become obsolete. Electronics, including not just amplification or distortion of traditional sounds, but the creation of synthetic sound itself have opened a new resource as significant as the emergence of the symphony orchestra roughly 200 years ago. Why bother shaking off the past when an almost infinite future lies invitingly ahead? Just as Stravinsky re-thought such fundamentals as the disposition of the notes of an E minor triad, Stockhausen has re-thought the fundamental principles of music itself, even moving into realms of mysticism in which he provides nothing but a concept which will emerge differently at every performance, the players producing the notes spontaneously by delving into their own minds. If this may seem to be a total abrogation of responsibility, it might also be said to be a contemporary equivalent to much seventeenth and eighteenth-century practice, in which keyboard parts in concerted music were normally confined to a single bass line—the right-hand part being supplied by the performer according to a code of numbers[1]—and when even the melodic line (especially in slow movements) was often written as a mere outline which the performer was expected to embellish freely according to his inventive skill.

---

[1] The 'figured' bass, in which numerical symbols were used to indicate harmonies: 6/4 would mean the notes a 6th and a 4th above the bass.

Now a century is a long time in music. In 1812 Beethoven wrote his Seventh and Eighth Symphonies, in 1912 Stravinsky was at work on *The Rite of Spring*. Presented in such blunt terms as this, one realizes the extreme vagueness of the categories so often used—eighteenth-century 'style', nineteenth-century 'style'. We all think we know what such labels mean; but we have seen from even a perfunctory survey of just four twentieth-century composers that they have little in common. Has this perhaps always been the case? Has the passage of time eroded differences which once were more striking; did Brahms and Wagner occupy positions as opposed to each other as Stravinsky and Schoenberg? The answer, need I say, is a qualified Yes.

We sometimes use words such as 'stream' or 'mainstream' in connection with the continuing flow of stylistic change. Let us enlarge the stream to a river and imagine the entire history of Western music to be like a river of immense length. Even the greatest rivers are narrow at their source and so it is with our musical river. Since music of any permanence was initially concentrated mainly on the church, it was united across national boundaries by the established ritual of the liturgy; plainsong was the common factor, a musical Pax Romana whose Latin texts and obligatory melodies enforced a unity that over-rode both the linguistic and melodic inflections arising from differences of nationality. For a time secular music was handed down rather than written down, co-existing with church music but not regarded as a serious art-form, a literal folk-music of a spontaneous and unsophisticated kind. Often it was used to narrate ballads of heroism or love, such epic songs being the stock-in-trade of the twelfth-century troubadours, who, far from being 'wandering minstrels', were often aristocrats of high renown. Nevertheless, the travelling band did exist, along with jugglers, acrobats and itinerant musicians; such parties were no doubt welcome in the spartan conditions of French châteaux or English castles. Literally hundreds of these early secular songs have been preserved, though the notation used gives only the rise and fall of the tune, not the rhythm. Purely instrumental music (for dancing) seems to have emerged in the thirteenth century, many of the instruments being Middle-Eastern in origin as a direct result of the crusades on the one hand or the Mohammedan conquests of Spain and Sicily on the other. Even drums, whether the military side-drum or the small tuned kettledrum, came to Europe from the East.

While in the initial stages vocal and instrumental music tended to go hand in hand, they also encouraged a degree of cross-fertilization; secular tunes filtered into the church's domain, snatches of Gregorian chant would appear, desanctified, as the basis of popular song. Gradually the division between secular and liturgical became more clearly defined, church music by its very nature tending to be less susceptible to change, secular music reflecting the more rapidly changing patterns of society, particularly aristocratic society where music could be enjoyed as a luxury denied to illiterate serfs. The first diatribe against 'modern' music, with its indecently fast speeds, excess of ornament, mingling of voices (polyphony) unnatural rhythms and other perversities which would lead to the corruption of its adherents was launched by Pope John XXII in a papal bull of 1324. It is a significant landmark showing that the face of music was changing sufficiently for the Church to feel it was time to call a halt.

Needless to say, such a gesture was in vain, and the fourteenth-century saw the emergence of national styles so that although France, Italy and Germany were still far from the political and geographical concepts we know today, French, Italian or Germanic music came to acquire clearly recognizable identities which reflected national temperaments. This was hardly surprising at a time when travel was arduous and slow; the average man lived out his days within an area of a few square miles, only venturing into distant parts when he was impressed into an army to fight some war whose motivation he may scarcely have understood. Once music was liberated from the uniformity imposed by its association with the Church, national traits were bound to develop.

The pace of life in the Middle Ages was slow and measured. Men were content to start to build great cathedrals knowing that they would not live to see their completion. The changes in musical idiom during this period were also slow to materialise when compared to the transitions of the nineteenth-century or the hectic pace of our own time. It was craftsmen as much as composers who helped to accelerate the change; men brought their inventive powers to the craft of instrument-making, and as early as 1323 a French writer, Jean de Muris, tells of several keyboard instruments, clear precursors of the clavichord and harpsichord which were to be the pre-eminent instruments for domestic music more than 350 years later. When we consider the gradual evolution of such instruments over a period of three centuries or more and then compare the enormous changes in instrumental resources brought about in the last seventy years, it gives us some idea of how the small stream that began our musical river swelled to a mighty flood (see p. 117).

This chapter does not pretend to be a condensed history of music; I leave that to scholars better qualified than I. But it is necessary to look at the distant past in order to comprehend the way in which those signs of musical personality which I call Idiom evolved. As music increasingly became 'composed' instead of being based on traditions, so it came to reflect the greatest artistic manifestation of the Middle Ages, architecture. The great mediaeval cathedral is the supreme example of the organization of space within man-made confines of stone. Such buildings need to be planned meticulously with an eye for symmetry and perspective, an awareness of the exact placing of every stone. Contemporaneously with the flowering of this great architectural style we find a comparable preoccupation with symmetry and precision of placing in music. Composers such as Guillaume de Machaut (1300–77) or Dufay (*c*. 1400–74) produced works of almost unbelievable intricacy in which virtually every part would be a reflection of another. 'Crab' canons, in which one voice spells out the same notes as another in reverse order, 'mirror' canons, where a vocal line would be fitted against itself inverted *and* reversed, combinations of a theme with itself in notes of half the duration or twice the duration, all these and other intellectual devices were freely used with complete mastery, laying the foundation for a tradition which was to culminate in the sheer genius of J. S. Bach's 'Musical Offering' (1747). It seems ironic that an approach to composition so cerebral was not to reappear until twentieth-century serialism. The building methods may be different, but perhaps the Gothic spire and the skyscraper may have more in common than at first appears; certainly a contemporary composer such as Peter Maxwell Davies openly acknowledges his debt to the fourteenth and fifteenth-centuries, and the parallels between serialism and the rigid canonic techniques of pre-Renaissance composers are close enough to make the attitude of the serial composer less contrary than is commonly supposed.

It is worth underlining that Western music evolved horizontally rather than vertically, by melodic lines rather than harmonies. Plainsong, as we have seen, was an unaccompanied strand of melody moving through a relatively small range of notes; organum was essentially the same concept except that one had two (or four) strands in parallel motion. The thinking that lay behind it was not harmonic, and the more elaborate developments in organum that were initiated in the Abbey of St. Martial in France during the twelfth century continued to be linear, consisting of a more fluid and decorative counterpoint to a slow-moving bass. Meanwhile popular music, too, placed more emphasis on melody than harmony and one of the finest examples, 'Sumer is icumen in', is an admirably contrived four-part canon superimposed on a two-part ground.

The point is worth stressing because even as polyphony (the combination of various melodic lines) developed, it tended to exploit the imitation of a single leading part. Thus Johannes Ockeghem (1430–95), one of the greatest Flemish masters, can begin an impassioned song about frustrated love with clear imitations between the top and bottom lines.

('Ma bouche rit')

(Davison & Apel: *Historical Anthology of Music*, O.U.P.)

The second part of the song begins with a similar imitation but with the lower line leading the way. The discipline imposed upon the three lines is by no means rigid, the middle part being something of a 'rogue', going its own way; but the gesture has been made almost automatically. It was a tradition that was to endure for centuries; we find it as a fundamental composing technique in the works of at least four centuries by composers as different in nationality and period as Josquin des Prés (1450–1521), Thomas Tallis (*c*. 1505–85), Morales (1500–53, Spanish), Andrea Gabrieli (1510–86) Palestrina (1525–94), Orlando di Lasso (1532–94), William Byrd (1543–1623), Carlo Gesualdo (1560–1614), Orlando Gibbons (1583–1625) and down through the entire school of English madrigalists to Purcell (1659–95) in his string Fantasias. It was to lead logically to the fugue which, in Bach's hands, became one of the glories of music. The line of descent is clear to see, and it is worth pausing for a moment to consider why this seemingly intellectual approach should have found such favour over so long a period.

There are at least two ways of building a wall; one (and I suspect this may be a primitive method) is to start at one end and build it up to a fair height before proceeding any distance. The other is to dig a foundation trench and work consistently along its line raising the wall a brick at a time along its entire length. To do this one must of course have a clear ground plan to start with. Now while the mediaeval mind coped miraculously well with architectural concepts in stone it was less adept at conceiving musical form as an entity. The composer was in the position of a bricklayer setting out to build a wall by eye alone with no clear concept of the ultimate shape of the building. In such circumstances the simple pragmatic method would be to lay down a line of bricks in the right direction (the *cantus firmus* or plainsong 'foundation') and then lay another line on top of them (the 'organal' or added part). Experience soon teaches the builder that walls built on this principle tend to fall over; he therefore develops a system of interlocking so that the cemented joins do not occur at the same vertical point.

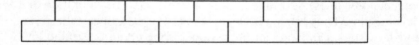

This is directly comparable to the obsession with canonic imitation that so pervaded early attempts at polyphony. To pursue the analogy further, let the direction of the wall be compared to the melodic line and its height (or depth) be equated with harmony. Once we develop a clear ground plan and with it a sense of form, we can reinforce the salient points with pillars or buttresses that enable the mason to indulge his skill more freely in the intervening spaces (see diagram on p. 95).

This is precisely what a composer such as Pachelbel (1653–1706) is doing in a passage such as this in a Chaconne, or Ciaconna as he calls it.

Early Keyboard Music, Schirmer

The solid foundation of harmony is clear to see, as is the essentially decorative function of the right-hand part. It represents an approach to composition that was virtually unthought of before the sixteenth century.

Perhaps the biggest single factor in bringing about such a change was the development and increasing availability of keyboard instruments. Lacking the sustaining qualities of wind or string instruments (or the human voice) they excelled in the provision of vertical blocks of sound or in swift running passages. The other factor of immense importance was the birth of opera that ensued a little later, in which the solo singer's expressive phrases were accompanied by relatively static harmonies. Such harmonies were, however, selected with considerable subtlety in order to bring out the emotional content of the words they accompanied. On its own a sequence of chords such as these has no outstanding merit.

But couple these harmonies, as Purcell did in *Dido and Aeneas* (1689), to a profoundly expressive vocal line which frequently sets up marked dissonances against the supporting chords, and you arrive at music of a high emotional order.

The notes marked with a cross are clearly at odds with the supporting harmony, and it is the tensions they create that give the music its poignancy.

Although *Dido* was the first true English opera,[2] the road had been well explored by the Italians from the dawn of the seventeenth century. The whole of the Renaissance in music might be described as a preparation for the emergence of opera and of the solo performer, whether singer or instrumentalist. With the exception of the Troubadour or Minnesinger (his German equivalent) mediaeval music-making had been almost entirely communal; moreover its close association with the Church or ceremony inevitably led to the suppression or effacement of the composer's ego. The Renaissance stood for the birth of a new, more human attitude to Art in all forms. If music lagged behind painting and sculpture in the realization of this new ideal, it was probably because it is easier to convey the human form visually than it is to translate human experience into the more abstract medium of music. Since the Renaissance vision aspired to a somewhat idealized expression of human feeling, it is not surprising that the first operas were invariably based on Classical mythology. In this way emotion could be

[2] Actually predated by *The Siege of Rhodes*, which however was composed by a sort of cooperative of five composers (Lawes, Cooke, Locke, Coleman and Hudson).

kept at a remove from a contemporary immediacy, symbolic figures from a remote past having an almost abstract quality not all that different from the detachment of church music. It was the performer, rather than the role he was playing, who became the emotional focus, and it might be argued that the greatest contribution that early opera had to make was neither spectacle nor play-acting, but the considerable increase in expressive demands it made upon the solo singer. It is true that many a late sixteenth-century madrigal expressed emotion with surprising intensity, but to sing of such passions in the company of a group of fellow-singers is not the same as sustaining a solo role for a sizeable length of time.

The development of harmony as a positive force in music can almost be directly correlated to the need to convey emotion in personal terms. Once composers began to explore emotions in the particular rather than the abstract they realized that harmony was a powerful weapon. Example 15(a) is a passage by no means ineffectual but relatively orthodox.

Ex. 15(a)

Compare it now to 15(b), which is what the English composer Weelkes (1576–1623) actually wrote in 1600.

Ex. 15(b)

Bar 4 brings a stunning shift of key, the E natural breaking violently away from the C minor established in the previous bar. Bar 6 appears to be heading for D major:

instead, the sharp thrusting ascent to A sharp in the tenor part twists the music into B minor, whose confirmation is not merely postponed by the G natural so skilfully placed in the penultimate bar but averted by the nearly as unpredictable D sharp–E–E–D sharp in the alto part.

The power of such harmony is undeniable; even today it strikes the ear as curiously 'modern' in that one senses the contradictions in which it abounds and which my bowdlerized version eschews. Inevitably, though, the sense of personal protest inherent in the words 'O Care thou wilt despatch me' or 'Hence, Care, thou art too cruel', is diminished by being set for five voices. Such communal distress becomes less credible than a solo aria; within a matter of years opera emerged as the proper medium for the expression of such emotions. It was a notable tributary to add its current to the slowly widening stream.

The example above raises an unavoidable issue whose solution proved to be a difficult problem, though its effects on the course of music were to be profound. While gifted singers with a sure sense of pitch could sing Weelkes's passionate cry in tune, it seems that many keyboard instruments of the time could scarcely have played it in such a way as to be acceptable to our ears today. This was due to the system of tuning then in use known as Mean-tone Temperament, a system that had been accurately tabulated only as late as 1562 and which was universally adopted in Western music by 1700. It endured longer than is usually thought, the 'Equal Temperament' tuning that displaced it being first applied to the Broadwood pianos manufactured in England in 1842, fifteen years after Beethoven's death. In this respect English piano manufacturers appear to have been somewhat behind the times though it is extremely difficult to give any precise date for the acceptance of Equal Temperament. It is known that the principles of dividing a scale into equal intervals had been established theoretically as early as 350 B.C. by Aristoxenus. Guitars were actually tuned according to such a system in the late fifteenth century; the Flemish composer Willaert espoused its cause in 1550. In 1722 J. S. Bach produced the justly famous first book of twenty-four Preludes and Fugues for the 'Well-tempered' (or well-tuned) keyboard. It appears, then, that the battle for the acceptance of Equal Temperament tuning was fought over a long period, presumably against conservatism and incomprehension. What was the problem?

For those who wish to dabble in some very detailed mathematics, the subject of tuning will be fully dealt with in any good book on Acoustics.

Without taking too obvious a refuge behind the phrase 'Take my word for it
. . .' I will try to simplify the essential facts; we need to know one measure-
ment, a *savart*, which is equal to one fiftieth of a whole tone or one twenty-
fifth of a semitone. No problems arise with the interval known as an octave
since the number of vibrations per second producing the sound will double at
each ascent. Thus if 'middle' C has a frequency of 264 vibrations per second,
the C an octave higher will have 528, the one a further octave higher 1,056
and so on. (If you are interested, the range of a piano is from twenty-seven
vibrations per second to 4,224.) However, once we start to think about
intervals such as major 3rds and minor 3rds, major 6ths and minor 6ths,
problems begin to arise since D sharp and E flat are not theoretically the
same, nor are F sharp/G flat, G sharp/A flat, or A sharp/B flat. As an added
complication the note F (in the scales of C, D flat, E flat, F, A flat or B flat)
becomes E sharp in the scales of C sharp or F sharp. So long as music moved
by relatively close non-chromatic intervals, 'true' intonation could be used,
particularly if the complication of harmony was avoided. Mean-tone temperament was the first generally accepted attempt to come to grips with the
problem of tuning, a problem that was becoming acute with the development of the organ in particular. If we represent the initial note of a hypothetical seven-note scale as zero the intervals between the notes measured in
savarts would be shown mathematically as follows:

Octave 300

Seventh 272·1

Sixth 221·1

Fifth 175·5

Fourth 124·5

Third 96·6

Second 51·0

Tonic note 0·0

Such was the scale devised by the pupils of Pythagoras in Ancient Greece
according to sound mathematical principles.

The compromise established by mean-tone tuning would mean flattening
the 2nd by 2·7 savarts to 48·3, sharpening the 4th by 1·4 savarts to 125·9,
flattening the 5th by 1·4 savarts to 174·1, sharpening the 6th by 1·3 savarts to
222·4, flattening the 7th by 1·4 to 270·7. Only the third and the octave would
remain exactly true, but a deviation of 1·4 savarts represents only one
thirty-fourth of a tone; on the other hand, the difference between E flat and
D sharp is 10·3 savarts, nearly a quarter-tone, which is clearly detectable.
With this system of 'modified' tuning one could play satisfactorily in a
limited number of keys; however, a complete change of tonality such as we
found in the Weelkes example would not have been practical. A further
compromise was needed. The solution was at least mathematically simple

since it involved dividing the scale into twelve equal semitones—hence the term, Equal Temperament. In such a scale the intervals measured in savarts would be spaced like this:

```
                                          Octave  300
                                  Seventh  275
                          Sixth  225
                  Fifth  175
          Fourth  125
      Third  100
  Second  50
Tonic  0·0
```

semitones being 25 savarts apart and tones 50. A comparison with the previous chart shows that the only notes now strictly in tune with a true scale are the initial Tonic and its octave; every other note is out of tune by varying degrees. Thus the 2nd is 1·0 savart flat, the 3rd 3·4 savarts sharp, the 4th 0·5 savarts sharp, the 5th 0·5 savarts flat, the 6th 3·9 savarts sharp and the 7th 2·9 savarts sharp. The strength of this compromise lies in the fact that the smallest deviation from true tuning (the barely measurable 0·5 of a savart) is to be found with the most important notes of the scale except for the Tonic, the Dominant (5th) and the Sub-Dominant (4th). Moreover, the two greatest deviations lie with the 3rd and 6th, both of which thus have their essentially *major* quality enhanced. (In the minor key both would be flattened.) Even the added sharpness of the 7th is to its advantage, underlining its inherent desire to rise to the semitone above, whence it derives its name 'Leading Note'.

Although these measurements are all very small as 'errors' of intonation go, they caused an enormous difference to the language of music, enabling composers to open up all the resources of chromatic harmony and to write in all tonalities. Theoretically of course it would have been possible to tune a spinet or organ so that it lay 'in' E flat major; but that would have made a modulation to a key such as B major impractical. In practice it seems that most keyboards were tuned 'in' C, thus giving keys containing a large number of sharps or flats a true sense of the unattainable. Even to this day one can count the number of symphonies, concertos or sonatas in keys such as E flat minor, B flat minor or G sharp minor on the fingers of a single musician. The legendary obscurity of such tonalities lived on long after equal temperament had made them accessible; they are awkward to finger on string, wind or brass instruments, and hard to read at the piano simply because we come across them so seldom.

Equal temperament tuning was most vital with keyboard instruments since they are most concerned with harmony. Before its invention and practical application musicians would almost certainly have tuned their instruments, as many harpsichordists do to this day. As keyboard suites were almost invariably composed in one key, I suspect that the instrument would indeed be tuned to suit. One does find Scarlatti writing in keys such as F sharp major, but I cannot imagine him immediately following with a piece in C. It seems more likely that he would have 'sharp' days and 'flat' days when the instrument would be tuned to accommodate the five or six related keys which Mean-tone tuning would make acceptable. As for Bach, it is certain that no *organ* he ever played was tuned to Equal Temperament. The 48 Preludes and Fugues for 'Well-tempered keyboard' were published in two parts; only Book I carries a reference to 'Well-tempered' on its title-page, while the first published edition (issued fifty years after his death) omits all reference to temperaments of any kind. It is possible that the work was written as propaganda for what Bach knew to be a worthwhile advance rather than as a celebration of its universal acceptance. Presumably all competent musicians tuned their own instruments, but to tune purely by ear is extremely difficult and those who succeeded must have known or devised some theoretical basis to work from. It is worth mentioning that in this respect the clavichord held considerable advantages over other keyboards since it is possible to modify its intonation by the amount of pressure exerted on the key.

Organs were consistently tuned in the compromise Mean-tone system well into the nineteenth century, while the piano that Broadwood sent to Beethoven as a gift in 1817 would have been tuned to Mean-tone. Presumably had he been able to hear he would have retuned it himself.

Even so, as early as 1590 an experimental harpsichord was made in Prague with nineteen notes to the octave, the raised notes equivalent to our black notes being split so as to give different sounds for C sharp, D flat, etc.—proof that instrument-makers had grappled with the problem for a long time.

With the issue of tuning now out of the way we can turn to the next great tributary to join the musical river, solo instrumental music. Needless to say, instrumental music had existed for centuries, but mostly as a complement to voices; indeed much of the concerted vocal music published in the sixteenth century carried suggestions of the instruments that might be used to double the voice parts if required—'da cantare ò toccare' (to be sung or played). This traditional tendency to look on instruments as a mere prop for singers hindered the development of a truly instrumental style. What purely instrumental music there was was mostly for 'consorts' or families of instruments such as the viols. In 1594 Hércole Bottrigari described a famous court ensemble in Ferrara that consisted entirely of girls—possibly a surprise to women's libbers of today. 'You would see them betake themselves in Indian file to a long table with a large harpsichord placed at one end of it. Silently they entered, each one with her instrument, whether string or wind, and gathered round the table without the slightest noise, some sitting, some standing . . . At last, the conductress faced the table from the other end and, after having ensured that the other sisters were ready, gave them noiselessly the signal to begin with a long, slender, well polished baton.'[3] The last point is particularly interesting since the use of a baton, or even a conductor, is normally ascribed to a considerably later period. It is also worth noting that string and wind instruments were blended, whereas the more normal sixteenth-century practice was to have a brass consort, a string consort or one of wind. (Mixed groups were called a 'broken' consort.)

Not surprisingly it was the keyboard instruments, able to provide both harmony and melody—in that order of importance—that made the first substantial development as soloists. The period from 1575 to 1625 was a particularly rich one in English musical creativity, and although a wide range of magnificent vocal music was produced, the keyboard music is perhaps historically even more important. Three collections of particular interest appeared, *My Ladye Nevells Booke* (1591)—a set of forty-two pieces by William Byrd (1543–1623), *Parthenia or the Maydenhead* (1611) described on the title-page as 'the first musicke that euer was printed for the Virginalls'[4] and the Fitzwilliam Virginal Book (*c*. 1621), a manuscript collection of nearly 300 pieces by a number of composers. Many of the pieces in these collections still belong to dance-forms such as the pavan, the galliard, or the jig; but others are sets of variations on popular songs of the day or free fantasias designed to display the technical skill of the performer.

Real virtuosity was called for, especially by the aptly named John Bull. Ornamentation was lavishly used to compensate for the lack of sustaining power in the smaller instruments as well as to provide accentuation. Contrary to general belief, the thumb was certainly used, as the following authentic example of fingering from 1652 shows.

Judging from instructions given by sources as varied as Frescobaldi (1583–1643) and Purcell (1659–95) frequent pairing of fingers was used in scale-playing, the performer's hand scuttling crabwise over the keyboard

Imagine applying this sort of technique to the elaborate runs called for in the Preludium by Orlando Gibbons (1583–1625), given in Ex. 16.

---

[3] Paraphrased from Curt Sachs: *A Short History of World Music* (London, 1956).
[4] Virginal, or virginals, was by this time a name used for either harpsichord or spinet.

Ex. 16

Here is a truly liberated style of keyboard writing bearing no relationship to voices or the consort music of a previous era.

The range of music covered in these historic collections is remarkable. 'Felix namque', composed by Thomas Tallis in 1564, is a vastly complex piece, starting contrapuntally in the vocal style it is true, but soon developing a rich resourcefulness in the handling of rhythm and a positively magisterial progress towards its final cadence. It is over 250 bars long, eleven pages packed with notes, and as elaborate in its way as a whole movement of a major sonata by Beethoven.

If on the other hand one seeks an expressive style with an emphasis on a right hand melody, such pieces as 'Giles Farnaby's Dreame' (Ex. 17) come to mind.

Ex. 17

Giles Farnaby (1566 - 1640).

From here to Schumann's 'Träumerei' may seem quite a journey, but the foundation has certainly been laid for the expressive miniatures we tend to associate exclusively with the nineteenth century. It would be a mistake, though, to assume that this early keyboard music is essentially fragile. Block harmonies were used to spirited effect as in *The Earle of Oxford's Marche* by William Byrd.

Despite the solidity of these harmonies, the notation shows how hard it was for composers such as Byrd, brought up on counterpoint, to escape from the habit of thinking in 'voices' or individual parts. Thus all the chords in the right hand are written with the top note as a separate entity even though the instrument precluded any possibility of 'bringing out the tune'.

It is dangerously easy to lump all 'olde musicke' into one dusty pigeonhole in our minds and to forget that this great heritage predates even the *births* of Bach and Scarlatti by seven decades or more. Assuming that much of the music in the Fitzwilliam Virginal Book was written some time before its actual collection in 1621 and that Bach and Scarlatti (both born in 1685) composed nothing of significance until they were about twenty, then a gulf of approximately 100 years separates them. Look back 100 years from our own time and see the vast changes that have overtaken music; the distance of time may have diminished our understanding of quite what was involved in the virtual creation of a fluid and varied keyboard style out of nothing, but the Elizabethans, adventurous explorers in more than one sense, were admirably equipped to do it.

Obviously, composers of other nationalities are not to be disregarded, but the most substantial contribution to the true dawn of keyboard writing came from England, just as the nursery of violin playing was Italy. If I seem to have spent an inordinately long time on a relatively obscure period it is because the whole repertoire of the keyboard rests on these foundations, for what these adventurers did was to shake off the implied restrictions of vocal music and invent a true keyboard idiom. The association between an instrument and the music written ideally for it is something that only a performer can truly understand. I once had the strange experience of sitting next to an internationally known guitarist while he played a Bach fugue that I knew well as a keyboard piece. There was no way in which I could relate the placing of the fingers of his left hand with the 'feel' of a piano; familiar passages took on a perverse appearance; what I might have played with my thumb he was playing with a fifth finger. Each instrument has its own 'feel' and the proper idiom for the keyboard is unlikely to be readily transferable to the cornet or the violin. We have all experienced how foreign well-known orchestral scores can sound when they are transcribed for military band, with passages that run naturally on violins sounding a hectic scramble on massed clarinets. Within the limitations of the early keyboards, the Elizabethans devised an idiom that was entirely proper to the instrument. The limitations of harmony, the restriction to a very small range of keys were dictated by the problems of tuning I have already elaborated. A preference for step-wise motion came about through the style of fingering adopted, while the tendency to let swift-running figurations be in one hand or the other (but seldom in both at once) reflected an understandable wish for clarity. Above all they produced music that was genuinely instrumental, not a vocal concept transferred to a keyboard.

The violin as a solo instrument followed a little behind the keyboard. The principle of bowed instruments had been established in the middle ages[5] with the rebec, but the violin itself did not emerge until about 1530. It should not be confused with nor even related to the viol. All viols are played on or between the performer's knees; the bow is held 'underhand' as opposed to the overhand hold on the violin-bow; viols have six strings as opposed to the violin's four; they are 'fretted' as the guitar is, giving the player landmarks to assist the accurate placement of the fingers.[6] On the other hand, it is almost as misleading to believe that the Stradivarius violin acquired for an astronomical sum by a present-day virtuoso is the real thing. I am not suggesting it is a forgery; however, it is not generally understood that because of the ever increasing demands of 'new' music over the centuries, as well as the spectacular advances in technical accomplishment, the noble instruments so lovingly made in Cremona by Antonio Stradivari in the seventeenth and eighteenth-centuries (he lived to be ninety-three) have been substantially modified. To use a vulgar automotive metaphor, the chassis and bodywork have been preserved but the suspension and engine have been improved. The black ebony fingerboard that lies under the four

[5] If one includes non-European and earlier civilizations, it dates back thousands of years.
[6] For a time the instruments co-existed. In *Orfeo* (1607) Monteverdi specifies an orchestra of viols *and* violins.

105

strings will have been lengthened to enable the player to reach much higher notes than were originally attainable, the bridge will be higher, increasing not just the tension but the playing length of the string, the soundpost that joins the back and belly of the instrument inside will have been thickened, the angle of the fingerboard changed, a chin-rest added, the bow altered. More than eighty pieces of wood go to the making of a violin and there is not a nail or screw to be found anywhere; it surely represents the apogee of the joiner's art.

The four strings are tuned a fifth apart:

a moment's thought gives us a good reason for this. Discounting the thumb, which holds the neck of the violin, the violinist has four fingers only at his disposal. If he begins on the 'open' string G and then places his first finger approximately an inch up the string he will find the note a tone higher, A; a further similar step will bring the next tone, B (2nd finger); a narrower step will produce a semitone, C (3rd finger); another wide step, significantly harder to place accurately and on the weakest *shortest* finger will produce the note D. How much simpler, then, to provide a new string for this note. In this way it is possible to play a G major scale through two octaves using all four strings but only three fingers to each string. I need hardly say that this is a gross over-simplification of violin technique but it serves to make two important points; first, that the violinist makes his own intonation and second that what he is actually doing is to shorten the string temporarily thereby raising its pitch. If we follow this second thought to its logical conclusion we realize that if the player continues his progress up the G string he will pass beyond the pitch of the adjacent string D. He does this by shifting his grip on the neck of the instrument and moving his entire hand to a new starting point. Such shifts are known as changing 'positions' and there are at least seven positions. Staying on the G string for the moment, the seven positions would produce the following notes, the semibreve representing what one might term the 'anchor' note that determines the position and the crotchet-heads the three further notes that can be obtained without a further shift.

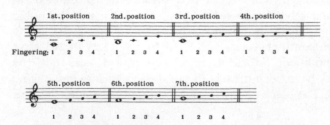

By this means we can find a compass of virtually an octave and a half on the one string, even more on the higher strings since the higher the pitch the narrower the intervals between the notes. Skilled players can climb to 8th or even 9th positions on the E string, at which altitude the fingers will lie so close together as almost to overlap. The secret of accurate intonation lies in exact placement of the fingers and the ability to shift positions fluently; what the layman fails to appreciate is that the relative distances between tones and semitones are subject to continual variation according to how far up the string the hand has travelled, the higher the narrower. Thus if a violinist plays a passage in octaves—

the distance between the two fingers playing the notes will be marginally different in every case. To make such fine adjustments accurately needs infinite patience and endless practice.

It may seem at first glance that such details belong to a violin tutor rather than a general book on musical appreciation; moreover have they anything to do with the matter of Idiom I am supposedly discussing?

Inevitably they have; let us take an absolutely basic example to make the point clear. One of the most elementary things it is possible to do on the violin is to draw the bow across the four open strings so as to produce this sound.

Yet to do this with a smooth legato touch with one hand on the piano is extremely hard; to use the fingering 1, 2, 3, 5 (1 representing the thumb) or 1, 2, 4, 5 stretches even the largest hand. Some such alternative as 2, 1, 2, 5 is almost as awkward. It is a combination of notes that no composer with the slightest feeling for the keyboard would use unless it were to be divided between the hands. Now let us take an alternative group of notes starting at the piano. A pattern such as this might easily occur in a toccata-like piece, and, providing your hands are large enough to stretch a 10th comfortably, it is perfectly easy yet will sound quite brilliant.

On the violin this would be so impracticable as to be literally impossible to bring off. Either 10th is possible, but the transition from the 2nd note (which has to be played on the D string) to the 3rd note (which must be 'found' in the 5th position on the E string) involves skipping over the A string, while the transition back from the 4th note (D) to the low G sharp again involves an awkward skip across the D string. Since the strings are not laid flat like those of a guitar but arranged in an arc, a literal 'bridge'-shape ⌣⌢⌣, smooth transitions are only possible if one travels through adjacent strings. A figuration such as the following example is ideal violin writing since the lowest two notes are 'stopped' by a single finger pressing on the G and D strings, the C sharp is played on the A string, the top note on the E.

The same passage would be downright awkward as the right-hand part of a piano piece.

We have already travelled a long road in this chapter but we have now arrived at a point where, because of the emergence of instruments as soloists in their own right, Medium and Idiom interact dramatically. I have stressed the important effect that the birth of opera had in widening the emotional range of song; the development of truly instrumental styles was just as significant an advance, but each instrument to a certain extent dictates the composer's thought. Writing for the flute is not the same as writing for the trumpet; even closely related instruments such as the violin and viola have clearly differentiated tones, as any listener to Mozart's exquisite Sinfonia Concertante* for violin, viola and orchestra (K.364) will appreciate. What the great Italian violin school of composers achieved was a comprehensive exploitation of those things that could be done supremely well by string instruments. Corelli (1653–1713), Vivaldi (1675–1741), Tartini (1692–1770) and Locatelli (1695–1764) all contributed to the establishment of a tradition of string writing (as opposed to string *playing*) that was hardly changed until Paganini (1782–1840) amazed the world with his innovatory techniques. Suppose that by some miraculous time-machine, Vivaldi had been able to see a copy of the Beethoven Violin Concerto, would he have been able to play it? Given a few days to practice and sort out the problems of living at a high altitude, he certainly could have done. The techniques involved are logical extensions of the groundwork laid by Vivaldi and his contemporaries. Would he have been able to play the Paganini concertos or caprices? No; he would have written them off as impractical, just as orchestral players of a later era were to reject Wagner's *Tristan and Isolde* as unplayable.

Now Vivaldi was a mere ten years older than Bach, close enough in period for them to have some characteristics in common. In particular, both make much use of pattern and sequence in music. Here for instance is Vivaldi soon after the first solo entrance in the Violin Concerto in D (op. 7 No. 12 in the old numbering, RV 214 in the new).

At first glance this seems to be monotonous note-spinning of a puerile order; look at it from a violinist's view, though, and we see that it is superbly written. The sequences in bars 1 to 4 are each enclosed within in an interval of a 4th. A pianist will think of each note as a separate finger action but a violinist simply holds his 1st finger on A throughout bar 1, using it as an 'anchor' from which the other notes can easily be reached; in bar 2 he shifts position so that G becomes the anchor note, in bar 3 he makes another shift to use F sharp as a new anchor and so on. The whole passage lies superbly under the fingers and in this respect it can be argued that the violin 'composed' the music almost as much as Vivaldi did. Even so, isn't the music itself feeble in invention? Not so much as one might imagine.

It is one of the marvels of musical scale formations that owing to the irregular distribution of tones and semitones, passages such as this are much more subtle than at first appears. The principal group in bar 1 (*ABAD*) consists of an alternation of a tone and a fourth; in bar 2 it is a tone and an *augmented* fourth (G–C sharp), in bar 3 a *semi*-tone and a fourth, in bar 4 a tone and a fourth. The intervals are therefore constantly changing, and while it is true that bars 1 and 4 seem to be identical with regard to intervals, their harmonic function is different: bar 1 establishes the Dominant as the point of departure, bar 4 establishes it as a point of arrival. Such subtleties may be lost to our modern ears but if we can make the imaginative effort to put ourselves back to a time when such music represented a new threshold of virtuosity, we begin to realize that such clichés were once valuable.

Here, now, is a sequence from a Bach organ work, the noble Prelude in F minor.

Obviously the same subtle variants are to be found with regard to the disposition of tones, semitones, minor 6ths, major 6ths, minor 7ths, major 7ths and the like; but what of the recurring A flats in bar 1, the Gs in bar 2, the Fs in bar 3 and the E flats in bar 4? It is tempting to think of them as directly comparable to what I described as Vivaldi's anchor-notes, but to do so would be misleading. Vivaldi's anchor-notes serve a primarily technical function; they are, as I put it, 'composed' by the violin since they are there for the convenience of the player. Bach's recurring notes serve a musical purpose, providing constantly varying harmonic tensions. Fuse each pair of notes into a chord and the degree of harmonic variation becomes more apparent.

Instead of Vivaldi's single harmony to each bar we find six changes varying from the violent clash of a minor 2nd to mellifluous 3rds or extended 7ths. Here is epitomized one of the causes for Bach's superiority over Vivaldi as a composer—his infinitely greater harmonic resource. When, as he frequently does, Bach uses constantly reiterated patterns, the continual shift of harmony which such patterns embellish is seldom without surprises or tensions.

Let us pursue this idea of patterns a little further, particularly in their relation to harmony. So well established was this relationship that rapidly moving figurations were frequently written out as seemingly static chords; for instance, a composer of the Vivaldi school might write a sequence such as this:

The performer would not dream of playing these as three-note chords but would simply continue a pattern previously established, using the chords as a framework.

A slight change of pattern such as the one in the final bar was quite acceptable, the musical justification here being a desire to bring out the resolution of the C natural to the ensuing B. Obviously it was far less trouble for the composer to jot down the shorthand version; if the performer wanted to demonstrate his virtuosity by packing more notes into the bar,

that was perfectly acceptable too, since the essentially harmonic function of the passage was not affected.

One of the most remarkable of such passages is to be found in Bach's Chromatic Fantasy, a work which clearly began life as an improvisation and in which the improvisatory element is deliberately preserved by Bach when he ceases to write specifically articulated notes and leaves us to deal as we like with this astonishing sequence of harmonies.

Ex. 18

The second chord of bar 5 is suspect, even in a context of such daring; it seems probable that by a slip of the quill Bach omitted a few accidentals and that he intended this harmony.

However, such textual speculation is irrelevant since the purpose of the example is to show a convention which was perfectly understood by performers of the time. Writing music by candle-light with quill-pens (using sand as blotting paper) was an arduous labour, and composers were glad to make use of any short cuts that ingenuity could devise. Mozart uses an even more drastic condensation in the coda of the C minor concerto (K.491) where we find four bars of arpeggios suddenly reduced to one note to the bar.

111

It is clearly ridiculous to break off the figuration in this way; the single dotted minims simply represent the outer extremities of a continuing pattern. An examination of the original manuscript reveals that the four bars in question are packed into the last inch and a half of the page and that it was physically impossible for Mozart to cram the notes into so confined a space unless he resorted to this expedient.

With such a tradition in mind, it is clear that any competent eighteenth-century keyboard-player would have realized, when he saw the sequence of chords in Ex. 19, that the one thing he would *not* play would be the notes as written. They would serve as a basis for some sort of arpeggio figuration whose precise disposition would be left to him.

Ex. 19

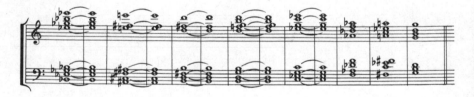

The abrupt change from flats to sharps in bar 3 looks a little strange, but apart from that we have here a sequence which could perfectly well appear in a Prelude by Bach or Handel (both of whom often used such condensed versions of essentially rapid figures) or one of their lesser contemporaries such as Krebs or Muffat. It comes as something of a jolt to realize that what we have before us is the stormiest section of the development in Beethoven's 'Waldstein' Sonata, op. 53. In essence, Beethoven is simply continuing a long-established convention, though to him the figuration has now become too important an aspect of the composition to be left to chance; what we find in the score (see Ex. 20) is a dramatic version of the harmonies in Ex. 19 whose frequent repetition has a positively battering effect.

Although the tradition of treating essentially harmonic sequences in this way extended back for some 200 years before Beethoven composed this sonata, its function was transformed in this context. The imposition of a positive rhythm, denying the performer the freedom of improvisation, created a totally new dramatic tension absent from either the Bach example (a

Ex. 20

contemplation of harmonic relationships) or the Mozart (a decoration thereof).

If we move forward a further step in the same direction we might arrive at the so-called 'Black-note' Study of Chopin, op. 10 No. 5. Reduced to its bare bones, the glittering right-hand part would consist of these chords:

What figuration Chopin chooses to decorate this framework is up to him; had he so wished he could have based the study on groups of four notes.

113

In fact the triplet figure he chose suits hand and keyboard particularly well, and a comparison with the chord-sequence above shows how strictly he keeps to a simple formula.

It might be said that here we are back in Vivaldi-land since to a large extent this figuration has been 'composed' by the keyboard just as Vivaldi's figuration was 'composed' by the violin. The Chopin studies are certainly far more demanding technically than Vivaldi concertos, but such a difference merely reflects the development of virtuosity that automatically came with the passage of time. The fundamental correlation of instrument and musical material remains the same, for while a pianist will derive a positively sensuous delight from the perfect disposition of Chopin's notes on the keyboard in relation to the hand, a violinist would find them a nightmare.

It would be wearisome to pursue this aspect of music in further detail; suffice it to say that a cello concerto, whether by Boccherini, Dvořák, Saint-Saëns or Shostakovich, will exploit those things which a cello does best; a piano concerto will not be the same in concept as a harpsichord concerto, nor will something written for flute be satisfactorily transferred to a clarinet. To this extent, and especially is this true of virtuoso works, Idiom and Medium are closely linked. How, then, is it that in a symphony we may well hear the same theme played by several different instruments at different times?

The full orchestra provides the composer with a rich palette of sound-colour which he will naturally wish to exploit; even so he will draw a clear line in his mind between themes which are susceptible to colour-variation for the sake of contrast and those whose coloration is integral. For instance the notoriously difficult horn solo that occurs near the beginning of Richard Strauss's *Till Eulenspiegel* would not readily transfer to any other instrument,[7] whereas the equally famous horn theme in the slow movement of Tchaikovsky's Fifth Symphony is entirely acceptable (even if different in colour) when he later gives it to the first violins.

Returning to my metaphor of the river, three main tributaries flowed into it in the course of the nineteenth-century: the remarkable dominance of the piano as a solo instrument, the emergence of the symphony orchestra as a

[7] He *develops* it on other instruments but never quotes it in its entirety.

permanent institution, and what I can only describe as the Wagnerian flood, which was to change not only the harmonic idiom of music but also its scale—in the sense of sheer size. Lengthy music in itself was not new, as the major religious works of Bach or the operas of Handel show readily enough; but such music was invariably divided into relatively short sections, arias, duets or choruses, complete in themselves. Beethoven significantly enlarged the span of his symphonies, concertos, quartets or sonatas, though still preserving the formula of four contrasting movements. Wagner elongated the span of his music to such a degree that a single act of an opera would last as long as an entire symphony of Beethoven. He aimed to abolish the set-piece aria of Italian opera which we find in Verdi even as late as Otello (1887); instead, he conceived opera in symphonic terms, the heart of the matter being in the orchestral pit rather than upon the stage. It was an approach to composition that was to have far-reaching effects, preparing the way for the symphonies of Mahler and Bruckner and even operas such as Berg's *Wozzeck* (1921) or *Lulu* (1929–35). Such a path could not be pursued indefinitely without leading to an impasse; a form of musical elephantiasis set in, Schoenberg's *Gurrelieder* (1900–11) being perhaps the ultimate manifestation beyond which it was impossible to go. It is scored for 4 piccolos, 4 flutes, 3 oboes, 2 cor anglais, 3 clarinets, 2 E flat clarinets, 2 bass-clarinets, 3 bassoons, 2 contra-bassoons, 10 horns, 4 small 'Wagner' tubas, 6 trumpets, 1 bass-trumpet, 1 alto-trombone, 4 tenor trombones, 1 bass-trombone, 1 contra-bass-trombone, 1 tuba, 6 timpani, a huge percussion section, 4 harps, celeste, a correspondingly large number of strings, 3 four-part male-voice choirs, an eight-part mixed choir, 5 solo singers and a narrator. No wonder the scoring and composition took some eleven years. Such works inevitably price themselves out of performance irrespective of their quality, even though special occasions such as the 1931 Leeds Festival may prompt a composer to make exceptional demands, as Walton did in *Belshazzar's Feast*.

In the twentieth century our river of music breaks up into a delta, largely caused by a sudden awareness that it was impossible to pursue a post-Wagnerian path any further. There was a spontaneous realization that a conscious solution needed to be found. Certain composers (Bartók, Vaughan Williams, Kodály, Sibelius, early Stravinsky) sought refuge in a folk-based idiom, exploiting national characteristics of melody in a more ambitious way than had been done previously in Slavonic Dances or Hungarian Rhapsodies. The use of folk-music in itself was nothing new, but its incorporation into large-scale symphonic conceptions was. Others, notably middle-period Stravinsky and Hindemith, divorced themselves from the nineteenth century by seeking a new partnership with the eighteenth, neo-classicism, as it came to be called. What might be termed the traditional stream of melody and harmony has gradually dried to a mere trickle, while a new source has emerged, 'Sound-sters' not Song-sters, starting with Varèse

(1885–1965) and leading on to Stockhausen, Boulez and the fascinating new sonorities opened up by electronics.

The stylistic divide which I have compared to a delta has been made more acute by the greatly increased awareness of the past that we now have and the sheer weight of material that lies behind us. Not only has a huge amount of music been written already, thus precluding the possibility of exploring those particular sound-combinations again, but through gramophone records we can experience the music of even remote eras as well as alien cultures. This was not always so, as the famous incident of Mendelssohn's re-discovery of Bach's St. Matthew Passion shows.[8] Today every composer knows only too well what his contemporaries are doing and the search for some individuality of language can easily drive him to ever more extreme experiment. There have always been changes of musical language; there is nearly as much difference between the style of Orlando Gibbons and Handel as there is between Brahms and Vaughan Williams. Inevitably, though, the pace of change has accelerated and the composer's task has never been so hard as it is now, when so many of the traditional resources have been used up.

[8] At the age of twenty he conducted the first performance given since Bach's death.

The River of Music

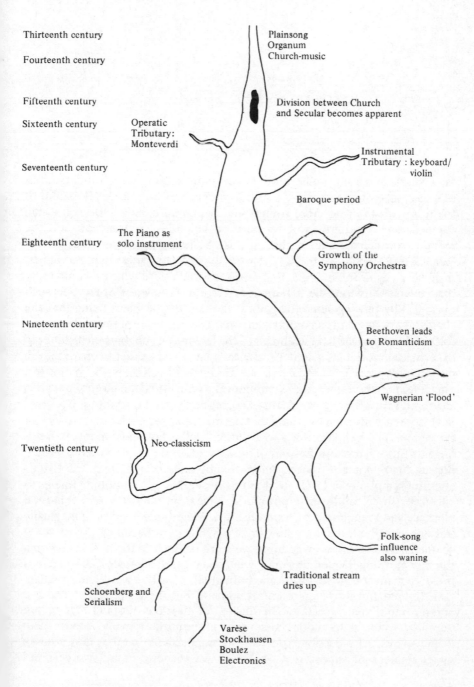

Thirteenth century

Fourteenth century

Fifteenth century

Sixteenth century

Seventeenth century

Eighteenth century

Nineteenth century

Twentieth century

Plainsong
Organum
Church-music

Division between Church
and Secular becomes apparent

Operatic
Tributary:
Monteverdi

Instrumental
Tributary : keyboard/
violin

Baroque period

The Piano as
solo instrument

Growth of the
Symphony Orchestra

Beethoven leads
to Romanticism

Wagnerian 'Flood'

Neo-classicism

Folk-song
influence
also waning

Traditional stream
dries up

Schoenberg and
Serialism

Varèse
Stockhausen
Boulez
Electronics

117

5　Purpose and Method

Having reached a stage where we have explored some of the fundamentals of music, including not only the sounds themselves but the development of the resources to bring those sounds into being, let us now move on to the composer and enquire into the purpose behind a composition and the method by which he achieves that purpose. Someone asked me the other day 'What is music actually *for*?' It is a harder question to answer than one at first imagines; a cynic might argue that music is valueless, to which I would reply that invaluable would be a fairer description. One must not evade such questions by playing semantic games, though, the problem being that the simple query demands a complex answer. The purposes of music are manifold; at the top of the list I would place the faculty that enables the listener to experience emotion at a higher plane than he would expect to encounter in everyday existence. The despair we share with Tchaikovsky in the last movement of his 'Pathétique' Symphony may not equal the intense pain of a shattered love-affair or the death of someone dearly loved, but it is a good deal more moving than anything that normally happens to us in the office or the home. The exhilaration and triumph of the last movement of Beethoven's Fifth Symphony is something we seldom if ever experience in real life, as for that matter is the happy exuberance of the finale of Bizet's youthful symphony in C. (Note that I have cited three symphonic finales to exemplify three totally different moods.) Next on the list would come the pleasure and stimulation of sound itself, whether voices echoing magically through a cathedral, an orchestra deploying its amazingly varied tone-colours, a solo violin re-awakening the spirit of Bach or the lark's song on a summer morning. Depending upon what you require of music so the order of preference must now vary with the individual. Myself, I would put intellectual stimulus far above mere entertainment, but there are those who ask nothing more than a catchy rhythm to set the toes tapping. There are 'top-line' listeners to whom melody is all-important, while others take delight in obscure pieces by little-known composers so that they may nourish secret feelings of superiority. So far as we respond at all, we respond inevitably to the purpose of the music, whether it be to soothe, to stimulate, to surprise, to challenge, to amuse, or to set us dancing.

The purpose of a work is largely conveyed by its title, though we may take it that a generic term, such as Symphony or Quartet, is multi-purpose while more specific definitions, such as Prelude, Fugue, Minuet or Caprice, channel our attention into one direction. A *reductio ad absurdum* will show you what I mean. Let us suppose for the moment a hypothetical nineteenth-century Russian composer called Chestikov. We know and like the few works of his that we have heard, an Overture called 'Kings and Pawns', a symphonic poem 'Source of the Volga' and a ballet-suite 'The Czar's Dream'. One day we see a performance of his piano concerto advertised; confident that it will be worth hearing we go to the concert. The soloist, Ivor Sorfinger, appears to tumultuous applause; the work begins. A huge and splendid orchestral tutti lasting eight minutes leads to the first piano entry; Sorfinger plays six chords and an arpeggio whereupon the orchestra takes over and plays for a further ten minutes; end of movement. Throughout the slow movement the piano part is confined to a left-hand accompaniment of great simplicity, above which various orchestral instruments extend sumptuous melodies; at the climax the soloist drops out completely. As for the last movement, it is all orchestra except for the final eight chords in which Sorfinger enthusiastically joins. It may seem a silly way to make a point, but however gorgeous Chestikov's melodies, however glorious the orchestral sound, such a work would inevitably leave the audience dissatisfied; led to expect a piano concerto they would feel deprived by the absence of any significant contribution from the soloist.

Let us now imagine the same work, this time billed as Chestikov's Symphony No. 1. No soloist enters but we see that there is a piano in the orchestra. 'That's unusual' the more knowledgeable members of the audience murmur to their friends, and try to think of a single nineteenth-century symphony that has a piano in the score. Ah yes, Berlioz did specify a piano as an alternative to the bells in the last movement of the *Symphonie Fantastique* but that was only as an undesirable option. We settle back and listen, wallowing in Chestikov's soaring themes and appreciating as we go the highly original splashes of pianistic colour in the rich score.[1] The identical music, a failure as a concerto, is hailed as a neglected masterwork under another name.

Titles are important then, but only insofar as they arouse expectation, telling us *how* to listen rather than *what* we should expect to hear. Works sharing a common title may be very different in substance and effect but the title tells us the purpose of the composition, whether it is an overture to *Macbeth*, the 'Gold and Silver Waltz' or 'Gruppen'.

---

[1] Stravinsky's use of a piano in his *Symphony in Three Movements* shows how effective it can be.

Purpose, then, is an integral part of the composer's original conception of a work; if he sets out to write a string quartet, the medium itself will be a stimulus for the musical material. We have already seen in the previous chapter how idiom and medium inter-react, but there is far more to composition than writing passages that lie well under the fingers. A composer must not only be able to imagine sound clearly, even complex combinations of many tone-colours, but he must also know how to organize them satisfactorily within the continuum of time. He does this partly by conscious manipulation of the material, partly by intuition. Some composers are clearly more intuitive than others; we hear a lot about Beethoven's sketch-books, those eloquent testaments to a long process of gestation, reworking themes from insignificant or trivial beginnings to sublime achievements. But what time did Mozart have for sketches when he wrote his last three great symphonies in a mere six weeks, what sketches did Schumann write for the Piano Quintet, composed and then copied in twenty days, or Dvořák for his Eighth symphony, composed between 6 and 23 September 1889? (In all fairness he did begin jotting down ideas for the work in August, but the creative juices seem to have flowed pretty freely once he committed himself to an actual score.) Such composers could not have had time for a detailed intellectual plan; instinct would lead them to shape a work satisfactorily, and one can sense that many of the happiest touches were literally inspirations of the moment, discovered at the actual point at which they occur. Now this does not mean that the intuitive composer need necessarily be deficient in what might be termed a feeling for musical architecture. To a composer of resource and experience the ground-plan of a movement is a relatively simple concept; it is the filling-in of the details that takes time. Obviously, the more intellectual challenge a work contains the longer its composition is likely to take. Even Bach, with his immeasurable skill in handling counterpoint, must have pored for many an hour over the intricate canons in the Musical Offering or the problems he deliberately set himself in the Art of Fugue, whereas many of the Preludes, being little more than decorations of a sequence of harmonies, could have been dashed off almost as quickly as the notes could be copied down.

It would be impossible to define the degrees of intuition and intellect involved in composition since they not only vary from composer to composer but also from work to work. The compositional process by which Schubert could write three exquisite songs in a single day would clearly be a different experience from writing the great String Quintet in C major, just as planting a window-box differs from cultivating a four-acre garden. Schubert is an interesting case in this respect since he had a certain *penchant* for putting pot-plants into the herbaceous border, to pursue the analogy. By this I mean that songs such as 'The Wanderer', 'The Trout' and 'Death and the Maiden' were transplanted into major instrumental works for which they were not originally designed. According to the accepted precepts of composition this was ill-advised since a song, by definition a complete entity, is unlikely to be suitable for development. As if tacitly admitting this, Schubert used them as themes for variations, which enabled him to preserve their integrity. In any event, such works are exceptional since Schubert's reason for incorporating songs into an instrumental context was almost certainly a desire to court a popularity inexplicably denied him. Only the songs were known (through Vogl's[2] advocacy), and Schubert must have felt that a song of proven popularity would help to 'sell' a chamber-work, rather on the 'book-of-the-film' principle beloved of publishers today.

There seems to me a real danger that too detailed an analysis of music may lead to misconceptions about the process of composition. I have been much impressed by Charles Rosen's penetrating study *The Classical Style*[3] in which he shows an almost frightening perceptivity about the subtlest relationships in music, both thematic and structural. As an instance I will quote his analysis of Mozart's Fantasia in C minor (K 475), a piece which I have played and discussed innumerable times without ever having seen it in these terms. According to Rosen it has six sections:

   I Tonic: C minor with the tonic weakened by immediate modulation going finally to B minor.
  II Dominant of the dominant: D major (since G major has been weakened, its dominant is used in its place).
 III Continuous modulation.
 IV Subdominant of the subdominant: B flat major (used as subdominant in place of F major, by analogy with section II).
  V Continuous modulation, affirmation of C minor.
 VI Tonic: C minor throughout. (p. 93)

As Rosen goes on to say,

> The symmetry is clear as is the relation of the form to the use of tonic, dominant and subdominant in [the] sonata. The music has the sound of improvisation and all the advantages of organized form: only in this way could it give such an impression of unity while sounding so rhapsodic.

The evidence is so convincingly presented that for a moment one is led to imagine Mozart seriously sitting down and planning a work whose second section should be in the 'dominant of the dominant' and whose fourth section should be in the 'subdominant of the subdominant'; furthermore, sections III and V, totally different in material, in tonality and in notation are supposedly slotted into an overall plan as complementary balances. However persuasive the analysis, I simply do not believe that Mozart worked in this way, though to be fair I am not completely sure that Rosen is implying that he did. It is my own belief that composers of the classical period had so inborn a sense of tonal relationships that they literally found their way into

---

[2] J. M. Vogl (1768–1840) the Austrian baritone who virtually came out of retirement to sing Schubert's songs.
[3] Published by Faber & Faber, 1971.

the proper key for a specific event rather than arriving at it by some such cerebral process as deciding to use the 'dominant of the dominant'. Similarly with form; there were no do-it-yourself charts of sonata form to which Mozart, Haydn or Beethoven complied. It was a handy structure to use precisely because it was adaptable and yet comprehensible. Once nineteenth-century theorists got their chilly grasp on it, they tried to freeze it into a semblance of rigidity, something which its greatest exponents would have regarded with scepticism and distaste.

I do not wish to give the impression that intuitive composers are inherently better at their job than those who are more intellectual. We do not know to what extent Beethoven was a special case owing to his deafness; would his method of work have seemed less laborious had he been able to hear? The curious thing is that his manuscripts show every sign of having been written at a great pace; it was the preliminary processes that seem to have taken the time. Brahms was another slow worker, while in the twentieth century composition has become so much more self-conscious a procedure that the prodigious output of eighteenth-century composers (often composing to a formula of sorts) is unlikely ever to be rivalled.

As always, any examples I choose must be highly selective, since every piece in existence could be analysed on the lines I propose. Let us therefore take a closer look at a few representative excerpts, considering them from the point of view of Purpose and Method. I begin with a little-known but wonderfully beautiful Prelude by Bach.

BACH: PRELUDE IN G MAJOR (BWV 902, 1)

Purpose: This is not what I have called a 'pattern' prelude since its style is essentially contrapuntal rather than harmonic. Bach's purpose is clearly to treat basically melodic ideas in such a way as to establish continually varying relationships between them. Sometimes one part will lead, another play a supporting role; even such supporting parts will contain an intrinsic interest that lifts them out of the category of mere accompaniment, *except*—but that is a surprise not to be anticipated . . . Let us examine the first two bars:

Notice that the right-hand tune in bar 1 becomes the left-hand tune in bar 2; similarly the left-hand tune in bar 1 becomes the right-hand tune in bar 2.

Which tune predominates? Neither, since both have equal claims to our attention. The Purpose is to display this equality of interest; the Method is to alternate the two strands of melody in this effortlessly graceful way, a dialogue so delicately poised that we hear two 'voices' without either of them disturbing the other.

In bar 3 it seems as though Bach has given up the intellectual challenge and allowed the right hand to take over the melodic lead:

but we are instantly proved wrong in this assumption by a beautifully placed echo in the left-hand in the very next bar.

I have deliberately omitted the right hand at this point since there is a trap we are supposed to fall into. If the melodic lines in bars 1 and 2 are interchangeable between the hands, we are not being wholly stupid if we assume it to be a game Bach will wish to continue. Apart from a mild and quite acceptable passing clash between G and F sharp it works perfectly well.

However, in Bach's eyes this has now become altogether too predictable a pattern.

What he does is far more subtle; bar 4 sees the introduction of a decorative shape which is in fact an inversion of a group that has already appeared in bar 1 (4th beat L.H.) and bar 2 (4th beat R.H.).

At this point sheer genius takes over from the height of mere craftsmanship. The left-hand phrase from bar 3 which I postulated as a probable right-hand for bar 4 (rightly rejected) now reappears in an unexpected place and is twice repeated, almost as though apologizing for having missed its entrance in the fourth bar.

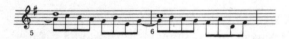

Against this we find an elegantly decorative counterpoint greatly extending the little inverted group I spoke of  and introducing a lovely rhythmic subtlety by arranging the notes so that they ascend in groups of five and three alternatively.

If we compare Bach's actual bar 6 with my proposed bar 4, we see the same quavers exactly; their significance has been marvellously changed, however, since they now represent the sharpest tension attained so far instead of a simple confirmation of what has gone before. Here is the implied harmony of 'my' version:

Thin gruel indeed compared to the rich spice of Bach's implied harmonization.

124

Within a couple of bars Bach has modulated to the dominant (D major) where he restates bars 1 and 2. The next bar (bar 11) exactly corresponds with bar 3.

We might therefore reasonably expect that bar 12 will correspond with bar 4; however, Bach has another subtle surprise for us, not only cancelling out the C sharp which was needed to establish D major but also introducing a new rhythmic element, a decorative triplet that he enjoys so much that he feels compelled to repeat it in the following bar.

And so the music goes on its elegant way, sometimes in two parts, sometimes three, sometimes four, but so designed that it flows without a

Ex. 21

perceptible break in its first twenty-eight bars. Bars 25–8 (Ex. 21) are particularly interesting, partly because several F naturals give a feeling that he is avoiding the predictable cadence into the dominant with some skill, partly because yet another pattern is introduced which is going to come to full flower in the second half of the prelude.

Now even the most cautious musical scholar would feel confident about laying a substantial bet as to what should follow. According to a hallowed convention the second half of a formal prelude of this type ought inevitably to begin with an exact duplication of the opening, transposed into the dominant. It was in every sense the 'done' thing.

Only if we are aware of this convention will we appreciate the extraordinary surprise Bach now has for us. You will remember that I said earlier that even supporting parts had a melodic interest *except*—and then broke off. It's important to have been aware of this, since up to this point the music has been conceived and presented as counterpoint throughout. Contrary to all precedent, Bach now changes the rules of the game; not only does he deny expectation by refusing to duplicate the opening bars, but he alters the concept of the piece, transforming it into a right-hand tune with a clearly subordinate left-hand accompaniment.

Having apparently established this new convention he immediately contradicts it by turning bar 30 into a two-part Invention*; bar 31 returns to melody-cum-accompaniment (transposing bar 29 above into A minor), and then he launches into an extravagantly decorated passage of two-part writing touching on various keys (E minor, A minor, G major, C major) before returning victoriously to the long-deferred reprise of the opening phrase, which he re-introduces in the Tonic key of G exactly as it was in bar 1. This unorthodox excursion has taken some twelve bars, which stem, if anything, from fragments of bars 26–7, but which are so free that they can legitimately be regarded as entirely new material. The Purpose was to foil expectation; the Method, to change the established style of the piece and to introduce new themes.

In a way, the prelude could be said to show a premonition of sonata form

126

the first twenty-eight bars being an Exposition, the central surprise section serving as a Development while bars 41–56 behave as a classic Recapitulation. It is worth stressing that the music is easy and agreeable to listen to; all the more profound pleasures to be derived from it are dependent on the listener's ability to appreciate the subtle interchange between the various parts as well as the unorthodoxy of the second half.

MOZART: PIANO SONATA IN C, K.309(1777) FIRST MOVEMENT

This sonata, at first glance something of a lightweight, is full of examples of Mozart's ingenunity in handling basically conventional ideas. The Purpose is clearly to produce an elegantly balanced structure based on sonata-form principles; the Method is to exploit contrasts of texture and volume and to lead us into supposing we can anticipate what is going to happen next —whereupon Mozart does something different . . .

Since the sonata is in C major, he feels it essential to establish the key unequivocally.

This barely disguised bugle-call, doh-soh-me-doh, is positive and masculine; it is instantly followed by a yielding, feminine response (Ex. 22) that serves to remind us of the essentially operatic nature of so much of Mozart's thought. Where the opening phrase commands, this beseeches.

Ex. 22

As you can see, the peremptory opening command reappears in bar 8; but notice how skilfully Mozart interpolates C sharps into bars 3, 6 and 7, a literal symbol of 'resistance' (a heroine's resistance?) to the dominance of C major. Again we have the pleading response, this time made more agitated by the addition of a few extra notes, followed by two bars which surely are eloquent of the hand-wringing anguish expected of distraught maidens.

Now the dynamics (louds and softs) so far have been clearly defined and are a significant factor in causing me to look on the music as a miniature opera by implication even if Mozart tells us that it is a piano sonata.

Bars 1–2 loud (Male)

　　　　　　　　　Bars 3–7 soft (Female)

Bars 8–9 loud (Male)

　　　　　　　　　Bars 10–12 soft (Female)

　　　　　　　　　Bars 13–14 intensified but still poignant.

It would be unkind to point out how much more long-winded the female appears to be though I feel Mozart would have been delighted by the idea.

Now, however, the drama quickens, as is clearly shown by the much closer alternation of dynamics. (I quote only the right-hand since the accompaniment is entirely subsidiary at this point.)

Continuing my little operatic fantasy, there is no doubting the heightened tension caused by these close juxtapositions of *f* and *p*. It is not hard to imagine a libretto of sorts:

GIRL:	Mercy!	Mercy!	—be still my trembling
Bar 15	16	17	
MAN: Get thee hence!	Get thee hence!		

GIRL: heart. Have pity!	Have pity!	—how can you be so	cruel?
18	19	20	21
MAN: Out I say!	Out I say!		

128

At which point she appears to rush upstairs!

If this is not strictly speaking analysis it is certainly 'interpretation'; if it seems intolerably frivolous I would call to my defence Mozart himself who, in an unfinished piano sonata, (K372a) actually wrote in the names of his sister-in-law and his wife on the manuscript, as though the piano were indeed singing an aria.

So - phie,   Con - stan - ze

Let us return to a more conventional approach. All that I have quoted so far would be classified as First Subject material despite its manifest duality. At bar 21 we reach a clearly recognizable Bridge Passage which in due course modulates into G, ending on a chord that might be mistaken for D major

but which in proper terms is indeed the dominant of the dominant. (How dull it all sounds after my operatic escapade!) Bars 33–4 establish a gently rocking accompaniment in the left-hand above which the Second Subject duly appears. Now apart from considerations of pitch, this too could certainly be thought of in operatic terms. I would not press the point if it were not for subsequent events, for once again we find what would otherwise be somewhat inexplicable interruptions. I begin this next quotation at bar 39, the previous 4 bars having been virtually identical, apart from a subtle difference of stress between ♪♪ ⅞ and ♪♪ .

Ex. 23

Bars 43 and 44 are reinforced with angrily dissonant semiquavers in the left-hand, quite different from the bland accompaniment in the preceding bars, proof it seems to me that an operatic analogy is again valid. Here, surely, is the angry male interrupting, here in bar 45 is the fluttering response of the heroine; bars 48 and 49 give every indication of a hammer-and-tongs argument with the accents thrown onto all the wrong beats, while the tense dissonance in bar 50, complete with thumping chords in the left-hand, is clearly the climax of the quarrel. The Codetta bears me out, bars 54 and 55 being placatory, bars 56–8 irate.

If the Exposition of this sonata appears to 'aspire towards the condition' of opera, the Development is a marvellous fusion of the essential principles of a sonata-form movement with a continuing operatic style. Just as Bach had a notable surprise for us after the double bar in his Prelude, so Mozart confounds expectation. Having just heard a very positive cadence in G major in bar 58, we have good cause to expect a continuation in that key; orthodoxy would demand this as the next move.

This is precisely why Mozart does not play this all too predictable card; instead he plunges us unexpectedly into G minor.

If we have absorbed the material of the Exposition properly (something the traditional repeat should have made easier for us) we should at this point be able to make a reasonably intelligent guess at what *ought* to come next: something like this perhaps:

In other words a fair match to bars 3–7.

What we get is a double surprise, not just the plunge into G minor but an unprecedented extension of the 'male' phrase, as though the minor key had destroyed all his arrogance.

In operatic terms this might easily be interpreted in two ways, as high drama or as comedy. Either it is our original male taking an even more severe attitude in bars 59–60 with our heroine cowering before his wrath in bars 61–2, or it is perhaps the sort of situation we might find in Figaro with the Count confronting Cherubino and Susanna with some incriminating evidence:

Bars 59–69 COUNT. Here's the scarf Sir!
Bars 61–2 { SUSANNA What shall we do?
{ CHERUBINO What shall we do?

Without words or a specific dramatic situation there is an ambivalence about the phrase that the performer must resolve for himself. Considering it in purely musical and instrumental terms provides a solution, for then all we have to do is to appreciate the surprise and the ingenuity of the extension. The dramatic function of Form is admirably illustrated, since the extension is only significant when compared to previous versions; but there is another surprise for us, a totally new theme, the most expressive we have had so far.

Reverting to my hypothetical opera, this is unquestionably the feminine character and again it could be serious or mock serious, since comedy is often a parody of tragedy. In instrumental terms, though, the music has an undeniable pathos; we should respond not only to its unexpectedness as a formal innovation but also to its emotional quality. It is immediately followed by a repetition of the masculine phrase, this time in D minor.

Once again we have a marvellous instance of the way form can be used as a vital element in the creation of surprise. Bars 59–62 have conditioned us to expect that if we hear the initial phrase in a *minor* key it will be extended by two further bars. In consequence we now expect this sequel.

Instead Mozart again heightens the emotional tension by moving immediately to the 'new' emotional rejoinder, intensifying it by the addition of extra notes and by widening the gap between the hands.

There follows a veritable storm in which the opening phrase of the sonata, initially so clear-cut in its delineation of a pure C major chord, is distorted into angular shapes above continually shifting harmonies. This is true development in that it totally changes the character of the music. The Purpose—to shed new light on a theme of rigid conformity; the Method—to distort its basic shape and to put four harmonies where initially there was only one.

Ex. 24

So intense is the fury unleashed in this outburst that after the first two phrases there is no longer time to spit out the minim octaves, emphatic though they may be; instead, Mozart twice repeats the suffix (bars 77–8) before exploding into the archetypal crisis chord, the diminished 7th (bars 79–81), whose angry progress is halted by a powerful cadence. We seem to have travelled a long way in terms of tonality, but whether by instinct or design, Mozart has actually brought us to A minor, the so-called relative minor to the proper key of the sonata, C major, since they share a common key-signature. Unexpectedly he interpolates the codetta from the Exposition (originally bars 54–8) with their alternation of pleading and anger made the more dramatic by transposition to a minor key.

(Before we move on, savour the dissonances marked with a cross in bars 83–4; how eloquently they express pathos.)

Back comes the initial theme, still in the minor version that has prevailed throughout the Development. This time it is followed by the two-bar extension, as in bars 59–62 (see page 131) with the same contrast of *f, p, pp*. To emphasize the (by now) critical need to restore the original tonality, Mozart repeats the pattern, adjusting the phrase so that in effect it becomes a dominant 7th ()—always a safe route home to the Tonic.

It is worth pointing out that this is the first and only time that the extended version (bars 59–62) appears twice consecutively, it being yet another structural change of significance.

We are now safely back on course with the Recapitulation and can afford to sit back and relax—or so we may assume. For seven bars precisely Mozart allows us this indulgence before jerking us back to attention by plunging us once more into the minor—C minor this time, the first appearance of a key especially calculated to upset the basic tonality of the movement. The response is touchingly emotional, the operatic implications once again being manifest in a phrase that melts the heart.

Ex. 25

From here on the differences are of detail rather than substance and those who wish to study them will be able to identify them easily enough without guidance from me. I cannot leave the movement, though, without stressing that to the casual listener this will seem a rather uneventful, even conventional eighteenth-century piano piece lacking the drama we find in Beethoven or the Romantics. In fact, as we have seen, it is *full* of drama, a miniature opera in which every move is skilfully plotted so as to bring us continual surprises. Am I therefore suggesting that before committing a note to paper Mozart prepared a sort of chart?

Bars	1–2	C major–*f*
„	3–7	Contrast. C sharps possibly to disorient tonality?
„	8–9	Repeat 1–2
„	10–14	Extend contrast.
„	15–21	Alternations of sub-dominant and tonic: close up contrasts to increase tension?
„	21–32	Must get into dominant somehow: take time though: spin out with scales.

The idea becomes more laughable the more one pursues it; this may be how examinations are passed, but it certainly is not how compositions are written. Yet I am confident that as he wrote it Mozart was acutely aware of the precise placing of every phrase, taking a keen delight in outwitting a potential audience by continually doing the unexpected. Such diversions take place because they seem right at the time, not because they have been planned in advance. For instance the sudden appearance of the initial phrase in the minor instead of the major at bar 101 would not have happened but for a retrospective glance at its several entries in various minor keys during the Development. The 'long-term planning' argument would presumably suggest that he put the theme into the minor at the start of the Development (bar 59) in order to prepare the listener for its appearance in the Tonic minor forty-two bars later, a contention I cannot believe.

Needless to say my entire operatic analogy is sheer fantasy, yet it accurately reflects the style of the movement, translating its inherent drama into more comprehensible terms than conventional analysis would be likely to do. It is an approach that might not get you through an O-level exam though it should considerably enhance both your understanding and enjoyment of the music. My next example enters a very different world.

BEETHOVEN: PIANO CONCERTO No. 4 IN G. Op. 58
Slow movement—*Andante con moto*. (N.B. not *Adagio* or *Largo*.)

Purpose: To write a very special slow movement whose content will symbolize the power of inner contemplation in overcoming aggression. Also a possible symbol of the isolation brought about by deafness.

Method: The juxtaposition of opposites; starkly aggressive unisons in strings (emphasized by the absence of harmony and the refusal to employ any other orchestral colour) as opposed to contemplative harmony supporting an expressive melodic line in solo piano part. Strings gradually reduced to silence in face of the soft answer that turneth away wrath.

If the Mozart movement we have just explored is a superb example of what might be termed spontaneous composition guided by an instinctive feeling for form, here as a contrast we have a movement that must have been planned as an entity from the start. The scheme is so clearly defined that it must have appeared to Beethoven as a vision; the drama is not quasi-operatic as Mozart's was, but quasi-balletic. By this I naturally do not mean that Beethoven visualized it as a ballet, but rather that it has the ritual quality of dance, dance used as a vehicle to express feelings bordering on a religious experience. As soon as one tries to be specific, to identify the 'ballet' as Job steadfast against adversity or Christ in the wilderness, the analogy crumbles; nevertheless, it is impossible to hear the movement without realizing that it must in some way be *about* something other than pure music. The word Concerto is derived from *concertare*, 'to strive with', an implication of conflict. Normally the soloist is a hero-figure conquering (literally in some concertos!) by force of arms. In this case the victory, if such it be, is spiritual. I find it almost incredible that a respected music-critic, A. E. F. Dickinson, should, in an entire book devoted to Beethoven, describe this movement as 'a witty dialogue between the strings and piano, the strings in ruthless unison, the piano seductive and Mendelssohn [*sic*]'.[4] Can musical perceptions really have altered so much since 1941 that this movement was ever thought 'witty'? Liszt was a good deal nearer the mark when he described it as Orpheus taming the wild beasts with his music, but even then the analogy suggests too direct a conflict. The true magic of this movement surely lies in the way the soloist withdraws into so private a world that he seems totally oblivious of the aggressive utterances of the orchestra.

The first five bars consist of a tough uncompromising statement given out by all the strings in unison. It is marked *f* and *sempre staccato*, an injunction that suggests not the light-footed steps of a ballerina but the incisive stentorian bark of a dictator in commanding mood.

(doubled at an octave and two octaves below)

As musical material goes, this invites development; by way of experiment let us try to develop it and see what happens. Suppose for the moment that a composer (not Beethoven) had hit upon this as an opening; suppose also that he had got as far as seeing the imaginative possibilities of giving the soloist a quiet entry. Almost certainly he would have felt the need to link this in some way, perhaps taking the last descending phrase and bending it to the soloist's will.

Ex. 26

[4] *Beethoven* (Nelson, 1941).

This is a tolerably convincing forgery; let us take its good points first. It begins with an imitation of the previous string phrase, albeit changed in dynamic (*p* instead of *f*) and character (counterpoint instead of unison). Bar 2 introduces the automatic suspense of a diminished 7th while cellos and basses mutter uneasy recollections of the opening rhythm. Bar 3 begins a modulation which progresses via G minor (bar 4) and a dominant 7th on B flat (bar 5) to the new key of E flat major—quite a shift from the E minor with which the music began. Bars 6 to 8 bring a solo version of the original opening, hovering interestingly between E flat major and E flat minor, with contrapuntal imitations between piano and woodwind extending through bars 9 to 10. The upward rising chromatic scale that in due course drags us out of E flat and back into the original key of E minor serves as a counterbalance to the descending scale of bar 5 which had served the exactly opposite purpose. The orchestral part throughout acts as a reminder of the original material, preventing the soloist from wandering too far into flights of fancy.

If we start to look for faults, the most glaring one is that this is palpably a Development rather than an Exposition. The shift to E flat, while convincing enough in the abstract, happens far too soon for comfort, while the imitative counterpoint in the woodwind is somewhat laboured. All the same, it's a feasible treatment, especially if it were to occur in the middle of the movement rather than on the first page.

Before we turn to Beethoven's own inspired solution let us try one more supposition; this time why not allow the soloist to pick up the gauntlet and fling it back in the orchestra's face? Having heard their challenge let him answer in ringing tones. He takes over their last three notes:

There is a certain inevitability about the suggested orchestral response as the stone-throwing begins in earnest. (I am reminded of the Brahms Piano Concerto No. 1.)

Now a crucial factor in the genesis of Beethoven's movement was that the piano he was writing for was literally incapable of making the sort of challenge I have just postulated. Such a response would have been self-defeating, a confession of impotence. In the entire first movement the direction *ff* appears only eleven times, mostly on single note runs where it indicates intensity rather than volume. The first physical show-down between piano and orchestra occurs in the Fifth concerto which was written for a different instrument, a new grand that came into Beethoven's possession in 1807. Even with his defective hearing he was able to size up its potential. In the Fourth Concerto it was politic to turn the other cheek in the event of a confrontation. From this purely mechanical consideration emerged the truly wonderful inspiration that has been handed down to us. That aggressive opening phrase from the orchestra is neither commented upon (as in my first hypothesis) nor contested (as in my second.) It is quite simply disregarded. In a rapt contemplation that verges towards mysticism the pianist conjures these magical chords from the keyboard.

Ex. 27

The use of the word 'magical' may leave the reader mildly baffled; what is so magical about this really rather ordinary progression of harmonies? The answer lies partly in their context. One should remember that this comes after a first movement in which there have been a multitude of notes in the bar, especially in its closing stages. Not only have we recently experienced the cadenza, with the inevitable virtuosity it entails, but also the final affirmations of G major from the orchestra, above which the pianist has extended curtains of scales. The impact of the slow movement is two-fold then, not just the drama implicit in the music itself, but the contrast with what has gone before.

Beautiful though the pianist's first phrase may be, the orchestra remains unaffected. Another angry statement breaks the spell, this time introducing C sharps so as to shift into D major. The pianist responds as before; this time he is not even allowed to finish before the strings break in with yet another interruption. Though still marked *f* and *sempre staccato*, something has happened to weaken their resolve, since their phrase is shortened from its previous five-bar length to two bars and a note. It evokes the gentlest of responses.

The tender warmth of harmonies such as these makes a wonderful contrast to the stark unisons in the orchestra, gestures of benediction against which the mailed fist falters. Two-bar phrases in the orchestra are reduced to two-note phrases, *f* becomes *p*, *sempre staccato* becomes *sempre diminuendo*. At last the strings are reduced to a single plucked note—at which moment a miracle of invention occurs. The most notable feature in the piano part up to this point has been control, a refusal to be baited into any direct response to the aggression of the orchestra. But now that that aggression has at last been stilled, now that this spiritual victory has been won, the control breaks down. The restrained chords give way to a phrase whose romantic eloquence looks forward to Chopin, as though tears flood out in sheer relief that the battle of wills is over.

Ex. 28

A brief cadenza more like cries of lamentation than a display of finger dexterity leads to the final bars, in which a reconciliation of sorts takes place even though grief is not dispelled. It is a movement that is totally unforgettable in its impact, Classic in its simplicity, Romantic in its conception. Let us move into the twentieth century.

DEBUSSY: VOILES (PRELUDES BOOK 1, No. 2)

Purpose: Tone-painting akin to Impressionism; the depiction of heat, languour, the gentle movement of a small sailing-boat, a sudden gust of breeze, 'going about', the splash of water against the bow.

Method: A nebulous absence of tonal definition brought about by using whole-tone scale: extremely subtle use of piano tone-colour constantly suggesting orchestral sound: avoidance of conventional pianistic figuration: considerable flexibility of tempo and avoidance of any strict rhythmic pulse.

Debussy's directions at the start of this Prelude read, 'Dans un rhythme sans rigeur et caressant', an instruction which puts me in mind of a wonderful piece by Froberger (1616–67), a *Tombeau* (literally 'Tombstone' but perhaps better translated as Epitaph), written as a memorial to a friend called Blancheroche who fell drunken down a staircase to an untimely end. Froberger said that his piece 'se joue fort lentement à la discretion sans observer aucune mesure'—that it should be played 'very slowly with freedom without observing any strict beat'. I simply mention this to show that expressive keyboard playing was not in itself anything new. What was new was Debussy's treatment of the piano as a surrogate orchestra; admittedly one often hears suggestions of orchestral sound in piano music from Haydn's day onwards, but the writing remains a keyboard conception. The orchestral paraphrases of Liszt are essentially pianistic, and though he often suggests drum-rolls, trumpet-calls or the brilliance of flutes and piccolos, it is done in the manner of one who says 'Look how splendidly I can imitate the orchestra', an attitude which paradoxically places the piano at a disadvantage in comparison to the real article. Debussy's approach is different since he is a master at inventing sonorities that one can mentally translate into orchestral colour while at the same time knowing that to do so would be a loss rather than a gain. His exploitation of the special haze that can be produced by imaginative pedalling is unequalled, as is his cultivation of the subtlest nuances of quiet tone. When Liszt writes orchestrally for piano he tends to go for big sounds, the thunder of drums, the blare of brass, the shrill voice of the woodwind or the sustained shimmer of strings tremolando. Debussy suggests low flutes, muted strings, soft pizzicato basses, quiet horns, seductive harp ripples. His curiously oblique harmony is admirably illustrated by almost every phrase in this evocative Prelude, never more subtly than in the haunting phrase with which he begins (see Ex. 29).

Before examining this in any detail let us try putting it into conventional harmonic terms—E major seems the obvious alternative.

p très doux   *p*   *più p*

Ex. 29

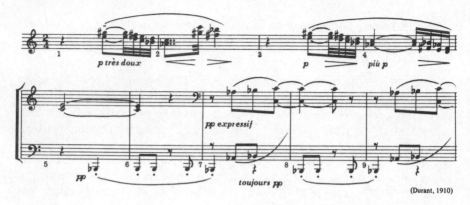

(Durant, 1910)

The loss of character is extraordinary; it is like a bad drawing as opposed to an exquisite water-colour. It might be tolerable on a pair of clarinets who could breathe a little life into the stagnant notes, but on the piano it is thin and inadequate. Yet turn back to Debussy's version and we find a sound that is so *right* for the piano that it is unthinkable that it could be as satisfying on flutes, oboes, clarinets or violins. Only the piano can envelop the sound in a soft haze.

If we turn our attention to the quiet repeated B flats low in the bass, every orchestral alternative is slightly wrong. There is certainly a suggestion of soft timpani beats but the pitch is too low; on the other hand a bass drum could not define the note with any exactitude. Pizzicato cellos could not descend so low, C being their bottom note; a pizzicato double bass is about the nearest but it would lack the bell-like resonance of the piano in this area. A harp? Possible, but we would be too aware of the string being plucked, whereas a pianist can produce the note almost without impact. It is a fusion of drum, of bell, of harp, of pizzicato bass, yet if one were to mix all these ingredients the sound would be disproportionately loud. Here then is a paradox, music that appears to be conceived in orchestral terms but which, on further thought, shows itself to be untranslatable; only the piano can produce the right sounds.

One of the secrets lies in Debussy's spacing of sound. Those strangely bare octaves in bars 7 to 9 (actually 7–14 if I quoted the whole piece) have a completely different timbre from the almost inaudible dabs of B flat in the bass or the floating thirds which he re-introduces above them. Instead of blending sound, he separates it, each strand having not only an individual content but a special and distinctive tone-colour.

In due course the bare octaves of the central part are raised an octave and enriched with whole-tone harmony (Ex. 30).

142

Ex. 30

To clarify the picture I have laid out the music on three staves*, enabling us to see the components, each having a positive individuality. When Bach writes three part counterpoint, the melodic threads produce harmony; here, though, we might say that Debussy is using harmony to produce counterpoint, even if the bass is static and the central part merely repetition. It is these very characteristics that give the music its feeling of stillness, a boat barely moving on a day when the sun is hot and there is little or no breeze. If the music seems to be getting nowhere it simply matches the yacht.

The ingenuity of Debussy's 'scoring' for the piano demands extreme sensitivity from the performer. In the following example we find a nice problem of touch; the sustained B flats in the bass force one to use the pedal, leading to something of a harmonic blur; yet the ascending whole-tone scale is marked staccato, a suggestion of drops of water, while the little flutters above are written in such a way as to suggest a dialogue of sorts, such as might occur between oboe and flute. Somehow a considerable variation of tone-colour needs to be found within a very narrow range of soft dynamics. This is how Debussy writes it:

Ex. 31

Again it is helpful to open up the score to see what is actually involved.

Ex. 32

Imagine the top line as a flute-part, line two as an oboe, and the third line as a harp perhaps duplicated by violins pizzicato (*pp*) on the two ascending scales and then by a solo violin (muted) in bars 3 and 4.[5] Looked at in this way the music is clearly counterpoint, yet the effect is a wash of harmony whose components merge by some alchemy. Incidentally, I wonder whether the figures in the top two parts of the third bar of this example represent gulls, the pattern of the notes being very similar to Benjamin Britten's undeniable gull-screech at the start of the first Sea Interlude from *Peter Grimes*.

The notation is very different but the effect is surprisingly similar.

In the whole course of Debussy's languorous Prelude there is only one climax, a passage which seems to me clearly to describe a sudden gust of breeze, the boom swinging out widely, taking the previously slack sail with it, and the helmsman 'going about' to go on another tack (bars 42–4). The wind drops almost instantly but for a while the boat dips and bobs on the water as gentle wavelets slap the bow. The music is so descriptive in every detail that I regard it as sheer perversity to argue (as has been suggested) that the title might mean 'Veils' instead of 'Sails'. The word 'Voiles' may be ambiguous but the music certainly is not. However, let us move from intuition and speculation to factual evidence; for my final example of Purpose and Method I turn to a contemporary work in which the composer himself has given us a detailed insight into what he calls his 'artistic kitchen'.

ANDRZEJ PANUFNIK: SINFONIA DI SFERE (SYMPHONY OF SPHERES, 1974–5)

I was present at the première of this symphony in London on 13 April 1976 and found it an exhilarating and inspiring occasion. The work received an ovation, and I remember a leading music critic remarking to me that it was indeed unusual to find a major new composition being greeted with such a genuinely emotional and enthusiastic response. In other words as a tonal experience the symphony unquestionably communicates directly to the audience. If at this stage you begin to wonder if there is any value in reading about music that you may not in fact have heard so far, be of good heart for the insight into the creative mind that Panufnik himself provides is something of a revelation. Since his name is scarcely as familiar as Bach, Mozart, Beethoven or Debussy a brief biographical sketch may be forgiven.

[5] I still make the reservation that this is essentially piano music and that such intrumentation, though apt, would destroy the effect.

Born in Poland in 1914, Panufnik was to become acknowledged in his own country as a composer of the very first rank. The political pressures of a Communist regime proved intolerable to him, however, though he had survived the horrors of the Warsaw holocaust and was in the deepest sense a true patriot. In 1954 he fled from Poland, coming to England with nothing but a suitcase full of compositions. He became conductor of the City of Birmingham orchestra but after two years relinquished the post so as to devote himself entirely to composition. He has written a piano concerto, a violin concerto, a number of orchestral pieces, sundry short works and a remarkable sequence of symphonies, each having a descriptive title rather than a number. These titles to a certain extent speak for themselves: *Sinfonia Rustica, Sinfonia Elegiaca, Sinfonia Sacra, Sinfonia Concertante, Sinfonia di Sfere* and, most recently, a newly coined word, *Metasinfonie*, fusing the idea of Metamorphosis and Symphony together.

The reason I choose to discuss the *Sinfonie di Sfere* as my final example in this chapter is because Panufnik's procedures are so fascinating in detail and so well documented by the composer himself. It is interesting, though, that he specifically asks that if a detailed programme-note be included at a performance of this symphony, it should not be read until *after* the work has been played; music first, analysis afterwards. However, I hope he will forgive me if, for the purposes of this chapter, I use his description of the process by which a remarkable work was brought into being.

Purpose: To write a work that would reflect in musical terms a sense of geometrical pattern and order, music which indirectly resembled the geometric symbolism of ancient temples and in particular the ritual geometric patterns used in early civilizations to promote meditation, patterns painted on tiles or walls or even drawn in the sand; the most significant and all-pervading figure to be the sphere, coupled with the number SIX.

Method: The meticulous planning of this work before a single note was actually committed to score is something that makes one think of an architect's blue-print. (Question: is a blue-print a picture, and if not why not?) Indeed Panufnik himself draws the analogy: 'If architecture can be described as frozen music, then this symphony could be said to be unfrozen architecture.' The starting point from which all else stems is a simple pattern of three spheres, each with a smaller concentric sphere within.

Panufnik visualized the symphony as a sort of journey through the three spheres, ascending through Sphere I to Sphere III. (see Spheres, fig. 1). Although music is normally (and properly) regarded as a temporal rather than a spatial art-form, he wanted to search for a new dimension of space through musical experience, a gradual penetration into what he describes as the 'soul' and the 'body' of the spheres, the 'soul' being the poetic content and the contemplative thought lying behind the notes, the 'body' being the

Spheres, fig. 1

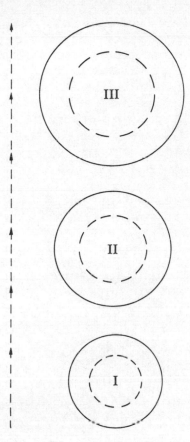

'chain of altering and recurrent feelings experienced through the framework of the musical material'.

Now I have already mentioned that the number SIX is also of great significance in this work, a number chosen for its unique mathematical properties:

$$1 \times 2 \times 3 = 6: 1 + 2 + 3 = 6: 2 \times 3 = 6: 3 + 3 = 6: 2 + 2 + 2 = 6.$$

These properties will be a constant, affecting all the basic materials of the work, rhythm, melody and harmony. Panufnik therefore decided to use six thematic groups disposed as shown in Spheres, fig. 2.

Seen this way the upper portion of each sphere is clearly the equivalent to a classical Recapitulation, repeating the lower portion after an intervention of time. The central subsidiary spheres however are not a Development but an Exposition of new material; as if to underline the essentially classical

147

Spheres, fig. 2

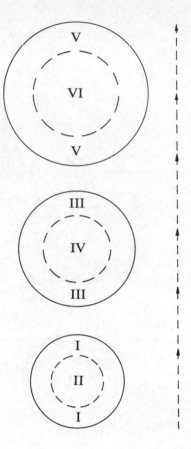

nature of the structure these subsidiary spheres are themselves repeated so that the 'journey' passes through 12 (2 × 6) phases in all.

```
↑      V
|      VI
|      VI
|      V
|
↑      III
|      IV
|      IV
|      III
|
↑      I
|      II
|      II
|      I
```

With this basic plan conceived, Panufnik next planned a more detailed exploration of the rhythmic melodic and harmonic aspects of the music, still relating to the number SIX. First he assessed some rhythmic possibilities.

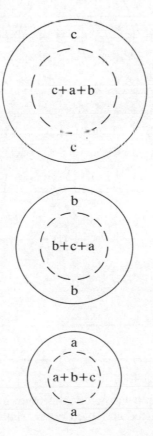

The most fruitful of these on consideration proved to be the first four equations, the first two being sufficiently alike to be coupled together. Panufnik decided to allocate Rhythm *a* to Sphere I, Rhythm *b* to Sphere II and Rhythm *c* to Sphere III.

Spheres, fig. 3

149

The inner spheres would contain three different permutations, thus providing both variety and unity since all sections are now inter-related. Running exactly in parallel with this rhythmic scheme he planned a comparable organization of notes, using a triad (3-note chord) with its two inversions.

By permutating these notes with great ingenuity Panufnik was able to produce SIX different horizontal lines of notes (not really 'melodies'), as well as what he calls SIX 'mixed' triads—combinations of notes from *a, b* and *c*. These he disposed of in an exactly similar way to the rhythmic patterns he had already decided upon (see Spheres, fig. 4).

Spheres, fig. 4 Rhythm   'Linear'
       Pattern   Pattern

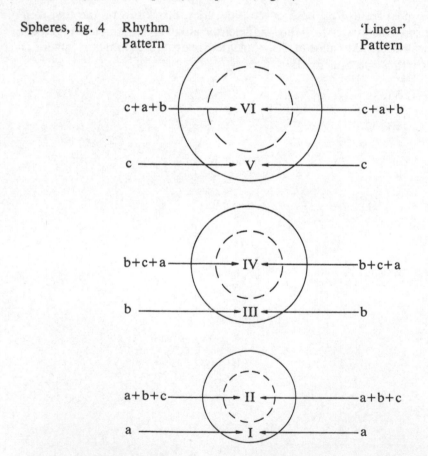

(Remember, though, that if we include the inherent repetitions each internal sphere is experienced twice and each outer 'rim' duplicated at the top.)

When he came to the Sphere of Harmony, Panufnik decided to use SIX chords of SIX notes; they are actually spelt out on the piano at the start of the coda near the end of the symphony, a fusion of essential elements as significant in its own musical language as the repetitions of an E flat major chord that we find at the end of Beethoven's Eroica symphony. Here are Panufnik's chords.

It will be seen that the groups of three chords are linked by stepping stones, notes common to chords 1–2, 2–3, 4–5, 5–6. Further, the chords in group A contain all 12 (2 × 6) semitones, as do the notes in group B.

By subjecting these harmonies to various procedures of transposition, breaking them into chains of intervals related to factors and fractions of SIX, Panufnik finds all the material he needs for the entire symphony. But other spheres of the music are similarly organized; for instance the dynamics are symmetrically planned so that the repetitions within the inner spheres show a reversal of loud and soft, while the dynamics on the two outer 'rims' of each sphere are also reversed (see Spheres, fig. 5).

Here, then, is a plan in which it seems nothing has been left to chance, an attitude of mind on the composer's part which may seem abhorrent to those romantic listeners who imagine all music to be a reflection of emotional experience, usually of an autobiographical nature. Yet the effect in performance is dramatic and exciting, especially in the brilliant way in which he uses three groups of four drums (12 = 2 × 6) placed at the left, the centre and the right of the orchestra. They communicate rhythmic messages to each other in a way that can be instantly comprehended by anyone who has ever seen John Wayne listening to Apache war-drums or Stewart Grainger sweating it out in the African jungle as the native drummers beat out their tribal morse code.

Now while it is true that composers of today have a tendency to intellectualize their music, quite often using extra-musical concepts as the basis for a composition,[6] it is quite mistaken to assume that this is an attitude exclusive to our century. The geometric plan of Panufnik's work is only different in degree from the controls exercised by composers as early as Machaut in the

---

[6] The Brazilian Villa-Lobos (1887–1959) actually composed a piece on the basis of a graph formed from the skyline of New York.

Spheres, fig. 5

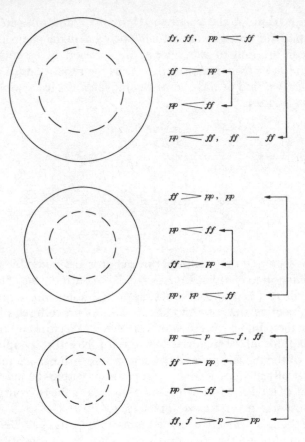

fourteenth century. One of Machaut's compositions, suitably called 'My End is my Beginning' is written in three-part polyphony; the outer parts are identical except that they travel in opposite directions, while the middle part reaches half-way before reversing itself. Expressed by an arbitrary sequence of numbers the scheme could be represented in this way:

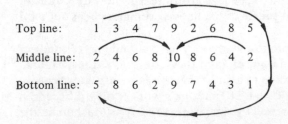

Top line:	1	3	4	7	9	2	6	8	5
Middle line:	2	4	6	8	10	8	6	4	2
Bottom line:	5	8	6	2	9	7	4	3	1

There are settings of the Mass from this early period which bristle with canons, inversions and retrogrades.

152

In the *Musical Offering* Bach devised canons of extraordinary complexity including one in which the central part (the 'King's Theme') is enclosed by two lines related to each other by augmentation and contrary motion; for example,

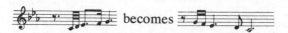 becomes

He sustains this intellectual tour de force throughout. Mozart wrote wonderfully ingenious canons in works such as the great Serenade in C minor for 13 wind instruments (K.388). He also wrote a *jeu d'esprit* consisting of what appears to be a violin solo. The joke is that it should be played by two violinists, one of whom starts at the beginning, the other at the end; the backward version of the music fits perfectly against the forward.

It is a composer's function to be a master of notes and his organization of those notes is a way of demonstrating that mastery. If emotion plays too dominant a part, there is a danger that he will lose control; conversely if intellect plays too great a part the music can be dry and cerebral. It is a measure of the achievement of composers such as Panufnik that although the material is rigourously controlled, the effect is not only dramatic but emotionally charged.

6 Interpreters

Language is a means of communication; music is a means of communication; ergo music is a language of sorts, a language transcribed into a code that needs to be interpreted. The artist whom we think of as a 'great interpreter' is one who best interprets the code, revealing subtleties that a less perceptive reading has failed to observe. Over the centuries composers have made ever-increasing efforts to bring greater precision to the notation of music, although it remains full of ambiguities. The advent of the virtually perfect gramophone record would, one might imagine, solve every query that future generations might raise about the music of our time. (How often one has wished that we might consult a record of Mozart actually playing his music; instead, we must use creative imagination coupled to scholarship and experience.) Surely a conductor of a Stravinsky work in the year 2050 will simply go to a record archive and listen to the composer's own definitive performance? Alas, even with such aids all problems will not be solved since recordings conducted by Stravinsky in his forties differ in many ways from those made in his seventies. Are the differences due to mature consideration or deteriorating powers? The decision will still lie in the hands of the interpreter, although obviously his task will be facilitated. Even today, though, no pianist playing Rakhmaninov's Piano Concertos will slavishly copy every facet of the composer's recordings, masterly though they are. For one thing he had a brusque way of playing his more seductive tunes, eschewing sentiment; the approach might not be too well received by audiences whose affection for Rakhmaninov is tinged by associations with weepy movies.

One of the beauties of music is that it is an art capable of constant renewal and revitalization; paintings, sculptures, books or poems remain essentially the same though the passage of time may discolour or erode them or cause their language to become obscure. Music, on the other hand, has its life rekindled with every performance; it is a magical time-machine enabling us to experience vividly the thoughts and emotions of people long dead. It is the interpreter who is responsible for breathing life into the page. The amount of help he gets from the composer varies enormously; in general, eighteenth-century composers (and needless to say their predecessors) were strangely

154

casual about indications of tempo, dynamics and the like. This was largely because they knew that they themselves would be in charge of the performance and that all such details could be explained by word of mouth. Nevertheless, even the indications of tempo that they did occasionally leave are susceptible to misinterpretation; Handel's conception of *allegro* (for instance) is not necessarily the same as Beethoven's or Liszt's. The further we progress along that river of music the more specific composers become in their instructions about performance. The notation of certain aspects of music is unfortunately very inexact; how loud is f, how quiet is p, how long is a pause, by how much does an *accelerando* increase the tempo or a *ritardando* decrease it, how short is a staccato minim, how much does a *crescendo* increase the volume, what does accent mean? The questions are legion and it is the interpreter who must find the answers. As a demonstration of the differing amounts of information made available by the composer I will quote brief extracts from two violin concertos; first the one in A minor by Bach, starting from the solo entry.

No tempo is indicated, no dynamic, no nuance, no phrasing; the actual notes (their pitch and rhythm) are clear, as is the bowing—some notes being slurred, others detached. To conclude from this that the music should be played as though composed at the typewriter is wholly false. Every phrase needs to dance, and it is the interpreter who will make the music airborne—or, if he is inept, leaden-footed.

By comparison Elgar seems practically to be standing beside the violinist issuing instructions in every bar.

(Novello)

It would be hard for the composer to be more explicit than he is here; yet if we listen to five different performances of this concerto by five violinists there will be innumerable small differences of tone-colour, of shading, of timing, even though each performer would stoutly maintain a fidelity to the spirit and the letter of the music.

Recent developments have enabled a composer to eliminate the performer entirely by putting sound directly on to tape. Is this the answer to the composer's prayer, an ultimate definitive performance for all time? Theoretically yes, though I do not believe I am being over-reactionary if I say that I doubt if it will prove an acceptable solution to the public—certainly not in concert-halls. To sit in rows listening to sounds emanating from a machine is a form of idol-worship (idle worship?) that is scarcely rewarding. The performer's contribution is not to be denied, though it may if anything be changed by a different sort of electronic aid. For instance the effect of 'wall-to-wall' television screens in a not too distant future may lead to hugely enlarged images of the conductor's or soloist's face and hands projected on a giant screen behind the orchestra. Audiences might feel deprived of the close-ups they had become accustomed to at home, though the prospect of silent slow-motion replays of passages where the soloist fluffed an octave or two is a depressing one.

In order to isolate a few of the more subtle aspects of the interpreter's art we can concentrate on quite small details. To my mind the most important word in the performer's vocabulary should be 'WHY'. For all too many players the fundamental question is 'HOW'—*How* shall I play this, *how* use the bow, *how* use my wrist, *how* finger the passage, *how* make it sound, etc. All these are perfectly valid and worthy questions that need to be answered, but they are of much less importance than the supremely interesting questions 'WHY'—*why* did the composer write these notes and no other, *why* did he use this notation, this register, this combination of instruments? 'HOW' questions are concerned with the technique of performance, 'WHY' questions are concerned with a true understanding of the meaning of the music.

Let us begin to explore some opening chords with this in mind. First a relatively obscure piece I have already mentioned in a different context (see p. 141), the *Tombeau* written by Froberger to lament the death of a friend. It is irrelevant for the moment to enter into a discussion as to whether it should be played on a clavichord, a harpsichord or even an organ. Historically incorrect it may be but I feel it is perfectly acceptable to play it on the piano if thereby we may receive the encoded message which Froberger floated down that river, ultimately to be washed up onto the shelves of a music shop in London where, beachcombing, I found it by chance. Delighted with my prize I took it home and sat down at the piano to read it through, to decode the message. The first chord I saw was this:

Instinctively, since it is a quite proper procedure in early music, I filled up the chord, thinking thereby to darken it, to increase the sombre quality implicit in the title.

I had asked myself the wrong question—HOW to make a dark funereal sound, not WHY Froberger had put such a wide space between the hands. I stress again that what I had done was in perfectly good taste and furthermore that it was done with the best of motives. I realized the error of my ways when I looked at the music a little more intelligently and saw that above that single low C in the bass Froberger had taken the trouble to put a rest, a positive admonishment *not* to do what I had just done.

Stick to these notes and the question How to play them is fairly easy to answer; the question Why did Froberger select these notes and warn us not to fill in the blank space is a much more fruitful one. What words are likely to come to mind to describe the sensation of suddenly and unexpectedly losing a close friend as the result of a fatal accident? We feel 'hollow', we feel the 'emptiness' of grief. The C minor harmony takes care of the grief but it is the space between the hands that eloquently tells of the deprivation. In terms of an instrument whose compass was much smaller than that of a modern keyboard, the gulf between the hands is considerable, symbolizing precisely (if unconsciously) the emptiness of grief I have described.

The idea may seem fanciful, so let us project it into a later period. Debussy at the start of his Prelude 'La Cathédrale Engloutie' wants to convey an impression of empty space, of a grey sea merging almost imperceptibly at the horizon with a grey sky. The observing eye sees this vast emptiness at a single glance; in a single chord Debussy captures not only the stillness but the width of the vision.

The dynamic (*pp*) helps to tell us of the stillness, but it is the wide gap between the hands that tells us of the emptiness of the scene. There is another Why question to be asked—Why is there no third in the chord, either major or minor? If you have a piano try putting first a B natural then a B flat into the right-hand chord; the B natural will bring the sun out, the B flat will darken the sky. Put a B flat into the left hand as well and there will be such a dark streak of cloud that a storm will seem to be brewing. It is the absence of either third that tells us the sky is grey, or at least colourless.

Here is a famous chord that has a totally different effect, the very opening sound of Beethoven's Fourth Piano Concerto (see p. 40).

Where Debussy gives us space, Beethoven gives us compression; the chord has a density that bespeaks a seriousness of purpose, yet it does not have to make its point with a blow or a clatter of notes. Debussy's chord makes us want to 'see through it' so aware of space does it make us; Beethoven's chord envelops us in its warmth, though its purity is such that we are aware of a very classic beauty devoid of sensuality. Imagine the impossibility of Beethoven electing to begin with this chord instead.

The sound is almost obscene by comparison.

There are times when the interpreter is faced with a real puzzle; here for instance in the slow movement of the Piano Sonata in E flat op. 7, Beethoven asks the impossible.

No pianist in the world can play this since no piano has yet been invented that can make a *crescendo* on a held note. An organ can, by opening the swell pedal; any string, wind or brass instrument can do so without difficulty. The piano cannot because once the hammer has struck the string, the sound will inevitably start to die. The performer who asks only 'How' will shrug his shoulders and say 'Can't be done . . .'

Let us place the note in its context.

There are a number of interpretative problems here; the pianist who simply asks 'How shall I play it?' will play bar 1 *f* as requested, play the 2nd and 3rd beats of bar 2 *pp* as requested, and then avoid the problem of Beethoen's *crescendo* in the third bar by playing this:

It is simply not the same; the question to ask therefore is not 'How shall I play it?', but 'Why did Beethoven demand something that on the face of it is impossible when he knew as well as anyone the limitations of the piano?' (Deafness is irrelevant; he was not deaf when he wrote this.) Here then is a tough code to crack; he must have had a reason for writing the *crescendo*. Is the pianist supposed to have a sort of balloon coming out of his head saying

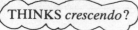

Clearly there must be more to it than that.

I have no guarantee that the solution I am about to offer is correct, nor are there any prizes to be won. I simply put on record a description of my own attempts to decipher the code. Now it is obvious that bars 1 and 2 of my example match or correspond to bars 3 and 4; the only difference seems to lie in the dynamics in bar 3, the $p < sf$. What is the *purpose* of the *crescendo*? Bar 1 is f, strong and austere (since there are no harmonies and the octaves strike the listener as strangely bleak after what has gone before). Bar 2 presents a huge contrast, a pathetic cry after the forbidding utterance of Bar 1. What does it mean—strong/weak? A contrast of timbre? A question-mark in musical terms? It certainly does not mean anything like 'Off with your head!' 'No . . . No . . .' There is no suggestion here of the quasi-operatic style that we found in Mozart's K.309 sonata. A suggestion of orchestral colour perhaps? More promising: the octaves in bar 1 are *like* horns and trombones even if the bottom notes are too low for Beethoven's brass. The pathetic little cries *could* be a flute or oboe; bird-calls perhaps, like those at the end of the slow movement of the Pastoral Symphony? Bear it in mind but think on; we have still not tackled the problem bar. WHY does it start p, which prevents it from being similar to bar 1? If it started f it wouldn't need the *crescendo*. Suppose for a moment we think not exactly in terms of opera but in terms of drama; it's certainly dramatic. Let's work on the strong/weak idea. Strong octaves, forlorn response. Touching quality of response softens the heart? Wait a minute—what *sort* of 'strong'? It isn't two people is it? It isn't a forbidding God-like figure and a small child. It's all happening *in one person*; that would make the octaves mean not 'I *am* strong' but 'I *must be* strong' which is quite different. So here is this man (Beethoven?) putting on a façade of toughness behind which is a terrible vulnerability; perhaps those tiny isolated sounds in bars 2 and 4 are more like tears than bird-calls. Despite the tough façade tears start to flow; in bar 3 does he perhaps say 'No, I must be strong' and then find tears continuing to spill? Certainly there's a lot of pain evident elsewhere in the move-ment—and a lot of evidence of control, reticence, even a virtual inability to speak. Is the $p \underline{\hspace{0.5cm}} sf$ like a great racking sob, then, a desperate attempt to establish control? (*I feel this is beginning to make dramatic sense but I still haven't solved the problem of WHY he wrote a crescendo, nor for that matter HOW to perform it.*) Let's think; what does a *crescendo* normally do? Obviously it makes the music get louder; what goes with louder? Quickening of the pulse . . . hang on—not *my* pulse but the music's pulse; quickening of the *beat*. Try shortening that first minim a little so that the silent quaver pulse I've been counting all along suddenly hurries a little; make a grab for the A flat like a gesture of desperation. That's it; it's a gesture! *Crescendo* here equals *accelerando*, only he couldn't write *accelerando* as it would have seemed even more idiotic since there's no obvious rhythm to accelerate with. However, accelerating the implicit rhythm creates a marvellous effect of emotional disturbance.

I cannot swear that this has been a verbatim description of an actual consecutive train of thought that passed through my mind between the hours of 14·35 and 14·40 on a wet Tuesday in November 1947; nevertheless it is a reasonably faithful reconstruction of a thought-process that gradually led me to my own particular solution to this seemingly small but quite knotty problem. If I were simply to say to a pupil, 'Shorten the minim in that bar, it makes a good effect,' I doubt if he or she could ever make it really convincing. Interpretation is a matter of making decisions, and in a case like this no amount of scholarship will help. One has got to be courageous enough to stick by one's intuition, but intuition is not just feeling. It is not enough to say 'I play it thus because I *feel* it that way.' That is the escapism of a romantic. One must be able to say, 'I play it thus because I know WHY I feel it that way.' Let us move on to an example with a few more notes.

The story of the first performance of the Beethoven Violin Concerto makes a nasty smudge on a page of musical history. It was read at sight, unrehearsed, by a violinist called Franz Clement; the opening movement was played in the first half of the concert, the subsequent two movements later in the second half of the programme. At some point between, Clement astounded the audience by performing one of his best party-pieces, a trick solo for one-stringed fiddle played upside-down—scarcely an ideal spiritual preparation for the sublime beauties of Beethoven's slow movement. The concert took place on 23 December 1806, and one can hardly believe the performance to have been a Christmas present Beethoven would have appreciated. What 'interpretation' could Clement have brought to a work of this quality when he did not even know what lay ahead of him let alone how he had survived what was behind? What for instance did he make of this opening cadenza, when he certainly would have been working out fingerings for any awkward-looking passages while the orchestra groped their way through the introduction?

Ex. 33

161

Harmonically this is nothing more than a hugely elaborated dominant 7th

a fact which Clement was probably capable of comprehending even at sight since such elaborations were a standard procedure. What he certainly failed to realize was the wealth of thematic significance Beethoven manages to bring in, making it not mere decoration but actual development. Just before the soloist's entry the violins have (for the first time) introduced a theme which evokes an instant response from cellos and basses.

The interchange is repeated as if to underline its importance and then, after two brief but emphatic phrases from the bass the tension goes out of the music in a descent of four notes which in its turn is echoed by the violins.

Now it is these last 4 notes marked with a square bracket that usher in the soloist, and his opening notes mirror them to beautiful effect, not only complementing and confirming the harmony but balancing the *two* phrases of cellos and then violins with a single extended phrase.

If you ask what this has to do with Interpretation, I reply 'a great deal', since it is an important part of the interpreter's function to reveal musical relationships such as these.

To continue, the next two phrases in the solo part are decorated versions of the last notes we had heard from the orchestral violins,

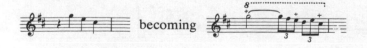

becoming

Beethoven now extends this into a long descent that is a skilfully disguised scale, the triplet rhythm effectively masking the underlying implication of *paired* notes.

The crotchets written small reveal the implied scale whose pairs of notes are subtly accelerated in the semiquaver ascent which follows.

Again the structure that lies behind this apparent finger-exercise is extremely subtle in its planning, a short ascent followed by a slightly longer one which is capped by the longest of all. Here is the framework:

At this point the upward progress of the run is halted briefly for a last reminder of the critical four notes that initiated the entire passage. Originally in a very simple form,

they ultimately reappear somewhat decorated

their importance being brought out by the fact that Beethoven here asks the player to give separate bows to all the remaining notes of the run. The feeling of acceleration without any real increase in speed is marvellously contrived by a sequence that begins with triplets with a suggestion of pairs, continues into paired semiquavers and finishes with separate semiquavers.

Now although this may have seemed like a return to analysis it is inseparable from Interpretation since the performer can scarcely give a running commentary pointing out the subtleties I have so laboriously revealed. It is his task to disclose the underlying secrets of the music in terms of sound alone, clarifying Beethoven's intent by the way he times each change of direction, each ambiguity of rhythm, each thematic allusion. Interpretation is so often (mistakenly) assumed to be primarily concerned with emotion; emotion is the easier aspect. The comprehension and revelation of musical

163

structure is the harder problem, yet one that is very much the performer's responsibility.

I do not want to seem insensitive or heartless when I say that the average listener over-rates emotion in music. Even to make such a suggestion will produce a reaction of outrage; 'Isn't emotion the be-all and end-all, the sole purpose of the operation?' I maintain that it is over estimated purely because it is so easy to produce. If I play a single note on the piano,

it will create a sort of pool of stillness, a clearly emotional effect brought about by the simplest possible means. If I play the same note a different way,

I create an entirely different emotion. *All* sound produces an instant response; loud, soft, high, low, growing, diminishing; the note I have just shown as a piano example would be a low note on the flute, a high note on the double bass, so that even a fixed note is susceptible to emotional change according to the instrument it is played on. Quick repeated chords are exciting; slow repeated chords are restful if quiet, majestic if loud. Emotion is an instant by-product, something the performer can scarcely evade.

Where the interpreter's art makes itself manifest is in the constant *gradation* of emotion, the shading of tone, the subtleties of timing, the beauty or vibrance of the sound he produces, the feeling of involvement and the comprehension of the substance of the music. A soloist can make his own decisions; a quartet will have to come to a corporate agreement, often the result of heated argument. Once we move to opera or full orchestras the conductor has the responsibility; if he is working with amateurs or children his authority will not be too hard to sustain; if, however, he is working with a top-class orchestra or star soloists, he can only earn respect and true co-operation by showing that he has outstanding perception. Every member of a great symphony orchestra is an accomplished musician; the older members have a huge reserve of experience to draw upon and will already have performed the standard repertory many times with a variety of conductors who between them will have discussed virtually every aspect of the music. On occasions when I have been rehearsing with the finest orchestras I have sometimes been amazed by the depth of knowledge of the whole score displayed by players, not just within their own section, but from one group to another. An oboe player will point out a marginally different phrasing in his part in a theme originally played by the violins. Should it be observed or changed so as to tally? String players constantly compare (and change) bowings, and much time is spent arguing the pros and cons of differences so subtle as to be unnoticed by all but a very select few of the audience. To the players such details matter; they really care and are quick to respond to suggestions that shed new light on a passage. Someone once wittily defined the difference between the amateur and the professional musician; however carefully rehearsed, the amateur, comes the hour of reckoning, will come unstuck somewhere; however *little* rehearsed, the professional will some-how manage to bring off a performance. It is a mite cynical and not wholly fair to the excellence nowadays achieved by so-called amateurs, especially the young; nevertheless there is an element of truth.

Imagination, involvement and insight are perhaps the three qualities most required from the interpreter—though I would hesitate to specify an order of importance. Technique, however essential, is but a means to an end and pays diminishing returns if it is not put to truly musical purpose. How, though, does the artist keep fresh performances of works that he plays many times in a long career? It is a measure of the quality of music as an art that it will stand such repetition; the secrets of great music are not easily deciphered; there are always new thoughts, new discoveries to be made, new perceptions. There is another factor and that is that the artist himself changes; the young artist, setting out to challenge the world in the full confidence of youth, will in time change to a man of fifty who has known disillusionment and sorrow. Both have something to offer, the exuberant passion of youth, the mature experience of age. Both will be qualified interpreters but they may not pass on the same message nor read the text with the same inflection.

7 Meanings

Having in the last two chapters looked at Purpose and Method, the composer's angle, and Interpretation, the performer's, perhaps it is a suitable moment to start to think about the Meaning of music. Despite some notable exceptions such as the *Symphonie Fantastique* or *The Sorcerer's Apprentice*, music is not a particularly good medium for either autobiography or narrative. I have already remarked that substantial sections of Tchaikovsky's *Romeo and Juliet* overture would transplant into a symphony; conversely the Lovers' theme from the same work would fire our imaginations just as much if it were to be called 'Dante and Beatrice', 'Tristan and Isolde' or even 'Antony and Cleopatra'; the love-story needs to be epic and tragic—the names are immaterial. On the other hand were it to be called 'Florence Higgs and Bertie Smallbone' it would no longer seem suitable, loath though I am to denigrate Bertie's undoubted passion for the amorous Flo. While the ardour in his breast may have seemed to him fully the equal of Romeo's, Tchaikovsky's music would seem to us too extravagant for what we might look down upon as a plebeian romance.

Mendelssohn once wrote:

> People often complain that music is too ambiguous; that what they should think when they hear it is so unclear, whereas everyone understands words. With me it is exactly the opposite, and not only with regard to an entire speech but also with individual words. These too seem to me so ambiguous, so vague, so easily misunderstood in comparison to genuine music which fills the soul with a thousand things better than words.[1]

It is an interesting viewpoint whose closing ambiguity does something to support his argument; is it the 'thousand things' that are better than words or does he really mean 'music which, better than words, fills the soul with a thousand things'? Much as I would like to agree with him I find it hard to do so, as a brief excursion into fiction should prove.

[1] Letter to Marc-André Souchay, 15 October 1842.

166

A sailor, half-seas over with drink is winding his way down the steep wet cobbles of a narrow street. A woman darts across his path. 'Excuse me,' he says. A street-urchin laughs derisively at him, but he's still bowing to the woman. And now a whole pack of children come streaming past, hair flying in the wind. Dazed, the sailor staggers along the quay to where his ship is anchored. There she lies, the *Arethusa*, her gilt figurehead straining towards the horizon even when, as now, her sails are furled. A proud sight she is, such as to make even a drunkard pause. There's an hour or two yet, though, before he's due on board and he sets off again into the town. In his fuddled state, he's not too sure of the way; his hat blows into the water but he doesn't even notice. As he reaches the main street he again bumps into a passer-by and, with the elaborate courtesy of the happily intoxicated he bows once more. Disregarding the laughter of the crowd he bows again and again. . . .

It may not be the most inspired prose but it is a passage I once used to show how easily music could be misinterpreted if we try to listen to it in terms of images and story-telling. The catch is that the music was specifically intended to be descriptive; it is the opening of Elgar's 'Falstaff' and has nothing to do with drunken sailors. Yet my narrative fitted the score so closely that were one to make a film of such a sequence and put Elgar's music in the background it would seem a perfect match. Even the hat blowing away is aptly described by a small flurry of notes. My vision of the *Arethusa* served splendidly for what Elgar clearly intended to be the Prince Hal theme, but it would have done as well for King Arthur, Francis Drake, a battleship, the river Thames or Trafalgar Square. If one had not been forewarned that the work was called *Falstaff* the chances of guessing that the theme was a portrait in miniature of Prince Hal would be extremely remote; one would recognize it as 'heroic', 'majestic' or 'grand', but little more.

When it comes to Meaning, music can cope with generalities rather than particulars; for instance it would not be hard to write a piece suggesting a church, but ask which church and bafflement sets in. St. Mary's, St. Andrew's, St. Peter's, St. Paul's? Music can suggest movement, the movement of waves, of wind, of birds flying, insects crawling, men marching, children playing. It can suggest locations, the desert, a dark forest, snowfields, cities. Obviously it can also convey emotions, excitement, anger, despair, contentment, happiness, innocence. It is precisely because it can express emotion so easily and so unmistakably that it becomes dangerous to interpret music in emotional terms. Can one seriously maintain that a composer needs to feel sad to write sad music and happy to write happy music? If this were true the first few pages of any classical sonata-form movement would have to be dismissed as the work of an irresponsible neurotic so rapidly do 'emotions' change. Indeed, if there is any correlation between the composer's state of mind and the music he writes it is more likely to go by opposites, since he may well write cheerful music as a form of therapy to drag himself out of a pit of despair. Of course the Romantics did use music as a means of self-projection; but if the finale of Tchaikovsky's

'Pathétique' Symphony is symptomatic of a state of mind, how is it that the previous movement seems so triumphant? Are we to presume total confidence from Monday to Thursday and total desolation from Friday to Sunday?

Do not misinterpret me; I am not saying that composers never allow their true feelings to spill into the music, but simply that it is a relatively unusual occurrence. In a way, composing is not unlike playing a part on the stage—the role can carry one away. Technically it shouldn't; the greatest actor can shed real tears to order six nights a week at a precise time and twice on Saturdays. It is a measure not so much of his depth of feeling but of his technical mastery. Composers, like actors, know perfectly well how to simulate tears or laughter, how to storm and rage, to soothe or languish. How otherwise could they set words to music in a true marriage? Present a composer with a situation that calls for music and his imagination will respond at once. He may take time to work out the details, but his reaction will be in terms of sound as surely as a dancer's reaction will find itself in bodily movement. I remember once discussing a film over the telephone; it was the first I had heard of the project and to begin with I did not even realize I was being asked to write the score. Before the end of the conversation I had 'heard' the opening title-music in my inner ear; I knew the sort of sound, the texture, the tempo. Months would pass before I committed a note to paper but that first reaction would continue to germinate.

Where do these sounds come from? That is a question I would hesitate to answer; suffice it to say that a composer 'thinks' sound as a sculptor thinks forms, a mathematician thinks equations or a film-director thinks images on a screen. One cannot help it, and the compulsive composers such as Mozart or Schubert who burnt themselves out with their labours could no more stop composing than you or I could stop envying someone more gifted. What do the sounds *mean* then? What is the significance of this cataract of notes spewed up out of the subconscious and poured by the guiding intelligence into the proper mould, be it sonata, symphony, quartet or opera?

In the beginning comes the urge, the urge to write—regardless of any outside stimulus such as a film-score or a commission for an anthem to commemorate the donation of a new stained-glass window to the Old School chapel. I speak now of the true composer whose compulsion dominates his life. It is, I suppose, not unlike a pregnancy; the work gestates, matures, ripens and is born, sometimes with labour, sometimes as effortlessly as fish spawn. I suspect that in most cases the basic conception comes first; one does not hear composers saying 'I thought of a wonderful idea the other day; I wonder whether to put it into a concerto or a sonata.' They say they're planning to write a symphony or a choral work, or that they've heard a wonderful singer and feel they *must* write something for her. At this point they have activated the subconscious and in due course sounds will start to emerge, bubbles coming to the surface. As the notes begin to form into more

coherent shapes a fascinating process begins which I have sometimes compared to wood-carving. Wood has a grain, and if the sculptor 'goes against
the grain' too violently the wood will split. In the battle of wills between the
wood's 'desire' to keep its shape and the sculptor's desire to change it, both
become casualties. While composition is not exactly comparable, there often
comes a moment when the musical substance seems to take on a life of its
own, to contest the composer's will or, for that matter, to nudge him in the
direction it naturally wants to go. (We have seen this at its most elementary
level during our exploration of basic harmony.) As a vivid example of what I
mean I would quote an early sonata of Beethoven, op. 10 No. 1 in C minor.

Ex. 34

The emotional characteristics here are very clearly defined, so much so that
they can be represented visually, the loud chords as solid blocks, the jagged
upthrust that follows a vivid contrast in its energetic movement, and then the
placatory gesture.

When Beethoven begins the Development he first modifies this by putting
it into C major. It is an obvious change even to an untrained ear.

169

And there, at the cross, is the conflict of wills. By all the rules of symmetry there *ought* to be a loud chord at that point. Look at the abstract pattern above and then cover up the second block with your little finger; how fundamentally it changes the appearance of the pattern, how eagerly the block seems to leap back into place when you remove the finger once more. Now while Beethoven can 'control' the loud chord by repressing it, he cannot de-energize that jagged ascending arpeggio. Like a horse tossing its head in the air and dragging a groom with it (who's leading whom?) the rising phrase asserts it strength. 'Be still' say the ensuing chords. 'To hell' says the arpeggio. We pick up from the last chord of the previous example.

From here on the development takes a strange course since Beethoven makes no further reference to any material from the Exposition. It's as if he says *to the music* 'If you say to Hell to me then I'll say to Hell with you!' And he metaphorically chucks the lot out of the window. His reason for this somewhat drastic action is clear; that jagged upward phrase is too positive an idea to be susceptible to development.[2] By comparison

is putty; you can do anything you want with it—play it loud or soft, turn it upside down, play it half-speed, put it into the major. It's so adaptable it can pervade an entire movement and spill over into some of the others as well.

Now if we don't allow our attention to be distracted by the magician's passes, all that Beethoven actually *says* in the course of the first five bars of the sonata is this:

_____

[2] Try playing it *p* and see how unconvincing it seems: to be quiet is contrary to its nature.

It is very hard to translate this into satisfactory non-musical terms; a domestic row seems hardly adequate even if the structure is right.

HUSBAND: (*f*) Hell! I *told* you not to move it.
WIFE: (*p*)   Shh dear, you'll wake the baby . . .
HUSBAND: (*f*) Hell! I told you not to move it.
WIFE: (*p*)   Shh dear, you'll wake the baby . . .

The dialogue is inane enough as a 'translation'; its repetition makes it ludicrous. Yet the repetition is satisfying, even necessary within a musical structure. If I try to improve things by upgrading my analogy—Jove hurling thunderbolts upon a cowering world?—the music seems inadequate. In a search for Meaning we are either driven to pedantry—the first three bars present an aggressive version of C minor: in bar 4 there is a contrasting shift to the second inversion of the dominant followed by a sharply accented diminished 7th on the supertonic, etc. etc.—or to a rather feeble (since obvious) statement that the music exploits the contrast between aggression and pathos. Since we seem to have reached something of an impasse let us turn to a different piece of evidence; perhaps it will help.

Here is Mozart at the start of his great sonata in C minor, K.457.

Although to a casual glance it may not look all that similar to the Beethoven, a closer examination shows that in musical terms they are almost identical. Mozart's rhythm is more measured than Beethoven's, which seems almost neurotic by comparison. The absence of harmony on the first beat gives an air of austerity to Mozart though, on the other hand, he makes a more poignant response. Both composers have felt the need to establish the tonality of C minor with a rising arpeggio: they even end on a similar note.

Both feel the need to contrast this with a pathetic rejoinder which must shift to the dominant—or a corruption thereof in the shape of this chord.

The marginal difference here is that Beethoven interrupts the pathos with the impatient interpolation of an accentuated chord; yet if we look at the larger structure this is quite proper, since both composers are thinking in terms of 4-bar units, Mozart's being 4 bars of 4/4, Beethoven's 4 bars of 3/4. (Incidentally the shorter bar plus a substantially quicker tempo combine to give a far more agitated character to Beethoven's movement.) If we pursue the comparison we find the two concepts continue their parallel course.

Now it seems highly unlikely that Beethoven had even the remotest inkling that he was treading so closely in Mozart's footsteps, although we do know that this particular sonata was in his repertoire and that therefore its proportions had presumably become embedded in his subconscious. The fact is that openings such as this were a standard procedure; Mozart used a very similar layout in his very first symphony, written at the age of eight. Examples of a strong unison proclaiming the Tonic key followed by a contrasting 'feminine' response shifting to the dominant are so numerous that they would fill a substantial catalogue on their own. They seem to meet a fundamental need somewhat akin to an architectural concept. The scale may change from compact to expansive, the material may be austere or ornate but the structure will remain similar. As an experiment, let me try extending the span of Mozart's opening phrases. First, take the initial rising octaves and extend them into a sequence; the idea is not all that far-fetched since he himself does something of the kind to most dramatic effect in the coda. Here, with deference, is my suggested alternative, whose purpose will become clear in due course.

Ex. 35

The next step is to pad this out a little, adding a few harmonies and allowing changes of harmony within the bar. The structure remains recognizably similar; the changes are of detail rather than principle.

Ex. 36

Certainly the last four bars are rather too physical in their impact for Mozart, but the preceding bars are perfectly feasible in Mozartian terms. Let

173

us now close the gaps up so as to get a majestic 3/4 sequence while keeping the framework essentially the same.

The purpose of this exercise becomes apparent when we now turn to the start of the massive Brahms Sonata in F minor, op. 5 (Ex. 37), whose Herculean beginning seems to be poles apart from Mozart; yet this relatively simple bridging process has brought them quite close together.

Ex. 37

Before I draw any final conclusions from this experiment I would like to take it a little further by applying a similar technique of extension to Mozart's second phrase—just this much in the original.

Suppose that he had written this:

Instead of two-and-a-half bars, we here find seven-and-a-half; instead of the subsequent octave phrase being in the dominant, it is in the tonic since we have wandered far enough away to need this restoration of stability. If we now revert to Brahms (Ex. 38), we will find him feeling the same need for a

Ex. 38

175

pathetic response to the opening challenge that both Mozart and Beethoven seem to have experienced. Needless to say, the scale has been extended—hence my 'stretched' version of the Mozart; but the function remains identical.

Just as my speculative Mozart example returned to the tonic for the reprise of the opening phrase so did Brahms, and for the same reason.

The conclusion to be drawn from this is that whatever superficial differences there may be, all three composers are in fact *making the same statement*; they are concerned with establishing a tonality, exploiting an immediate emotional contrast, balancing phrases one against the other. If these things sound somewhat pedestrian, that is the penalty we must pay for trying to express musical meaning in prose. Mozart expresses his version with the greatest economy, Brahms with the greatest rhetoric. Now size is not to be denied a certain value. No less an authority than Henry Moore said 'Physical size has an emotional meaning. A reduced model of Stonehenge would lose all its impressiveness.' The Brahms sonata *is* impressive because of its size, and audiences will always find it easier to perceive as 'great' music. Does this mean then that the Mozart example is 'small' music? To the imperceptive ear Mozart does often seem small-scale; we need to make an imaginative effort to understand how notably he stretches his resources. Economy of utterance need not mean poverty of thought. Let us turn for a moment to language again for an analogy.

> As he stood there alone at the castle-top the beauty of the scene that extended beneath him scarcely registered on his mind. The setting sun tinged the shallow waters a delicate pink so that it seemed almost as though they were scented with some exotic fragrance. A few birds still hung almost immobile in the evening sky poised to swoop on a careless fish, their black pinhead eyes searching the water with a systematic thoroughness. His hand, resting on the rough stone, absently scratched at a small growth of lichen. If only he could rub out the events of the past few months as easily. At the foot of the tower there were rocks, their sharp serrated edges looking in the rapidly diminishing light like the spines on the back of sleeping monsters from an infinitely remote past. How easy it would be to make that small leap and leave gravity to do the rest; no use to scream; he would swoop as silently as any marauding gull and the rocks would put an end to his despair. For a moment he pictured himself there spreadeagled on the murderous rock, his brains splattered, body torn. The gulls would come flocking then, grateful for a last supper. Last supper . . . he grunted at the irony. No, he couldn't do it; it would take more courage than he could muster. Slowly he turned towards the arch, a last ray of sun flecking his cheek. He must go down and face her once again. The thought appalled him; he was sick of pretending deference to a woman he so despised. 'Yes mother, no mother, I will mother, as you say mother.' The words seemed to echo through the archway mocking him with their hypocrisy. How long could he keep up this monstrous deceit when he'd gladly have watched her die?

Well, that passed the time didn't it, though it was a lengthy way of saying 'To be or not to be'. Now Shakespeare is not always economical in his use of language, but it is interesting to note that whenever there is a moment of crucial action he pares words down to the minimum. 'To be or not to be' is perhaps the most remarkable instance of compression, a man caught in a moment of indecision on the threshold of suicide. But think of 'It is too late' as Othello stifles Desdemona, 'Out vile jelly' as Gloucester is blinded, Lady Macbeth's 'Give me the daggers'—all direct statements using simple words, tonic chords as one might say, though all in a minor key. My prose elaboration of 'To be or not to be' was what might be termed a late romantic treatment of a classic idea, as is the start of the Brahms F minor sonata. Mozart's economy is comparable to Shakespeare's concise use of words at turning-points.

In case you feel I have made too special a plea by a careful selection of somewhat rigged evidence let me establish an even more improbable link. One would think there could scarcely be two composers further apart from each other than Mozart and Liszt. Here now is a brief extract from the Fantasia, K.475, which is usually coupled with Mozart's C minor sonata.

Notice how skilfully Mozart 'winds up the spring' by tautening the rhythm in the left hand until, like a catapult, it releases that chain of descending 3rds. Meantime the right hand has been executing a *tremolando*, a literal shaking of the hand that is often used as a pianistic substitute for orchestral sound. (In fact as a keyboard device it certainly goes back to Bach's time, but that is immaterial.) Liszt, being orchestrally minded in his piano writing, often falls back on the tremolando as an effect. To 'translate' Mozart into Liszt a necessary intermediate step would be to extend the tremolando and make the left hand a little more dramatic, agitating its rhythm and maybe indulging in wider leaps than the semitone which is enough for Mozart's purpose. As for the descending 3rds, he would find them irresistible as a vehicle for exhibitionism; they would be transformed into a virtuoso octave passage. Do not be dazzled by appearances; the content is the same even if the fabric is stretched (Ex. 39).

Admittedly this is a much more athletic exercise than Mozart's but it serves to underline the fact that once something has been done simply he

Ex. 39

who would follow must take the harder way. The element of virtuosity in music did not increase merely because people enjoyed showing off, though that unquestionably played a part. At a much more profound level composers were driven continually to stretch technical resources because their predecessors had already found the direct way of reaching any particular goal. My model for my pseudo-Liszt example is partly taken from his monumental Piano Sonata where he uses the identical components that Mozart had once employed to such purpose, a tremolando in the right hand, octaves in the left. The high register of the piano that he uses for his glittering right-hand part simply did not exist in Mozart's day (Ex. 40).

Here again then we find two widely differing composers saying *the same thing*; only the degree of rhetoric differs. Ask *what* they are saying and Mendelssohn would say with some justification 'it's too obvious for words'. If you don't get the message in both cases then music is not for you; the important thing is to realize that both composers are at full stretch and that therefore Mozart is not 'smaller' than Liszt. Perhaps my prime reason for placing Mozart above all others is that in his music I find everything that I require; passion, intensity, dramatic contrast, humour, delight, sorrow, profundity, daring and humanity all expressed with fewer notes and less effort than anyone else needed.

Ex. 40

If we are looking for a divide that cannot be crossed, we need to go into regions where the whole concept of the function of music changes. Let me again start from Mozart to make the point, although this time it must be hypothetical Mozart since he did not write the exact notes I require. The figuration is entirely characteristic; only the key of D flat makes it extremely suspect.

Look at those first four notes, unsupported by harmony and quite able to manage without it. They draw us into the subsequent melody effortlessly, but instinctively we appreciate that they are *en route* for some further destination. Here are the same four notes being used for a very different purpose.

The first time I came across these harmonies (at the age of sixteen) I found them literally incredible. I had not known that sounds so beautiful could exist and I explored them repeatedly with the untiring ardour of a lover at last permitted to caress the body of his beloved. Each chord needed to be tasted like some delicious sweet, lingering in the hand and the ear rather than on the tongue and the palate. The quotation is from Debussy's *Reflets dans l'eau*, as exquisite a tone-painting as has ever been devised. Here at least we have music with a specific meaning; those isolated notes high in the treble that follow the rich sequence of harmonies are obviously raindrops falling after a passing shower from boughs that overhang the water. But what of the harmonies? Can they really be only the slow heave of water on the lake, or are they, as I felt instinctively in those heady adolescent hours, something altogether more sensual? A couple lying on the bank in some idyllic dream? In those less permissive days I was too innocent to specify the details, nor would even Debussy have wished me to. In this piece we meet the dilemma of descriptive music; we know so clearly what it *means*; every flurry of wind, every ripple, each drop of water can be identified and yet if we sit back and think for even a moment, it is palpably unreal. However beautiful the depiction of detail, the time-scale is completely wrong. The entire piece takes less than five minutes to play and yet in that time a huge storm gets up, raising such immense waves as few lakes have ever known, only to die to an evening of immense stillness and beauty. It is clearly impossible in Nature, though entirely convincing in music. Like one of those films in which we see the growth of a plant compressed into seconds or an hour's movement of a cloudscape made into a brief ballet, Debussy has taken the sound and motion of Nature herself and bent them to his will.

If we were to try to convert every piece of music into a verbal meaning we should find the task too frustrating. Music is primarily *about* sounds and their continually changing relationships to each other; it is about tension and relaxation, energy and inertia. In the long run the sole reason for the precise placing of any note on a score is that the composer felt that that was literally the proper place for it. Asked once to give a definition of the act of composing, I described it as the 'identification of sounds half-heard'. So far as I know, it is tolerably true of the majority of composers. Sounds appear in his mind, sometimes sharply defined, sometimes obscure. He must dig them out of his brain and put them down on the page; he knows when he finds the 'right' sound because everything else has seemed wrong. Composition involves huge amounts of rejection; one is constantly turning sounds away because they do not fit the pre-conceived (if sometimes barely comprehended) vision. The surer one's technique, the easier the process is likely to be; the danger, then, is too great a facility, a road which has truly been the primrose path that has led to the virtual extinction of many a composer much lauded in his day. Time is a ruthless sieve whose cruel mesh entangles many a worthy talent. Those who survive the filtering process have qualities that are truly enduring. Their precise meaning may not be understood by all, but they communicate none the less; their language is eloquent enough.

8 Challenges

I have been too occupied in trying to acquire some small literacy in music to be able to have found time to do as much for literature. I have never read *War and Peace* though I would not dream of questioning its rank as a masterpiece; however what with films, serial versions on television and articles in the Sunday supplements I feel I have a sort of familiarity with it; it is part of the litter that lies around in the back-streets of my mind. If I have avoided reading it, it is not because I doubt its worth but because I know that it would be a serious task, not lightly undertaken—a challenge.

It is for this reason that I have chosen to call this chapter Challenges; it is an admission that there are a number of works that are not easy of access, even sometimes to the trained musician. Composers are specialists in what during the course of this book we have discovered to be a highly specialized language. Now, I speak English reasonably fluently and have a fair vocabulary: yet I know that there are many books far more demanding even than *War and Peace*, books dealing with abstruse subjects whose fundamentals I have not grasped, books on astronomy, surgery, mathematics, molecular biology, chess, company law, even (crowning irony) certain books on music. To an astronomer, a surgeon, a mathematician, a biologist, a chess-player, a solicitor or a music critic such books may demand a degree of concentration, but they will certainly not be incomprehensible. Why should we expect, then, that all music should be equally comprehensible? In fact we don't; all the same there is no doubt that many lovers of music are genuinely baffled by compositions that seem to be meaningless and incoherent. They feel that there should be something for them there but are swamped in a flood of sounds, most of which seem not only puzzling but disagreeable.

Some time ago I had given a talk to a music-club somewhere; as I was packing up to leave an elderly but pleasantly alert man came up to me.

> I've never played an instrument in my life [he said], but I've always loved music Now that I've retired I listen to it for hours a day on the gramophone; we've a good record library and I get several works out a week. I'm determined not to be left behind like an old fogey so I make a point of listening to a fair amount of

modern music; I've been having a real go at Stockhausen lately. I can't say I like it, but it does make Webern seem very tuneful.

What an exemplary attitude; and what a profound truth there was in his last words. Since, as I have said, composers are specialists it is hardly surprising that their use of musical language goes beyond the accepted norm of any period they happen to live in. 'Modern' music in the pejorative sense is not a new phenomenon exclusive to our age; there has always been modern music and audiences have always taken time to catch up with it. The finale of Beethoven's Second Symphony was described by a contemporary critic at its first performance as 'a gross enormity, an immense wounded snake, unwilling to die but writhing in its last agonies and bleeding to death.' They don't write criticisms like that any more.

Some time ago I had the good fortune to conduct four performances of Beethoven's 'Grosse Fuge' in the version arranged for string orchestra by Weingartner. Originally composed as the finale to the String Quartet, op. 130, Beethoven was forced to provide an easier alternative since publisher and players alike felt that his demands were too taxing. The movement was, in a word, regarded as 'impossible'. It so happened that when I came to rehearse it with an admirable chamber orchestra very few of the players had actually played it in either version; rehearsals were both exhilarating and exhausting, demanding arduous repetition of passage after passage just to get the notes under the fingers. As it gradually began to fuse into a coherent performance we came to feel a huge sense of achievement, something akin (I should imagine) to that felt by mountaineers when, after having spent painful hours with their faces inches from the rock-face, they at last emerge onto the peak and see extended before them a view of epic grandeur. Yet perhaps the most gratifying reward was when, after a performance, a woman came to me and said, 'Thank you so much for the Beethoven; a musical friend told me he'd had an off-day when he composed it and that I wouldn't enjoy it much. It was overwhelming and marvellous; I want to go straight out and buy a record so that I can listen to it again and again.' In this chapter I propose to deal in some detail with three musical challenges; let Beethoven's 'Grosse Fuge' be the first.

BEETHOVEN: GROSSE FUGE (GRAND FUGUE) Op. 133
Composed 1825, two years before his death.

Adjectives such as gargantuan, Homeric, thorny, complex, or heroic tend to be scattered around fairly freely when this work is written about in programme notes. Systematic analysis of its musical structure is more likely to lead to bewilderment than enlightenment. The French composer Vincent d'Indy once produced what must be regarded as a definitive guided tour of the work. It begins:

'It is a fugue with two subjects and variations. The work is unified by a principal theme, the counter-subject of the first fugue, which is used as the subject of the second. For the purposes of analysis the work can be divided into six main sections, each subdivided again.'

He than analyses in turn the Introduction, the First Fugue (with three variations), the Second Fugue (also with three variations), the Development of the two fugues in three sections, the Re-exposition in the principal tonality and lastly the Conclusion.

Charts such as these (and in detail it makes pretty turgid reading) have about as much relevance to the beauty or power of the work as a map does to the beauty of a landscape. Look at a map and one can tell if the terrain is flat or hilly, town or country, inland or coastal; but does it tell us if the fields shine gold with buttercups, if willows droop over the stream where king-fishers dart or if the craggy rocks emerge from beds of purple heather like ancient monoliths? The map maker would claim that that is not his business; similarly the musical analyst will maintain that all he is concerned with is the anatomy of the music. Nevertheless, I remain very sceptical about how helpful the average listener finds it to be told that in the second section, 'Variation I of the First Fugue gives us the return of the theme in one part only, this time appearing as the answer, not as the subject, leading on through the statement of the answer, transformed, to an exposition of the answer in the relative key.' If this is the price of clarification I would rather be left in the dark.

In fact Beethoven himself supplies us with a map of sorts, not unlike those chapter headings one finds in Victorian novels giving a brief résumé of the contents. Before we attempt to explore the fugue let us look at the very last bar of the movement which preceded it when it originally appeared as part of a quartet. The fugue comes after a slow movement which must unquestionably be described as one of the most profoundly expressive movements he ever wrote; the final chord is, however, written in an intriguingly un-orthodox way.

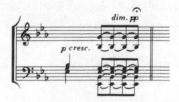

Now Beethoven was not so foolish as to be unaware that four quavers *tied* ♩♩♩♩ equal one minim (♩). Why, therefore, did he not write a minim and a *diminuendo*? We return to the concept of music as a code to be deciphered. He must have intended some special effect here, a *diminuendo* that could be measured by stages perhaps; imagine a room illuminated by four candles. As we leave it, the host snuffs out each in turn so that the light diminishes by stages, three candles, two, one, and then darkness. It seems to me a possible explanation of the effect he had in mind in terms of sound, altogether different from a slow continuous fade. Notice, though, that the top note of the chord is G, and it is that G that he now proclaims *f*, a blaze of sound designed to jerk us out of the mood engendered by the heartfelt beauty of the slow movement. He then spells out the notes of the main fugue subject, each note accented and all the instruments in unison. As proclamations go it could scarcely be stated in more positive and unequivocal terms.

Note that he uses the word 'Overtura' to make clear that this is an introduction; notice also how the monumental character of the first few notes is changed into something more athletic by the speeding up in bar 9 and the literal sting-in-the-tail in bar 10. The initial top G is simply a 'wake-up' note; the fugue subject begins on the up-beat to bar 3, but its first note is artificially lengthened, as though reluctant to drag itself into the new tempo. Thus the phrase can be seen to have both the solid strength given it by the accented unisons as well as a forward impulse that is like a disguised *accelerando*. This effect is heightened by the very next two phrases, two compressed versions of the same subject now put into a galloping rhythm that changes its character completely.

The significant pauses that separate these three opening statements from each other serve a two-fold function. Dramatically they are what is often referred to as a 'stunned' silence, our breath taken away by the forcefulness of the statement; intellectually they are designed to enable us to take in the substance of what has been played, as though Beethoven was saying 'Got it?' after each phrase. Incidentally those who regard twelve-note music and serialism as a twentieth-century perversion should note that Beethoven has got well on the way to creating a tone-row here, since between them these two phrases use up 11 of the 12 available notes in the chromatic scale: G, G sharp, F, E, A, F sharp, B, C, B flat, C sharp and D. Only E flat is missing, and you can attach what significance you like to the fact that the previous movement was in E flat major and that therefore this near-chaotic passage (tonally) is partly designed to expunge all memories of E flat from our minds.

There follows a complete change of mood and tempo. The same melodic contour that has already been presented in two guises, monumental or athletic, now becomes expressive and melancholy.

During this revelation the cellist has remained spellbound on a single held note; having witnessed such beauty, though, he cannot resist taking it for himself. As he does so, the other three players in turn offer a gentle caress of a phrase touched with an extraordinary compassion.

The tempo changes back to *Allegro*, the first violin now offering a ghost-like version of the theme, broken by silences between the notes and written in a similarly enigmatic way to the final chord of the previous movement that I have already discussed.

Now so far we have had not only a number of separate phrases but also three key signatures (G, F and B flat), three time signatures (6/8, 2/4, C or 4/4) and three tempo indications; *allegro, meno mosso e moderato* and *allegro* again. In addition we have had four clearly defined moods; monumental, athletic, contemplative/wistful and ghostly. Why? What is Beethoven doing?

If we think of fugues in general the subject matter will as a rule be constant in appearance and in tempo. Fugues are cumulative, as we have seen (pp. 61–3), but the subject itself rarely changes fundamentally except according to the rules of augmentation or diminution ♩ ♩♩ becomes 𝅝 ♩♩ or ♩ ♪♪ . What, in effect, Beethoven is telling us in this opening is that we should change our ideas of how a fugal subject is likely to be treated, that we

186

must be prepared to accept it in any one of these different guises. The 'ghostly' version is the most problematic since it is hard to say precisely what he means; certainly the implication is that the coloration of the tone should be subtly changed in some way. To use my candle analogy again, if the candles were extinguished at the end of the slow movement, are they here being re-lighted? When one lights a candle the flame has to be teased into life; it starts small and then suddenly glows, taking a tulip-like shape which has a distinct core to it. Are these notes, so tentatively proffered, like individual candles, pinpoints of light in an enveloping darkness? It is only an analogy, not a suggestion that Beethoven had such an image in mind. At any rate, the introduction or Overtura is now ended and the Fugue proper begins, a landmark Beethoven makes perfectly clear by writing the word Fuga on the score. The first violin presents us with a leaping, angular theme that is energy personified.

This theme has been both ridiculed and abused by critics who should know better. In order to understand it fully we need to make a couple of forays into earlier Beethoven.

During our brief exploration of some aspects of the C minor sonata, op. 10 (pp. 169–71) we saw how in essence the jagged upthrusting phrase which begins the sonata is simply an energetic activation of the chord of C minor. Since the energy is applied to something as basic as a single chord, the rhythm is the prime factor in establishing an emotional character, it being relatively unimportant whether the chord is major or minor, consonant or dissonant. If we move on to another more famous C minor piece, the Fifth Symphony, we find something much more subtle, for here the activation process is applied to something that has not only a positive emotional character of its own but one that is in opposition to the rhythmic drive. Part of the music wants to express a rather forlorn melancholy since it consists of a series of sighs of the 'Ah woe is me' type.

There is no denying the potentially expressive even pathetic character of these languishing phrases; yet the rhythmic element in the symphony refuses to countenance such self-indulgent woe and drives the music forward with a ruthless disregard for its desire to dwell upon its sorrows. Instead of the *alternation* of moods so clearly established at the start of the early sonata we find a *simultaneous* expression of two opposing moods, the forward impulse of the rhythm, the lingering expressiveness of both the harmony and the implied melodic line. Notice how slowly the harmonies change in comparison to the rapid tattoo of repeated quavers. (I have simplified the notation to show the effect.)

It is the fusion of conflicting and opposing elements that is largely responsible for the eternal fascination of such music.

If we now return to the Grosse Fuge, we can discern comparable subtleties since, for all its driving energy and relentless rhythm, there is an underlying harmonic scheme of considerable expressive potential. Suppose for a moment that without prior knowledge we happened upon a fragment of music on these lines:

Without any indication of tempo or expression we would automatically adopt an expressive style of playing, using a legato touch at a moderate speed. Now though the lower part in the right hand is an indulgence put in for the sake of euphony, the two outer parts are derived closely from the Grosse Fuge; they show the heart that is concealed behind a rough and aggressive manner. Apart from the difference of notation (♩ instead of ♫) the left hand of the example above shows the actual fugue subject. If you ask me why the notes are placed on the theoretically weaker beats of the bar (2nd and 4th instead of 1st and 3rd), I would offer two possible answers; 'physically' they reinforce those parts of the bar that tend to relax, which means that Beethoven is strengthening the rhythmic pulse without resorting to the tactics of Sousa; 'spiritually' this displacement has a much more subtle meaning because the mere facts that the notes appear in the 'wrong' part of the bar instils in them a longing to be allowed to go into the 'right' part. The combination of a driving rhythm, potentially expressive harmony and displaced accents gives us a complex of emotions that is powerful and challenging, but it is the inherent contradictions that give the music its special quality, as they did in the Fifth Symphony.

To analyse the whole fugue in this detail would become wearisome; suffice it to say that this first fugue is worked out with tremendous energy and an increasing emotional intensity that is eloquently conveyed by the simple procedure of closing the gaps between the notes of the main subject and throwing them still further off the beat.

The texture is made more turbulent by the addition of a veritable hailstorm of triplets; and then, with a suddenness that takes us completely by surprise, all movement stops. The strings seem to freeze on a chord of G flat major. Out of this dramatic pause comes a marvellously poetic interlude, an extensive development of that tiny compassionate phrase that we had glimpsed frustratingly briefly in bars 22 to 24. The fusion of ideas here is masterly. First, Beethoven gives us a link between the main fugue subject and the smoothly gliding figuration which he is now going to employ as a contrast to the relentlessly jagged rhythms that have dominated his thought for so long. As though God with a single gesture had halted a flight of demons, the music takes on an air of absolute serenity.

Ex. 41

As you can see, the fugue subject has reappeared, its demonic force exorcised. Beethoven several times warns the players not to be carried away by the sheer beauty of this section, exhorting them to stay *pp*. Only once, towards the end of this twilight interlude does he allow a sudden glow of warmth to creep in, like a shaft of golden sunlight flooding a garden before the veil of night is finally drawn.

Having lulled us almost to sleep with a gently rocking cadence, Beethoven plunges us without warning into what could be regarded as a miniature scherzo following what (in effect) has been a brief slow movement. The Grosse Fuge is not simply a fugue on the grandest scale but a marvellous fusion of fugue, variation *and* sonata form all within the span of a single movement, a symbolic culmination of a life's work. The scherzo, if I may call it that, is based on the second version of the fugue that he had revealed to us in the Introduction, the one in a quick 6/8. It is the cellist who gives the music its new impetus.

For perhaps half a minute, no more, the music dances carefree, light-footed and punctuated by little trills that are almost like suppressed laughter. Then, and again the shock is sudden, the very first version reappears, its giant strides accompanied by angry downward gestures that turn violin bows into slashing swords.

Time after time this immensely dramatic version of the fugue subject is hurled at us while its final trill—the sting-in-the-tail—becomes ever more waspish. In due course the leaping tenths and jagged rhythms from the original fugue reappear until again the music is brought to a stop and we are allowed one last glimpse of that celestial garden. Ominous clouds gather, strange chords separated by long silences, with growling trills in the cello suggesting the rumble of thunder growing ever more distant. Beethoven is now ready for a final survey of the material. He looks for a while at what I called the miniature scherzo, offers us a wonderful and quite new vision of the main fugue theme, remote and still, next flickering memories of the fragments from the first page, and then a coda that, having initially filled us with awe and then shown us a sight of Paradise, ends gloriously with the fugue triumphant, the throbbing chords that accompany it looking forward to a positively Wagnerian ecstasy.

Now I am convinced that all the troubles that this fugue has caused to listeners stem from a misguided determination to concentrate on the form rather than the music. Beyond all else it is a drama, possibly the most dramatic single movement that Beethoven ever wrote. If one is in a boat tossed about amongst huge waves, its sails torn and the tiller broken, it is little use looking at a chart to determine where you are. Leave that to the navigator, but only if you are proposing to abandon ship. The charts of this tremendous movement that have been prepared by well-meaning but seemingly unimaginative souls deserve to be thrown overboard until such time as you have been truly overwhelmed by its impact. Once that has happened, preferably several times, you may glance at a map or two if you wish. It is infinitely better, though, to accept the guidance that Beethoven thoughtfully gives us in his Introduction and then let him take the helm. No matter how rough the waters he knows the way.

STRAVINSKY: LE SACRE DU PRINTEMPS
Ballet composed 1910–13

The musical climate has changed so dramatically in the last two decades that the inclusion of *The Rite of Spring* as a challenging work may come as a surprise to some. The score which caused a riot in 1913 at its first performance has now been successfully tackled by youth orchestras; the music that outraged a sophisticated audience in Paris was incorporated into *Fantasia* twenty-eight years later by Walt Disney and was experienced without complaint by millions who would never have dreamt of going to a concert. Watching rather crude animations of prehistoric monsters gouging each other to death or volcanic lava spurting across imaginary landscapes they found the music in no way disturbing, if not as immediately appealing as the Bach-Gounod *Ave Maria* sung by a Hollywood choir at the tail-end of

Moussorgsky's *Night on a Bare Mountain*. At the time of writing it Stravinsky had two enormously successful ballets behind him; *The Firebird* and *Petrushka*. Both can be seen to be in a direct line of descent from the colourful nationalist music of nineteenth-century Russian composers such as Rimsky-Korsakov (Stravinsky's teacher) and Borodin, even though harmonically and rhythmically they were far more adventurous. In *The Rite of Spring* Stravinsky severed all connections with his predecessors, casting a link back to a primitive and unchronicled time. The work is pagan in character, built from surprisingly simple materials for the most part, though the effect is often dazzlingly complex. It is designed to celebrate in ritual the victory of spring over winter, something of more significance in Russia than in England, where the two merge together almost imperceptibly. In Russia the spring thaw is a convulsion of nature that must have seemed a recurring and longed-for miracle to primitive man. Not only nature but human life itself is symbolically regenerated in the ballet through the medium of human sacrifice.

The music is organized on totally different lines from a symphony; a ballet is a form of narrative, though here there is not such a detailed plot as we find in the two earlier ballets. Rather it is like a series of *tableaux vivants*, episodes which could even be played in a different order without undue artistic loss, though Stravinsky's ghost might rise Petrushka-like from the grave were anyone to attempt to do it.

The late Pierre Monteux, who conducted the first performance, recalled on the sleeve-note of his recording his first encounter with the music

> With only Diaghilef and myself as audience, Stravinsky sat down to play a piano reduction of the entire score. Before he got very far I was convinced he was raving mad. Heard this way, without the colour of the orchestra which is one of its greatest distinctions, the crudity of the rhythms was emphasized, its stark primitiveness underlined. The very walls resounded as Stravinsky pounded away, occasionally stamping his feet and jumping up and down to accentuate the force of the music . . .[1]

(No doubt had Beethoven endeavoured to play the Grosse Fuge on the piano he would have behaved in a very similar way.) Monteux went on to say that he was more astounded by Stravinsky's performance than shocked by the score; indeed to see that small and gnome-like figure thus belabouring the keyboard must have been almost surrealistic.

One phrase of Monteux's sticks out as crucial to an appreciation of this twentieth-century landmark, the orchestration 'which is one of its greatest distinctions'. It is important to realize that in listening to such music we need to approach it very differently from any nineteenth-century composition. For much of the time we are confronted by sound in the raw; we must forget the rich blending of sound which had become the aim of late nineteenth-

---

[1] Copyright RCA 1957 (Record No. RB 16007).

century orchestrators, which in turn had led to the brilliant colouring of Richard Strauss's music or the pastel shades of Delius. Here was the musical equivalent of the savage attack Picasso was to make on traditional concepts of figure-painting. The music was not so much conjured forth as hacked out, and the violence it did to all preconceptions of musical propriety was hard to accept.

If in these introductory words I have given a suggestion that Stravinsky was a crude manipulator of sound, then I have misled you. Both *Firebird* and *Petrushka* had shown him to be one of the supreme orchestrators of all time; his ear was extraordinarily acute. Despite the huge orchestra, despite the welter of sound that engulfs us, I doubt if there is a note in the score that was not precisely weighed in his mind before it was allowed on to the page.

The work begins with a famous, if not notorious, bassoon solo.

Now this could as well be played on the cor anglais, the clarinet (a little unsuitable since it involves crossing an awkward area known as the 'break') the alto flute, a trumpet—presumably muted—or an oboe. Why then did Stravinsky choose the bassoon when he must have known that any conventional bassoonist would rather be seen dead than playing up there? It epitomizes his approach to the orchestra; the sound is unique and totally unforgettable, as explorations of uncharted territory tend to be. Precisely because he was pushing the instrument to its outer limit and stretching the player's technique to the utmost he was able to create this absolutely individual sound. In fact the melody is the one authentic folk-tune in the whole ballet, coming from Lithuania; its circular repetitions, seeming to permutate the notes with something of the enthusiasm of a pools addict, give us a vital clue to one of Stravinsky's most characteristic hallmarks. The repetition of patterns and the permutation of rhythms pervade the entire score.

The whole introduction is an evocation of bird and animal sounds translated into orchestral terms. When we think of Beethoven's well-schooled nightingale, quail and cuckoo in the Pastoral Symphony we accept that they are not realistic but as stylized as the pretty, rustic figures in a Fragonard painting. Stravinsky aims at a much closer approximation to jungle sounds and our enjoyment might almost be measured according to our ability to imagine fantastic creatures, birds with brilliant plumage, giant frogs, insects that click and hiss and rustle, a growing cacophony of the wild that builds into a primeval dawn chorus. I always find it an incongruous experience to hear such music being performed by solemn gentlemen in evening dress; the least the orchestra could do would be to wear furs and paint themselves with woad, for man, once he appears upon the scene, is truly primitive, stamping the earth and grunting like his forebear the ape (see p. 24). Above this thud of footsteps we find chords composed of heaped-up 5ths on trumpets, like some giant metallic violin

and woodwind skirls which demonstrate an often-used trick of Stravinsky's. What he does is to reshape a very conventional pattern of notes as though passing light through a crystal. These five-notes which any child could play

are split apart so that in their simplest transformation they become

What was previously smooth becomes angular, yet there is perfect logic behind the reasoning. The next stage is to decorate this new version so that it becomes altogether more nimble.

Add sparkle with a pair of piccolos and the effect is as brilliant as sun on water.

Soon he builds the score into a mosaic of patterns, each simple in itself but seeming in total marvellously intricate. Ex.42 is a typical page of score; cast your eye along each line in turn and see how he exploits repetition. It doesn't matter if you can't read music; the patterns are as clear to the eye as to the trained ear.

Virtually every page involving full orchestra is built on similar principles. One's instinctive reaction is to feel that such repetitions must lead to boredom, yet boring is one word that does not come to mind during this astonishing piece. Partly it is the brilliance of the orchestral colouring that continually excites the ear, partly the asymmetrical rhythms. For example in the next sequence, 'Jeu du Rapt' or 'Dance of Abduction', we find orthodox 9/8

Ex. 42

B. & H. 19441

patterns

combined with alternate 4 + 5   or 5 + 4

The rhythms collide against each other as people do in a jostling crowd. A typical sequence of rhythms reads like this:

one hears its pulsation as an irregular pattern of long and short beats as shown in my 'morse-code' version beneath.

The ensuing 'Spring Rounds' is built from massive chords exploiting in a radical way the principles of parallel movement that date right back to the organum of the twelfth-century or earlier. It is a nice irony that a fundamental aspect of early Christian music should here be diverted to pagan purposes, though the deliberately rough-hewn harmony effectively disguises the music's remote ancestry.

The parallel 4ths and 5ths continue to tread heavily throughout this section building up to a climax of extreme dissonance, albeit attained by perfectly logical means. If you find the sound literally overwhelming it is entirely proper—Stravinsky obviously meant you to.

The combination of rhythms I have already mentioned; we also find the combination of tonalities known as bitonality (two keys simultaneously) or polytonality (several keys at once). For instance opposite is a fusion of three completely orthodox passages, the upper part clearly in C major, the middle line as clearly in F, while the bass is undeniably in E major.

(The bass line has been modified slightly here since Stravinsky alternates cello and double bass so rapidly that the figuration actually covers a wider range. The harmonic implications remain unaltered.)

Those who regard Stravinsky's score as intolerably complex should look at these examples in order to see how essentially simple much of his material is.

Much of the music moves at a prodigious speed, and it is in the spheres of rhythm and tempo that the orchestra is perhaps most severely taxed. At times the drumming is frenzied, whipping up a truly barbaric excitement which is hard to resist unless one has incurably conservative ideas of what the function of music ought to be. Even so, one can see a fairly clear line of descent through the 'Witches' Sabbath' in the Berlioz *Symphonie Fantasti-*

que through Mussorgsky's *Night on a Bare Mountain* and the 'Prince Igor' dances of Borodin down to *The Rite of Spring*; Stravinsky might have disowned such ancestry but it is there.

Much of the music is deliberately brutal in impact and I can remember feeling a slight incredulity when I first read that Debussy (surely at the opposite pole) had much admired the work at his first hearing. Composers do not always appreciate the compositions of their contemporaries. Yet though Debussy himself would have disdained to use the materials from which so much of it is built, he would have realized how much Stravinsky and he had in common in their virtuoso use of orchestral colour. This is most easily observed in the Introduction to Part II, whose translucent texture and gently shifting harmonies are very close to the technique and spirit of Debussy. Needless to say, there are many more such passages in *Firebird* and *Petrushka*; Debussy was perceptive enough to realize that *The Rite* was not sheer iconoclasm and that threads from the earlier ballets do exist.

An important aspect of *The Rite of Spring* worth underlining is the extensive use of percussion. During previous centuries it had been the most neglected area of the orchestra, confined even in big romantic symphonies to timpani, side-drum, bass-drum, cymbals and triangle with occasional rare excursions into such exotica as tubular bells. Rather like builders, whose instinct if they see a patch of neglected land is to say 'Develop it', twentieth-century composers have exploited percussion in a way that would have been literally unimaginable in Beethoven's day since many of the instruments now in use did not even exist then. There is a significant photograph of Stravinsky as a young man in his Paris studio; he is surrounded by percussion instruments, sitting on shelves like a row of cats in a witch's hovel, waiting to leap into action. Stravinsky uses two players with two full sets of timpani as well as a huge range of percussion instruments to be played by several other stalwarts, each of whom must be a genius at counting. They lead an almost independent existence as this next example shows. The conductor's beat varies between 5/4 and 6/4 but the two timpanists, with the sort of mutual interplay one might expect from members of a string quartet, continue resolutely in 2/4. Notice the way Stravinsky writes the part so that each player is aware of his musical relationship to the other.

'If you can keep your head when all about you
Are playing fives when you are playing twos . . .'

(This, however, is child's play in comparison to the demands to be found in scores from more recent years.) Rhythmic complexity is pushed to what (in 1913) must have seemed an ultimate frontier in the final section of the ballet, the 'Danse Sacrale' or sacrificial dance. Here the conductor must keep an absolutely rigid control of the beat if things are not to come seriously adrift; time-signatures alternate with daunting frequency:

$$\frac{2}{16} \left| \frac{3}{16} \right| \quad \left| \frac{2}{8} \right| \frac{2}{16} \left| \frac{3}{16} \right| \quad \frac{2}{8} \left| \frac{3}{16} \right| \quad \left| \quad \right| \frac{5}{16} \left| \frac{2}{8} \right| \frac{3}{16} \left| \frac{2}{8} \right| \frac{5}{16} \left| \quad \right| \quad \left| \right.$$
$$\qquad\qquad\qquad\qquad (3+2) \qquad\qquad\quad (2+3)(3+2)$$

and so on virtually through the entire section. The explosive chords usually occur *after* the beat rather than on it so that the conductor seems to be thrashing a monstrous animal that yelps after each blow. In the measured scale below, the dots represent the constant unit (semiquavers) while the arrows above show the placing of the conductor's beat, the accents below showing the orchestral accents. As will be seen they rarely synchronize.

If you simply try counting out loud at an absolutely constant speed, accenting the larger numerals, you will get a small idea of what is involved.

$1_2 1_{23} 1_{23} 1_2 3_4 1_2 1_{23} 1_{23} 1_2 3_4 1_{23} 1_{23} 1_2 3_{45} 1_2 3_4 1_{23} 1_2 3_4 1_{23} 4_5 1_2 3_{45}$

If you wish to make a game out of it, get someone else to count against you at exactly the same speed but with this accentuation.

$1 2_1 2_{31} 2_{31} 2 3 4_1 2_1 2_{31} 2_{31} 2 3 4_1 2_{31} 2_3 1_{23} 4_{51} 2_3 4_1 2_{31} 2 3 4 1 2 3_4 5 1_2 3_4 5$

Hours of innocent merriment may be derived from this simple approximation to one brief extract from this historic score (pp. 112–13).

For my third Challenge I turn to the opposite extreme; if Stravinsky's violence at times reaches the threshold of pain, here we stand at the threshold of inaudibility.

WEBERN: 6 BAGATELLES FOR STRING QUARTET, Op. 9, No. 1. (composed 1913.)

The influence of Webern on latter-day composers has been of infinitely greater importance than his impact on audiences. Even now, accustomed as we have become to every kind of musical experimentation, these brief musical aphorisms cause us unease. The total duration of the 6 Bagatelles is some three-and-a-half minutes. As Schoenberg said in their defence, 'Consider what moderation is required to express oneself so briefly. You can stretch every glance out into a poem, every sigh into a novel. But to express a novel in a single gesture, a joy in a breath—such concentration can only be present in proportion to the absence of self-pity.'[2]

It was the painter Paul Klee who stated 'To become more precise, you have to impoverish.' We have already seen (p. 164) how a single note can instantly evoke an emotional response, depending upon its volume and duration. Webern more than any other composer felt the significance of this evident truth. Imagine for a moment a poem consisting of individual words.

```
            Field
                        Green
                                    Evening
                                    Shadow
                        Dark
            Whisper
                        Soft
                                    Mouth
                                    Kiss
                        Tender
            Pulse
                        Throbbing
                                    Hands
                                    Clutch.
```

[2] Preface to the score (Universal Edition, UE 7575, 1924. Copyright renewed 1952 *Anton Webern's Erben*.

There can be no doubt what the poem means nor what it describes, even though it depends wholly on the evocative power of single words. The placing of the words is more significant than we realize at a first glance. Column I has three nouns; column II five adjectives; column III six words that are closely related in a way that the words in the other two columns are not. Similarly the number of syllables accumulates column by column; column I has four, column II seven and column III eight. Thus column I is notably more sparse than III, III is more dense than I. This is the *Form* of the poem, a form emphasized by diagonal or vertical relationships between words.

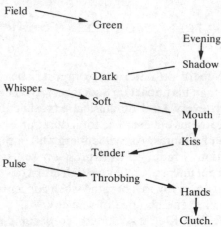

Field → Green

Evening ↓ Shadow

Dark → Shadow

Whisper → Soft

Soft → Mouth

Mouth ↓ Kiss

Tender ← Kiss

Pulse → Throbbing

Throbbing → Hands

Hands ↓ Clutch.

Let us now try to translate these words into music. Some are harder to deal with than others, but on the whole the content of each word is so positive that it should not be too difficult.

A 'field' is an open space so let us choose a bare 5th.

'Green' is harder to translate but I see it as a 'central' colour neither extremely dark or light. I therefore choose notes in the middle of the keyboard but a chord that has a touch of richness to it. It qualifies 'field' so we will allow the two sounds to overlap.

'Evening' is obviously a dark sound though not to the point of obscurity: however, 'shadow' darkens it, so again the secondary sound can modify the primary one.

'Dark' must obviously create a pool of darker sound.

200

'Whisper' is easy, a little rustle of notes; just for fun let us make it a tiny dialogue.

'Soft' is self-evident.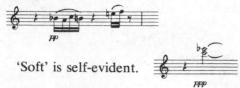

The transition from 'mouth' to 'kiss' is symbolized by choosing two adjacent notes for 'mouth' (the two lips) and merging them into a suitably sensuous chord, very properly lingering as time stands still.

'Tender' becomes an expressive phrase based on the 'kiss' chord.

'Pulse' is simple enough as is the idea of 'throbbing'. (Note that it is clearly a male pulse!)

'Hands' have five fingers so let us have two five-note chords spread out like hands entwining, and then cause them to 'clutch' by sounding together with a nice squeezing effect of *crescendo-diminuendo*.

The 'translation' of the entire poem will thus emerge as a piece of music whose every sound has a function, nothing being elaborated more than is strictly necessary (see Ex. 43).

The orchestration and dynamics are an added luxury designed to make the meaning of the individual sounds more apparent. The relationship between

Ex. 43

poem and music is now very close; it has little to do with composition but a great deal to do with the evocative power of single sounds, whether verbal or musical. The tempo enables one to savour each sound just as, if one were to recite the poem, one would need to punctuate it with long pauses.

My reason for this preliminary diversion is that Webern works to a notably different time-scale from most composers, a time-scale so compressed that unless we concentrate fully, a piece can be over almost before we realize it has started. He represents the most extreme reaction against the Wagnerian (and later Mahlerian) time-span. Within such a scale every sound must of necessity be significant since nothing can be wasted. Where earlier composers might have been obsessed with the expressive power of a melodic phrase or a sequence of harmonies, Webern explores the potential of a single note. Thus the first bar of the first Bagatelle consists at first glance of a three-note harmony, built up progressively.

Even to think of it as a harmony is misleading; it is a series of separate experiences. Each of the three notes has its individual expressive marking

When a meal looks as though it is going to be really frugal one tastes every morsel with relish. As we look closer at the score we begin to see how much thought has gone into the smallest detail. The first note is not the D we assume but what is called a harmonic, produced by touching the open D string (an octave lower) so delicately at its half-way point as to make it emit a sort of ghost voice. The second note, not even a full crotchet, lasts less than a second according to Webern's metronome mark, yet in that brief space he asks for $<pp>$ which by implication means three dynamic levels, $ppp<pp>ppp$. The clash between the three notes D. E flat, C sharp, which in *The Rite of Spring* might be thumped into us by three brass instruments, is treated here as an almost imperceptible nudge, one sleeve brushing against another as strangers pass.

In bar 2 the 2nd violin has a brief sigh

(the resemblance to my 'green' chord being merely coincidental) while the viola has a hollow rustle produced by playing very near the bridge of the instrument.

Only the 1st violin extends a wide arc of sound,

which in turn is mirrored by an even wider arc from the cello.

Now it is hard for the conservative listener to find anything like traditional concepts of melody or harmony here; the more he tries to do so the more

203

Ex. 44

No. 1 of Webern's Six Bagatelles for String Quartet, Op. 9.

frustrated he will become. Just as my poem consisted of isolated but evocative words so this music consists of a number of minute musical happenings; a dab, a sigh, a rustle, a shudder, a stretch, a blow, a whisper, a cry; it is a series of gestures as eloquent as a ballet-dancer's. But there are four 'dancers', four string-players, and though their gestures may almost unconsciously reflect those of a neighbour, they tend to move quite independently, four figures in a room each wrapped in his own thoughts. We, the observers, need to note the smallest move since even a mere flicker is important.

The next problem for the listener is that Webern tends to use very extreme, even distorted sounds; he has a great fondness for harmonics and *ponticello* (near the bridge) effects which deprive the sound of any richness of tone. No wallowing on the G string here; in fact so concerned is he about very quiet sounds that an apocryphal story grew up about a quartet rehearsing a piece of his under his direction. One of the players raised his hand in polite query. 'Herr von Webern', he enquired; 'I have here a note marked *pensato*; how do you want me to play it?' '*Pensato*?' said Webern; 'that means you don't play the note, you merely think it . . .' (The joke loses some of its savour when we realize that Stockhausen asks his performers to do that very thing on occasion.)

Webern's reason for avoiding the lush potential of string sound is to evade past associations, to escape from what might be termed a Max Bruch hangover. Nevertheless, a shout makes a great effect when the conversation is mainly conducted in a whisper, and the occasional stab of *ff* has an unbelievable cutting force considering that it is rarely sustained for more than a second or two. In a period of excess Webern preached a gospel of austerity, teaching others the value of individual sounds. The significance of what he did was profound; his music, seemingly abstract and cerebral, is full of emotion, virtually every note having an expressive indication attached to it. According to the belief of mystics, asceticism is a road to spiritual ecstacy; it is a belief Webern seems to have carried into music, nor does he lack eloquence though he speaks in aphorisms. Even today many listeners find his music difficult, not so much because too little happens but that too much happens in a short space of time. One can be excited or overwhelmed by the Grosse Fuge or *The Rite of Spring* without understanding them; Webern speaks to us with such reticence that we need to go a long way to meet him and to understand his aesthetic philosophy.

205

9   Words and Music

The relationship between words and music is a subject so vast that to devote a single chapter to it seems a sort of madness. Though I suspect that no words were involved the first time a human being ever sang, nevertheless, as we have seen, the earliest Western music was predominantly vocal. Even in the early stages of musical evolution certain basic truths about singing emerged—that if you wish to sustain a sound, vowels are more useful than consonants, and that singing enables a syllable to be extended in a way that would be unacceptable in normal speech. To take a very simple example, the sentiment 'I love you' could never be expressed in speech as eloquently as in song.

To extend the spoken word in this way would seem like a serious impediment of speech, while to sing it on the consonants L or V would be intolerable. Composers were quick to see the musically expressive possibilities of such extension; where a clear line must be drawn is between decorative passages that serve a descriptive function and those which are designed to show the virtuosity of the singer. Like instrumentalists, singers who have worked hard to acquire a fine technique welcome opportunities to demonstrate it; whether the end result sounds like music or vocal acrobatics is partly dependent on their artistry, partly on the quality of the music. Thus in the final scene of Monteverdi's *Orfeo* (1607) we find Apollo and Orfeo ascending into heaven singing (*cantando*) as they go. The characteristic embellishment of the word *cantando* is entirely relevant to its meaning, and while it demands a fine technique, it is artistically justified.

206

d'al — Cie - - - lo,

(J. W. Chester)

In the same opera Monteverdi shows a sense of practicality rare in composers by supplying two alternatives in a deeply expressive passage where Orfeo meditates on the prospect of death and the soul quitting the body ('alma da corpo sciolta'). The first version is for a singer of limited capabilities, a Grade I Orfeo, though presumably able to add some ornamentation.

al - ma da cor - po sciol - ta in-van pre - su - me.

The alternative is lavishly embellished, interesting not just as an authentic example of the sort of elaboration that was acceptable at the time but as a confirmation that singers capable of executing such roulades were not always available.

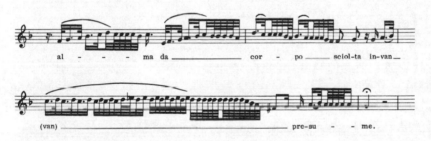

al - - - ma da ——— cor - po —— sciol-ta in-van—

(van) ——————————————————— pre-su - - me.

Note the literal shaking of the head on the word *invan* (in vain) and the typical rapid reiteration of a single note, often used by Monteverdi as a simulation of bird-song at its most vibrant. It is worth noting that a tradition for this style of singing is still maintained in genuine Flamenco; Manuel da Falla's opera *La Vida Breve* contains one aria which closely resembles the passage quoted above in its use of swift twirls of notes, rapid trills and the like.

Although Monteverdi uses harmony to wonderful effect in his madrigals, the emphasis in the operas is concentrated on the voice; the passage above would be almost as effective unaccompanied. This is not always the case. Some six years before *Orfeo* was composed John Dowland, one of England's greatest song-writers, wrote a song of extraordinary emotional intensity, 'I saw my lady weep'. Even if the singer decorated the vocal line spontaneously, we find no hint of embellishment in the voice-part since the heart of the matter lies in the lute accompaniment and the tensions set up between the slow-moving voice and the more disturbed rhythms that clash with it. If one

207

pinpoints the dissonances by picking them out of context they are remarkable, chords such as these:

Dowland is not so crude as to confront us with these undisguised, except for the first one. They are arrived at by a process, technically known as 'suspensions', whereby one note is 'suspended' from a previous harmony in such a way as to create a feeling of tension. You will see these pressure-points marked with a cross.

Ex. 45

(*English Ayres.* Ed. Peter Warlock. O.U.P.)

Dowland excelled in songs of melancholy, and no collection of the 100 Greatest Songs so beloved of anthologists could afford to omit such masterpieces as 'Sorrow, stay', 'In darkness let me dwell' and 'I saw my lady weep'.

We have already seen the part that words can play in dictating rhythm. Elizabethan music, being unhampered by bar-lines, demonstrates this particularly well, changes of time-signature being mostly the work of editors aiming to provide landmarks for performers today. The rhythms are often so subtle as to pose problems of ambiguity. For instance 'Whither runneth my sweet heart?' by Robert Jones (1601) is based on a quick running figure which admirably suggests the patter of flying footsteps.

However, the natural stress of the *words* would be 'Whither rúnneth my swéet heart' which would fit more comfortably into 3/2.

While this flows more naturally, it fails to allow for the counterpoint established between voice-part and accompaniment, no academic device but a symbol of the lover pursuing his nimble prey.

Ex. 46

(*English Ayres.* Ed. Peter Warlock. O.U.P.)

The song illustrates the rhythmic subtlety of so much of the music of its period in that the singer should avoid first-beat accentuation, treating the music as though it was in 3/2 yet allowing for the fact that mathematically such an approach would not add up. Later in the song a comparable flexibility is demanded in this phrase:

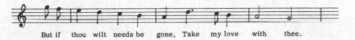

But if thou wilt needs be gone, Take my love with thee.

which should properly be phrased:

This degree of rhythmic freedom is often to be found in madrigals, where the stresses will occur in different places simultaneously, each singer having to establish an independent rhythmic pulse.

Nearly a century later, Henry Purcell (1659–95) brought English song to a peak of sophistication that has never really been surpassed. In his 'Ode on St. Cecilia's Day' (1692) we find one air in particular which shows him combining words and music with extraordinary inventiveness. The extension of words is elaborately done but virtually always germane to their content. Example 47 shows a few examples, all taken from the male alto solo ''Tis Nature's Voice'.

Ex. 47

'Movement':

thro' all the mo - - - - - - - ving wood.

'Aggression':

or strike, or strike _____ the __ heart.

'Grief':

and straight we grieve _____

'Joy':

re-joice _____

210

In case the symbolism of this last example seems obscure, it is surely meant to suggest coils (like literal coils of rope) with which Music 'captivates the mind'. As to the setting of the word 'Rejoice' it is interesting to compare its continuous pattern of semiquavers with Handel's treatment of the same word in his *Messiah*.

Here the voice is treated more as an instrument than as a bearer of a verbal message and the part would readily transfer to an oboe or violin without loss of meaning, something that is less true of Purcell. Although Handel almost certainly learned from Purcell's example (one aria in a Chandos anthem written a few years after his arrival in England is full of Purcellian mannerisms), it is not surprising that his settings of English are less perceptive in tone. Indeed several choruses in the *Messiah* are transplanted from earlier secular works, and he may have permitted himself a smile when he used the music he had composed for an Italian love-duet to set the words 'For unto us a child is born'.

Although we tend to think of Handel as a composer of oratorio, he actually wrote some thirty-nine operas, and it was in opera that the most striking developments in the setting of words to music were destined to occur. A problem that vexed a number of composers was how to reconcile the egocentric demands of the singers with some degree of dramatic realism. If operatic plots were often absurd it was partly because of a set of rules so strict that they might have been designed by a convention of militant trade unionists. Their purpose was to ensure that the singers were given an adequate vehicle to show off their different skills, but not in such a way as to allow one soloist to have more than his fair share of the glory. Each principal

211

soloist would expect five arias of differentiated styles to be allotted to him, or her.[1] (The cast would consist of six singers, three male, three female, though since the men were often *castrati* the music tended to be somewhat top-heavy.) These arias were invariably in *A-B-A* form which, since it involves a return to the opening material, scarcely helps the plot on its way. However, since the arias were planned to exploit various emotions and styles in an almost abstract way, they were not expected to have any narrative value. Needless to say, the reprise would be elaborately ornamented to draw further attention to the singer's (not the composer's) skills. No singer could have two arias consecutively, and each artist would invariably leave the stage after an aria was completed. Arias of dramatic importance had to be placed at the end of acts so as to ensure the greatest applause, while the only ensemble would have to come at the end of the entire opera. Duets, trios or quartets were virtually unknown, such was the vanity of singers. Handel for the most part accepted the appalling handicap of these conventions although occasionally, as in *Radamisto*, we do find a quartet. It was Gluck (1714–87) who fought most strongly for reform, seeking for greater dramatic truth and a more artistic ideal. But if Gluck deserves the credit historically, it is Mozart who for audiences today holds the crown. His achievement as an operatic composer did not come easily and there are a number of incomplete or unsuccessful operas to balance against the masterpieces of his maturity. While he continued to observe the convention of *recitative* (singing at the speed of speech to minimal accompaniment so as to move the plot forward) and *aria* (a solo song in which the action stays more or less static), he excelled in his ensembles in which he brilliantly combines different characters while allowing each to preserve a musical identity. While his letters indicate that he found the need to get all his characters onto the stage at the end of an act an artificial device, he rose to its challenge so skilfully that we are hardly aware of the virtuosity involved.

One of the most fascinating indications of Mozart's complete mastery of opera is the way in which, by the clear allocation of a *musical* personality to his characters, he is able to imply their relationships to each other and the change in those relationships brought about by the development of the plot. As an instance of his genius I would quote the trio involving the Count, Don Basilio and Susanna in Act I of *The Marriage of Figaro*. At the start of the scene the Count is ordering Don Basilio (a singing teacher) to go and seek out Cherubino, a young lad who is causing considerable troubles in the household. The Count has no idea that Cherubino is hidden in the very same room, having been hastily concealed in a deep armchair by Susanna, who, with characteristically quick wit, has flung a dress over him hoping thereby to shield him from the Count's questing eyes. As the Count tells Basilio that Cherubino the seducer must be banished, we can tell from the accompani-

---

[1] *Aria cantabile; aria di portamento; aria di mezzo carattere; aria parlante; aria di bravura.*

ment that he is stepping forward pace by pace, while the silences that punctuate his remarks suggest an attempt to gain control of an inner fury. Here the accompaniment, instead of merely supporting or underlining the content of the voice part, actually adds information about action and behaviour.

Ex. 48

I do not think it too far-fetched to assume that the first chord here (marked *p* and scored for wind) represents Susanna and Basilio quailing before the Count's wrath; they are literally 'windy'. Next we have the footsteps, while the sudden loud upward scale in the ninth bar represents the Count's anger spilling over, the subsequent breathless syncopations being Susanna's consequent panic. Immediately Don Basilio pours oil on troubled waters with some phrases whose unction would not come amiss from Uriah Heep himself.

It is now Susanna's turn, and her music expresses her confusion and dismay with a marvellous blend of artifice and realism.

Here in compressed form we have three of the five representative styles demanded in opera of Handel's time, the Count's music being an *aria parlante*, Don Basilio's an *aria cantabile*, while Susanna's is clearly an *aria di mezzo carattere*. They were styles familiar to Mozart as a child, proof of which comes in an interesting eye-witness account describing him as an eight-year old in London improvising a Song of Rage, a Song of Love, or an aria on the single word 'Perfido', during which 'he worked himself up to such a pitch that he beat his harpsichord like a person possessed, rising sometimes in his chair'. (Shades of Stravinsky playing *The Rite of Spring* to Monteux!)

The mixture of such contrasting ideas is remarkable in itself, but what is even more striking is the way in which Mozart exploits the differences for dramatic ends. Each character maintains a clear identity; yet when Susanna has a strategic fainting-fit the two men are for the first time united in their joint concern. Even here, though, Mozart shows that he was a born producer in the theatrical sense. Basilio knows that Susanna's swoon is put on; he therefore supports her in her play-acting by drawing attention to it. 'Ah poor girl she's fainting' he sings. It takes a moment for the Count to remember his manners and respond to a maiden's distress, his reaction *following* Basilio's. Notice too the exquisite humour with which Mozart depicts them jointly taking her pulse, its beat being slightly irregular such is her agitation.

No one has ever surpassed Mozart's mastery of ensemble, that most artificial of contrivances; on the face of it, it is ridiculous to have five or six people singing at the same time, often pretending that they can neither hear nor be heard by those who share the stage with them. Yet just as the string quartet is regarded as one of the severest tests of a composer's ability, so the ensemble is a challenge no operatic composer can refuse to accept. If I had to cite three examples by composers other than Mozart I should select the canon quartet from *Fidelio*, one of Beethoven's most perfect inspirations, the amazing septet (with chorus) that Verdi placed towards the end of *Otello*, and the justly famous quintet from Wagner's *Meistersinger*. Each is a perfect demonstration of technical skill combined with profound emotion; each represents an unforgettable highspot of operatic craft that lingers in the mind long after one has left the theatre.

To attempt a potted history of opera is outside the scope of a chapter such as this; I am concerned with the relationship between words and music, not music and the stage. All the same it is one of music's greatest ironies that the supreme composer of song, Schubert, should have found the opera-house a quicksand in which he floundered helplessly. It is a sad story, confirming that it is not enough simply to be a great composer if you want to succeed in the theatre. Although Schubert could divine the essence of a poem in a flash and translate it into supremely suitable music, he had little liking for the grand rhetoric that was demanded on the operatic stage by the 1820s. His genius lay in supplying an inexhaustible wealth of melody with accompaniments that were both apposite and inventive. His first song, 'Hagars Klage' (Hagar's Lament) written when he was a mere fourteen, is a lengthy rambling structure that aspires to operatic stature. Three years later he produced three songs that must rank as masterpieces. The least ambitious, 'Haiden-Röslein', is deceptive in its simplicity.

In less skilled hands the accompaniment could have degenerated into the tritest formula (see Ex. 49).

Schubert uses the formula but lifts it out of the music-hall pit and onto the concert-platform by the subtlety of his harmonization. Notice too his skilful

Ex. 49

Ex. 50

avoidance of the dominant (D) in the bass, which does not appear until the second beat of bar 10. (In my pedestrian alternative it plods its way onto every second beat.) The song (see Ex. 50) has the enchanting simplicity that one finds at times in Mozart, though to be so memorable with such economy bespeaks a special type of genius.

If 'Haiden-Röslein' looks back to Mozart, 'Erlkönig' might be said to look forward to Wagner. Look at the voice-part on its own (Ex. 51) and compare it to the folk-song quality of Haiden-Röslein; they seem to come from different worlds.

Ex. 51

Now any reasonably competent hack accompanist, presented with the voice-line only of Haiden-Röslein, would be able to cobble up a piano part that might bear a resemblance to Schubert's own, even if it turned out to be as banal as the one I briefly projected. With 'Erlkönig' things are very different; I do not believe that anybody, no matter how talented, would produce the remotest approximation to Schubert's accompaniment without prior knowledge. In the first place there are fourteen bars of intensely dramatic accompaniment before the voice even begins; in the second Schubert completely avoids the most probable harmonization of the opening phrase.

Instead of this orthodox treatment, he keeps us poised above a dominant bass, thereby, like a good story-teller, keeping us in suspense. The galloping triplets in the piano-part (easier on a piano of 1814 with its much lighter touch than present-day instruments) keep on relentlessly as the horse's hooves thunder on through the gathering darkness. The left hand is given a phrase whose threatening quality is out of all proportion to the simplicity with which it is achieved. Six notes of a G minor scale and three notes of a G minor triad do not on the face of it seem very alarming, yet in this context their effect is overwhelmingly sinister. Notice too how the phrases close up in bars 24 to 28, giving the impression that the dread figure of the Erl King is already beginning to overtake the father in this ride to the death (Ex. 52).

There was absolutely no precedent for the seventeen-year-old Schubert to draw upon in writing a song of this dramatic intensity;[2] not Beethoven

Ex. 52

[2] It was sung for the very first time by a fourteen-year-old boy!

himself had ventured so far into the realms of dramatic word-setting. Yet in the same year Schubert was to produce another masterpiece of a totally different kind, poignant instead of dramatic. Again the piano-part is crucial in its descriptive role. Here we have a spinning-wheel rotating monotonously; even the action of the foot-treadle is captured in the reiterated quavers in the left hand. Schubert has 'seen' the action of the poem as clearly as Mozart 'saw' his characters moving around the stage. It must have needed considerable courage to keep the accompaniment rigidly to its repeated patterns, potentially boring as they might seem to a young composer; but spinning is a boring task, nor is Gretchen's mind upon her work. All her thoughts are upon her absent lover and as her vision of him grows ever more intense Schubert embarks on a wonderful sequence of modulations taking us through F major, G minor, A flat major, B flat major (disturbed by anguished G sharps) until at the climatic moment she remembers the sweetness of his kiss. Then, and only then, does she stop spinning; she pauses on a chord tinged with sorrow, and then, so reluctantly, drags herself back to her task. Here is the section I have just described.

Ex. 53

In selecting three songs from his adolescence to represent Schubert's 600 or more I may seem to be doing him an injustice, yet here are the sure foundations on which he could build for the rest of his tragically brief life. In 'Haiden-Röslein' we find innocent and effortless beauty of line, in 'Erlkönig' intense drama, in 'Gretchen' a wonderfully inventive and suitable figuration to enhance the harmonic structure.

The fundamentals of good word-setting have scarcely changed in the last three centuries. Even the extremes of vocal range demanded by avant-garde composers today are little more than an extension of the compass Mozart expected of his singers. In Stravinsky's opera *The Rake's Progress* we find clear evidence that he had studied closely the best eighteenth-century models. Purcell would instantly have acknowledged a vocal line such as that given in Ex. 54 as expressive and musically proper, even if at times he might have thought the supporting harmony curiously spaced.

Ex. 54

(Tom)

Or - phe - us   Strike from thy lyre ___ a swan - -

- - - like mu - sic   and weep ___

ye ___ nymphs and _ shep - herds of _ these Sty - gian fields ___

etc.

Stravinsky: *The Rake's Progress*   (Boosey & Hawkes, 1951)

It may be argued with some justification that this is a deliberate pastiche and as such scarcely a fair example to illustrate the point I am making. But if we turn to Michael Tippett's opera *The Midsummer Marriage* (1954) we find ecstatic lines that are surely derived from Monteverdi; here, in the character of Mark, we find a latter-day Orfeo.

Ex. 55

(lento)   (a tempo)

And like the   lark ___   I _   sing, ___   I   sing ___   for _   joy ___

cresc. poco a poco

be - cause I   love ___

calando

e rit. molto

(Schott & Co., 1954)

Tippett's avoidance of an obvious tear-away climax here gives the music a special quality that can only be described as true rapture.

Both Tippett and Britten clearly acknowledge an inheritance from the past, but here too we need to recognize when the musical symbolism resides in the voice-part or the accompaniment. In the preceding example the voice conveyed the ecstacy; here, in a quotation from Britten's *War Requiem*, it is in the orchestral part that we find the great barrel of the cannon being raised (Ex. 56).

Ex. 56

(p. 56 fig. 49 – p. 57 b. 3)

(Boosey & Hawkes, 1962)

On the other hand, the isolated crotchets that the chorus sings in the *Lacrimosa* are clearly teardrops linked with sighs of grief.

Compare this to similar 'tears' in *The Rakes's Progress*

The musical imagery is the same whether written from the heart, as in the *War Requiem*, or stylized as in Stravinsky's opera.

I do not claim to be a composer of significance myself though I must have set many thousands of words. However, I cannot resist ending this chapter with a brief quotation from my own little opera 'Three's Company'. It is one of the few examples of a genuine musical pun that I know, a joke sufficiently obscure to pass unheeded in performance, yet incorporated into the score because I felt it was the only possible way to set the line. The accompaniment

223

is for piano alone; the joke would not be valid if it were scored for anything other than a keyboard.

10   Listening

It is all too easy nowadays to *hear* music; the lady from Banbury Cross would no longer need rings on her fingers nor bells on her toes to provide her with music wherever she goes. It would accompany her through supermarket and boutique, in café or cinema, in airport or railway station; at home she could have a virtually continuous stream of music washing over her as she dusted, ironed, cooked, made beds, fed children,—even (if she took her transistor or cassette-player down to the stable) while she groomed her white horse. The very availability of music encourages us to take it for granted as a background to living, yet hearing is not listening. To *listen*, according to the dictionary that comes nearest to hand, is 'to attentively exercise the sense of hearing, to direct one's hearing towards, pay aural attention to, take notice of . . .' Miss Banbury Cross is doing none of these as she flits around doing her chores; for her, music is a touch of aural sunshine made more notable by its absence than its presence.

Now I would not like to be thought such an intellectual snob as utterly to condemn such an attitude, any more than I would condemn myself for reading paper-back thrillers to pass the time on plane journeys. I do not delude myself that I am widening my literary horizons when I turn each action-packed page; I know that two days afterwards I shall hardly remember the hero's name, let alone how he managed to escape from the burning warehouse where he had found the heroin (no E nowadays) only to be recaptured and taken by submarine to the secret island where mad General Long Wun has a nuclear rocket aimed directly at the Carlton Club. On the other hand, on the rare occasions that I do read what I refer to as grown-up books I approach them very differently, being happy to go over a paragraph again for the sheer pleasure of appreciating the quality of the writing. I do not regard it as unreasonable that music should be treated in the same way; by all means let those who wish be fed with aural pap. My plea is that music that deserves respect should be treated with respect.

I am not violent by nature but I nearly smashed my television set the other day when, during some light entertainment programme, the compère announced that four dancers whose names I have fortunately forgotten would interpret a special arrangement of Rakhmaninov's 'Variation on a theme by Paggerninny'. I had not realized that Rakhmaninov was so incompetent as to need the assistance of Les, Fred or whoever it was, but ·my rage mounted as the monstrous travesty got under way. Instead of Rakhmaninov's elegantly curved phrase, we were subjected to this:

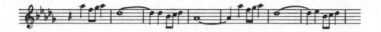

needless to say there was the inevitable beat in the background, while the strings poured gratuitous slush over the pianist—whose touch suggested a long apprenticeship in a smithy. This outrage, which should have been booed off the stage, was greeted with the rapturous applause that a certain type of audience saves for the special occasions when it knows it has experienced Great Art. Doubtless Les or Fred will be forgotten and Rakhmaninov will survive, but every such assault tends further to depreciate the musical currency. I would have thought that if publishers had any moral duty it was to preserve the integrity of the works of composers no longer able to protect them themselves. The trustees of the Rakhmaninov estate cannot be so hard up that they need Les or Fred's ordure to fertilize the assets; why then is such a perversion allowed? I know not, but I certainly care.

Now it is my belief that if music was treated with a proper respect, the public would recognize abominations of this nature and reject them. The degradation of great music must be a sign of decadence, and I do not accept the contention that hearing a syrupy version of the 'Moonlight' Sonata on singing strings complete with a vocal backing will make someone want to rush out and buy a record of Arrau playing it. The adolescents who respond to that sort of depraved version do not actually listen since almost certainly they will be eating an ice in a cinema at the time, nor would they be able to identify the piece in order to buy it. The corruption of music to commercial ends is not new; Mozart himself accepted that café bands would play tunes from 'Figaro' much as nowadays we might hear a medley from *My Fair Lady* or *Evita*. But there is no doubt that the ever-growing popularity of the gramophone and tape-recorder encourages such corruption; is one reason for the challenging and discordant nature of much contemporary concert-music a subconscious dread of the wrong sort of popularity? Do composers perhaps write tuneless music because they do not want their tunes to be prostituted as Rakhminanov's have been less than forty years after his death?

Hearing music is a passive process; listening to it is an active one. Let me try to postulate some of the qualities I would look for in an ideal listener. First, must come a response to sound itself, a sufficient awareness of music to be able to tell not merely one tune from another but one chord from another, to appreciate the tonal difference between a note played on a violin and the identical note played on a cello, to recognize rhythms when they reappear, to relate sounds across a span of time. Second, I think I would put a sense of period; it may seem surprising to place it so high but I feel it is an essential. If we have any appreciation at all of painting, architecture or literature it inevitably involves some feeling for period, however superficial it may be. It is not enough to know that something is 'old', neither is it necessary to know that it was begun in 1423 and finished in 1471. All the same we do need a rough chart to give us our bearings, since one of the greatest pleasures of listening is to sense how a composer stretches the resources of his period. Courage is a quality we can all admire, and it is inspiring to realize the courage of great composers when they break through barriers established by convention. The start of the last movement of Berlioz's *Symphonie Fantastique* may not be great music but it is awe-inspiring in its invention; there is hardly a bar that has any sort of precedent, and every time I hear it I marvel again at its sheer daring. Had it been written sixty years later it would not give the same *frisson*. In a rather different way I am amazed at the virtuosity of the sixteen-year-old Mendelssohn in the Octet for Strings; the absolute confidence with which he steers his way through the final fugue has the same effect on me as watching a child gymnast performing prodigious feats in the Olympic Games—one cannot believe in such perfection but the evidence is there. Again the reaction would not be the same had Mendelssohn written it at thirty-five; one expects a mature composer to be able to accomplish such feats. When Liszt begins his *Totentanz* with a passage that sounds almost exactly like Bartók I derive added pleasure from imagining how an audience in the 1860s would have reacted to such revolutionary sounds.

By a sense of period I really mean the ability to put oneself back into the period in which the music was written, to cleanse one's ears of the sounds from intervening years or centuries, to listen to Haydn as though we were present in the Esterhazy household, as though Beethoven was still unknown. Ideally all music should sound 'modern' since all music once was. If we can train ourselves to make the imaginative effort to move back in time it is astonishing how fresh every sound begins to seem.

I have been to many great archaeological sites in my travels and I dread the guide who reels off a string of names and dates that become increasingly meaningless as they multiply. I like to sit alone amongst the ancient stones and *listen*; somehow I believe that if I listen long and hard I will catch some echo of voices centuries dead. Once I climbed the Great Pyramid in the heat of the midday sun, and as I clambered up the great waist-high stepping-stones I almost felt the lash upon my back so closely did I find myself identifying with the sweating slaves who built so everlasting a monument to their suffering. I am unsure which Pharaoh was entombed within it, but I have felt the stone with my hands and feel I *know* the pyramid in a way that no book could describe.

227

It is the same with music; one's experience of it needs to be direct rather than remote. The gramophone and radio are wonderful inventions, but they are in my opinion no substitute for live performance. I know all the arguments about listening in privacy, about having to put up with a barrage of coughing in concert-halls, about the piano in the local hall being less than adequate and so on; nevertheless, a renewal of life through performance is an essential part of music's existence and I would even defend bad performances since they give us some insight into what makes good performances. Third in my list, then, would go a willingness to attend concerts; it is an act of homage worth paying.

So much stress is laid on analysis in programme notes that many a potential music-lover is put off, feeling inadequate when he fails to recognize the special moment when 'the theme appears in inversion and augmentation simultaneously above a sustained pedal-point on the flattened leading-note'. I am so sceptical about the value of information of this sort that I would not put the ability to stick the correct labels onto fragments of music very high on my list of desirables. What one unquestionably does need is awareness, an awareness of the 'special moment' even if one does not know precisely what is happening. I can clearly remember several such moments even from my childhood days, a sudden dawning of comprehension. The first time I ever heard Schubert's Unfinished Symphony was out-of-doors in Austria when I was fifteen and a half. There was no orchestra, simply an old-fashioned wind-up portable gramophone and a set of rather scratched seventy-eights. One could not hear much of the opening, what with the surface hiss, the scratches and competition from the birds; but came the second subject and I was ravished.

Ex. 57

At this point the violins take over the tune and I was probably too bewitched to notice the little sighs of approval with which the cellos listen to their colleagues, sighs that are relevant to the melody since they are derived from its first two notes.

This is such a cliché that it takes a moment to appreciate how Schubert has magically transformed it into an invention, as though it has never been used before.

What I obviously did appreciate was the way the tune breaks off, to be interrupted after a brief silence by a thunder-clap of a chord; I felt no particular virtue in doing so since the gesture is overtly theatrical and could scarcely fail to register. The moment of revelation came a little later when Schubert returns to his second subject and extends it unforgettably.

I didn't appreciate it specifically as three-part counterpoint nor did I follow the exact course of the modulations; what I did know was that this was a special moment indeed, something to haunt the memory. The sweet pain of the dissonance in the fourth bar was almost more than my young heart could bear and I was near to tears with the beauty of it.

Such appreciation is not greatly helped by the label-sticking process of analysis. It was years before I went a significant step further by realizing that in composer's terms Schubert has made a surprise move by putting this blissful tune into an unexpected key. By the laws of musical propriety it *ought* to be in D major, the relative major of B minor—the key in which the symphony began. With the assurance that comes with genius Schubert avoids the conventional solution and moves a 3rd *down* to G major instead of a 3rd *up* to D; subtleties of this kind are an added pleasure that comes with a greater knowledge of music. Simply to be told that the second subject is based on the sub-mediant rather than the relative major is not enough.

My next moment of revelation came at a concert which marked a turning-point in my life. I was seventeen and had just had a week's holiday rowing up the Thames from Oxford camping out each night by the riverside. Having a little money left over I and the friend who had shared the holiday decided to go to a Prom. The late Cyril Smith was to play Rakhmaninov's Third Piano Concerto; I had never heard of the pianist or the work. Two bars of gently rustling string chords led into a long tune for the pianist expressed with a simplicity that I found hard to believe. My knowledge of the concerto repertoire was minimal but at least I instinctively realized that such reticence was unusual.

p   (Left hand simply duplicates an octave lower.)

I was transported into a magic world in which I scarcely knew which was affecting me the most, the dazzling performance or the sumptuous music. The second movement begins as an expressive *adagio* but later changes to a mercurial scherzo; it was during this that I suddenly hugged myself with delight. Through the scintillating glitter of the piano-writing I heard a clarinet playing this strangely syncopated waltz.

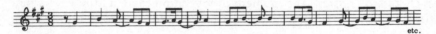

Though I had no prior knowledge of the work, I recognized this as a transformation of the opening theme, brilliantly distorted. It was the first time in my life that I had become aware of such a relationship without having it pointed out to me, a symbolic break-through that was like a sort of musical coming-of-age. Had I been told at the time that I would become a pupil of Cyril Smith's or that years later I would find myself conducting the concerto, I would have regarded the predictions as the wildest fantasy.

Here, then, we have the next requirement for the listener, the ability to store up material in the mind so as to be able to recognize it when it reappears whether in its original form or in disguise. A classic example would be the moment when Beethoven reintroduces the theme of the scherzo during the finale of the Fifth Symphony. It is like a ghostly apparition, and I have sometimes wondered whether he had Banquo in mind, since one of the projects he left unfinished was some incidental music to Macbeth. The passage would seem very suitable. On a much larger scale I would cite Mahler's Sixth Symphony, whose last movement is largely a re-assessment of material from the previous movements; if the listener fails to pick up the links the music is almost meaningless.

If the comprehension of such links over a large span of time might be termed horizontal listening, we should not discount the value of vertical listening, the appreciation of the beauty or power of individual harmonies. Here is a passage whose melodic interest is almost nil.

A spark of interest creeps in with the penultimate note but otherwise it is not a tune to be proud of. Now the composer, Manuel de Falla, must have known this perfectly well; in fact he is not thinking in terms of melody but playing with harmonies, harmonies which constantly shed new light on the B flat–G cadence.

(J. W. Chester)

From being downright boring as a melody the music becomes fascinating as a sequence of harmonies, the final B natural coming as an extraordinary relief, as positive as a ray of sunshine piercing the shadow of a cloister.

Now I have only to hear that to be reminded of a strikingly similar passage in Verdi's *Otello*, similar at least with regard to the falling minor thirds and the final twist to the major.

(Ricordi)

Notice though that Verdi does *not* vary his two-chord pattern; does this make him less accomplished or less interesting a composer than Manuel de Falla? The answer is 'No' since the function of the chords is different. They are deliberately similar because they represent Desdemona's sighs during the pathetic little 'Willow Song'; but what is more important as a musical difference is that they support a profoundly expressive phrase from the singer (Ex. 58).

Ex. 58

Io per a - mar - - - - lo e per mo - rir. -

(Ricordi)

231

The voice-part may not look all that interesting but the expressive potential of the phrase is enormous, the *crescendo* and *diminuendo* against the wan little repetitions in the orchestra being a crucial factor. If the singer has the artistry, there will not be all that number of dry eyes in the house.

This brief operatic excursion has disclosed two more assets the listener should seek to acquire—a knowledge of the repertoire wide enough to be able to make instructive cross-references (not necessarily as esoteric as this) and an appreciation of the part the performer plays in bringing the music to life. We need little encouragement in this respect since only too often we listen to performers rather than to what is being performed. The big box-office names will draw their audiences almost regardless of what they play, while an unknown but brilliantly gifted student will play Beethoven's op. 109 exquisitely to twenty or thirty people at a small music club in the provinces.

While we may accept this as a fact of life, it is hard to pinpoint precisely the qualities that make a performance great. If I had to pick a single word I would be hard-pressed to choose between Insight and Involvement. Insight has the greater appeal for the knowledgable, Involvement impresses the less initiated. As a player gains in maturity so he can afford increasingly to let the music speak for itself. One of the fascinating things about Rubinstein's playing was the way in which he seemed to let his hands get on with actually playing the notes while he sat outside, like a reticent conductor keeping an eye on a well-rehearsed orchestra. Rakhmaninov had the same uncanny detachment. At the opposite extreme we find a superb artist like Kyung-Wha Chung who attacks her violin with the ferocity of a young tigress; such involvement is immensely exciting. Incidentally string players tend to be more physically involved than pianists since the instrument is almost like another limb. Conductors too can be divided into the same categories, the extroverts whose gestures border on choreography and the statuesque who bring in cohorts of brass with the flick of an eyebrow.

I am sometimes asked whether it is possible to develop one's faculty for listening and if so, how. Apart from the obvious advice to keep at it, there are one or two more constructive suggestions I would make. If you want to learn about music, rehearsals give better value than concerts, as the huge success of master-class or workshop programmes on television has shown. I realize that to attend rehearsals with a professional orchestra is difficult to arrange; moreover the times are usually inconvenient for the nine-to-five worker. However, a great deal can be learned from sitting-in at rehearsals of any tolerably good amateur orchestra including, need I say, the numerous excellent youth orchestras that are to be found in town and country. In a way you will learn more from listening to amateurs since the birth-pangs of a performance are likely to be more prolonged. Most such orchestras are delighted to find an outsider taking an interest in their work and it could well be that you will find yourself on a committee; don't let the risk deter you. Ask around until you discover where and when they rehearse, explain that you are an earnest seeker after truth, and you are unlikely to be turned away. If you do get a chance to hear the same passage through several times, focus your attention on a different section of the orchestra at each repetition so that first you listen to the cellos, then the clarinets, then the *second* violins and so on. Don't just follow the tune; any fool can do that. Teach your ear to disentangle some of the more obscure threads.

Similarly if you go to concerts fairly regularly try not to sit in the same seats every time; get a different view of the orchestra so that one evening you concentrate on the woodwind, another on the middle strings. If the hall is not all that full slip discreetly into different seats for the second half; the ushers are not likely to notice, and if they do try to move you back tell them that your neighbour had a terrible cough and that you had to escape. Personally I find a score an invaluable aid to comprehension, but it will only be a hindrance if you find difficulty in reading it. If all this sounds as though I am turning what was once a pleasure into a chore, I would simply point out that an appreciation of the finer points enhances enjoyment in any field whether it be football, motor-racing, tennis, drama, poetry, cooking, drinking or the perennially fascinating observation of the opposite sex. In the course of my own life as a professional musician I have widened my range of musical appreciation enormously. I was brought up on an extremely conservative diet of Gilbert and Sullivan and Hymns more Ancient than Modern; as a student I had little sympathy or liking for anything written since World War I. I emerged from the Royal College of Music with a huge amount of ground to make up; it was the beginning of a voyage of discovery which has never checked.

The resources of music are limitless; no one person could ever hear all that has been written since the supply is continually being re-charged. I described it in an earlier chapter as a river, but it is a river that is inexhaustible; one can dip into its waters at any point and come out refreshed. It is an enrichment of life not to be lightly dismissed since it can widen our emotional experience and thereby cause us to grow spiritually. Let the final words be Beethoven's. 'Those who understand it must be freed from the miseries others drag about with them.'

Appendix

p. 13: A 3rd is known as an interval, a way of measuring the distance between two notes. If we think of a chromatic scale as a ladder progressing through the immediately adjacent notes on a keyboard (using both black and white), it would look like this.

13(a)

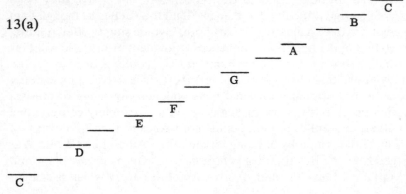

(I have chosen to start on C simply because the notes lettered CDEFGAB correspond with the scale of C major which consists entirely of white notes on the piano.) The distance between E–F or B–C is called a semitone (adjacent 'rungs'), the distance between C–D, D–E, F–G, G–A, A–B is a tone (skip a rung.) A scale using all the rungs (equal steps of a semitone) is called CHROMATIC: a scale using only those notes with letters under them is called DIATONIC. Whereas the chromatic scale proceeds by equal steps of a semitone, the diatonic scale is somewhat irregular, rising by a tone, a tone, a semitone, a tone, a tone, a tone, a semitone, each step being an *interval*.

13(b)

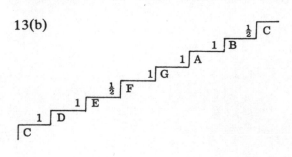

Certain rungs in the ladder 13(a) have been left unlettered; they are easily recognized as the black notes on the piano, but their identification depends upon whether we think of them as rising from the rung below or falling from the rung above. The intervening step between C and D can thus be called either C *sharp* or D *flat*, that between F and G either F sharp or G flat and so on. But since all diatonic scales are constructed on the same pattern as the ladder 13(b) and since logically the letter-names of the scale should each be represented in sequence, we soon discover logical reasons for deciding whether to call a chromatic note a sharp or a flat. Here is the ladder called the scale of D flat

13(c)

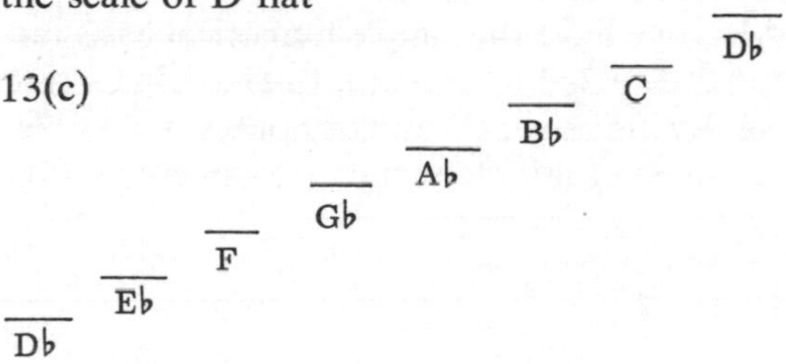

                                               ‾‾ Db
                                  ‾‾ C
                          ‾‾ Bb
                   ‾‾ Ab
          ‾‾ Gb
    ‾‾ F
‾‾ Eb
Db

The identical notes on the piano may be alternatively labelled.

13(d)

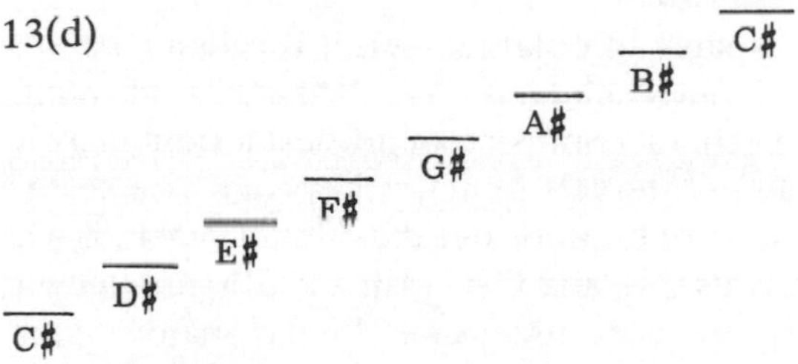

                                               ‾‾ C#
                                  ‾‾ B#
                          ‾‾ A#
                   ‾‾ G#
          ‾‾ F#
    ‾‾ E#
‾‾ D#
C#

In neither case has the alphabetical sequence been disturbed, but in order to preserve that sequence the note we originally thought of as F has had to be re-named E sharp; similarly C has become B sharp. It would obviously be chaotic to use sharp and flat symbols at random.

13(e)

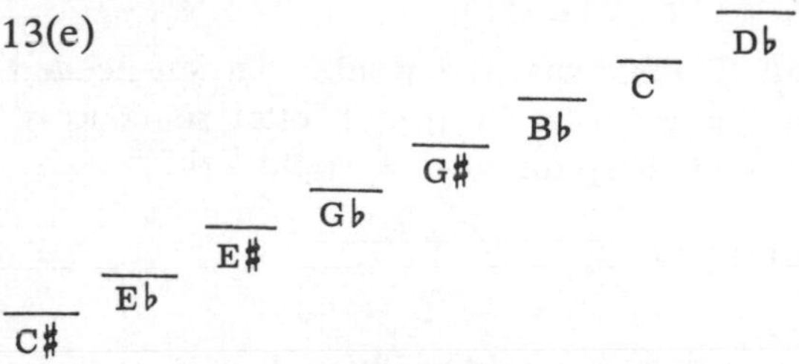

                                               ‾‾ Db
                                  ‾‾ C
                          ‾‾ Bb
                   ‾‾ G#
          ‾‾ Gb
    ‾‾ E#
‾‾ Eb
C#

The notes in this ladder would *sound* the same as 13(c) and 13(d) but the effect to the eye in musical notation would be bewildering:

though it may sound like a scale it certainly does not look like one. Incidentally, the symbol before the penultimate note is called a *natural* and its function is to cancel out other accidentals. There are also double-sharps (✗) which raise the written note by a tone, and double-flats (♭♭) which lower it by a tone; their function will become clear as we now explore INTERVALS.

If we number the rungs of the ladder in 13(b) 1 2 3 4 5 6 7 8 to correspond with the letters CDEFGABC, we have the simple numerical basis for naming intervals. C to D is a 2nd C–E a 3rd, C–F a 4th, C–G a 5th, C–A a 6th, C–B a 7th and C–C an octave. By the use of chromatic notes it is possible to modify these intervals, thus changing their character. If I select the 3rd, E–G

I can enlarge it, either by flattening the lower note

or sharpening the upper one:

Since in its initial state it is capable of enlargement, it is called a *minor* interval (in the sense of 'lesser'); once enlarged it is called *major*, meaning greater. I stress this since in the general confusion of musical terminology it is perfectly possible to have minor intervals in major keys and vice versa. Diagram 13(b) represents the scale of C *major* but the intervals D–F, E–G, A–C are *minor* thirds. The intervals C–F and C–G (4th and 5th) are known as *perfect* intervals since they are not susceptible to the major-minor ambiguity that is to be found with 3rds 6ths and 7ths. Nevertheless *all* intervals, even perfect ones, may be distorted by stretching (augmentation) or shrinking (diminishing).

Thus C–F sharp

is an augmented 4th, while C–G flat

(same sound) is a diminished 5th. Double-sharps or double-flats are needed at times to preserve the identity of intervals or the proper 'letter' sequence of notes in a scale passage. Thus in G sharp minor one would write:

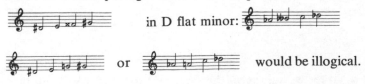

in D flat minor:

or   would be illogical.

One of the most interesting chords is the harmony known as the diminished 7th consisting of three super-imposed minor 3rds

If one omits the two interior notes and plays only the F sharp–E flat interval, it will *sound* like the major 6th F sharp–D sharp. This different 'flavour' will be enhanced if we give the chord a different centre (see pp. 34 et seq.).

The diminished 7th is invaluable as a suspense chord since it belongs to no particular key and may be used to modulate in a number of directions (see pp. 45–6). It is a chord traditionally associated with tension and was much favoured by Classical and Romantic composers at moments of climax.

p. 14: Note values and their notation
Although notation of music dates back certainly to Ancient Greece, the earliest period which need concern us as being related to our own method stems from approximately the fourteenth century, by which time the following symbols had emerged after considerable experiment, red coloration also being used to indicate duple time.

During the fifteenth century the same symbols were used but in white instead of black, e.g.

The change to modern notation was gradual and spread over more than 200 years: the first two symbols above became obsolete, leaving:

The corresponding values in rests or silences are:

Notes of duration less than a crotchet may be grouped together by a bridge whose lines correspond to the 'tails' on individual symbols; thus two quavers

may be written either as  or , four semiquavers as  or . Normally each bridge spans the number of notes necessary to make up one main beat, e.g.:

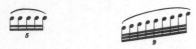

Irregular groupings usually have a slur  with the number of notes indicated numerically:

Putting a dot to the right-hand side of a note-head adds half its value. The same applies to rests.

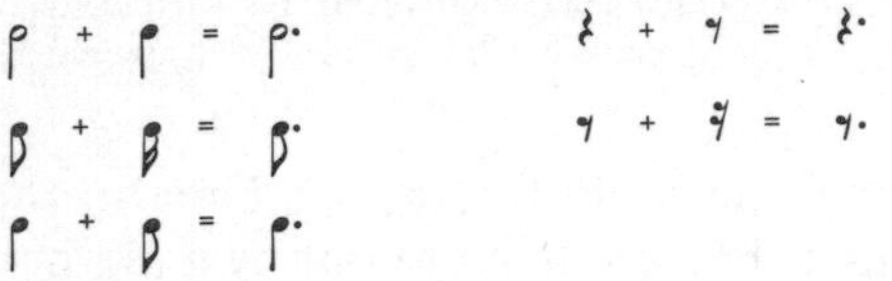

Stems descend from the note-head on the left-side, ascend from the right.

Time-signatures

Applying the principles established on p. 13 one can draw up a table of time-signatures (see pp. 239–40). The correct labels are given but do not need to be remembered; what matters is to understand the significance of the numerals.

Note that the examples for 4/2 and 4/4 *sound* the same but look different. One of the subtler aspects of notation is the choice the composer makes when faced with such alternatives; partly it reflects conventions of the period, early music tending to be written in 'longer' units (not necessarily slower thereby) while Beethoven had a tendency to use unnecessarily 'short' units in his slow movements, producing pages that look alarmingly dense with a multitude of hemidemisemiquavers (64th notes) but whose basic pulse is extremely slow. The difference between 6/4 and 3/2 is often misunderstood, and even composers of quality sometimes get it wrong. For instance in the Poulenc Organ concerto a number of bars are shown as 6/4

DUPLE TIME

$\frac{24}{16}$ and $\frac{36}{64}$ are theoretical possibilities but unlikely to be encountered.

TRIPLE TIME

$\frac{18}{8}$ $\frac{18}{16}$ and $\frac{27}{32}$ are also theoretical possibilities.

(𝅗𝅥. + 𝅗𝅥.) when actually they should be 3/2 (𝅗𝅥 + 𝅗𝅥 + 𝅗𝅥) The same problem does not seem to arise over 6/8 and 3/4, though nowadays we often find them interchangeable; in a passage such as this it would be irritating to alternate time-signatures:

But note the quite different effect this would have in a consistent 3/4, the second bar being syncopated instead of gliding along.

3rd.beat
falls here.

When the beat is flexible as in the earlier of those two examples, the composer will sometimes write a double signature, thus:

$\frac{3}{4}\Big|\frac{6}{8}$

240

This technique is also used if one has a consistent pattern of bars of unequal lengths. $\frac{3}{4}|\frac{2}{4}$ would mean alternate bars of 3 and 2.

5/4 is usually regarded as 2 + 3 ($\downarrow$ + $\downarrow$.) but often changes its internal stress to 3 + 2 ($\downarrow$. + $\downarrow$) Sometimes composers will indicate the rhythmic stress within a complex and irregular bar by a multiple fraction such as $\frac{3+3+2+3}{8}$ which would mean $\downarrow$. + $\downarrow$. + $\downarrow$ + $\downarrow$.

$\frac{11}{8}$ would add up to the same thing but would not indicate the disposition of the accents so clearly. In such a case one could 'beat' 4 with a 'limping' or shortened 3rd beat.

An alternative sometimes used is to substitute a musical notation for the lower figure in the time-signature, for instance $\frac{3}{2}$ becoming $\frac{3}{}$, $\frac{7}{4}$ being shown as $\frac{7}{}$

p. 19: Arpeggio (from the Italian 'arpeggiare', to play the harp.)
A technique of playing the notes of a chord individually instead of as a single unit while still conveying their essentially 'chordal' quality. Originally written as actual chords preceded by a wavy line,

they are more usually written out in full.

Notable examples are to be found in the Chopin studies, op. 10 Nos. 1, 8 and 11 and op. 25 Nos. 1 and 12.

p. 24: Aleatoric (more properly aleatory)
The term used to describe music in which a random effect is produced as a means of escaping the more rigid traditional methods of notation. The chance element may be so free that the performer is left to decide the order in which he plays a series of proffered fragments (which will vary from one performance to another); or the composer may instruct players to develop a given pattern of notes in their own way or play such patterns at marginally differing tempos so that they are not exactly synchronized. Effectively used by composers such as Ligeti, Lutosławski, Penderecki and Stockhausen.

p. 25: Minor
The scale shown in the first entry in the Appendix is what is known as a major scale. Any 'ladder' formation of notes is a scale but there are a number of alternatives according to the different distributions of tones and semitones. The minor scale is the second most important scale in the vast bulk of Western music, but it is somewhat enigmatic since it exists in two forms,

Melodic and Harmonic. Since the Melodic form also varies according to whether it is rising or falling one can see that music in a minor key has a less defined sense of tonality than that in major keys.

The Harmonic minor scale is shaped in this way:

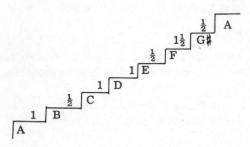

Note the very wide 'step' of one-and-a-half semitones between F natural and G sharp. This is not sheer perversity on some theoretician's part; the basic harmonies that would establish the key or tonality of A minor (see Chapter 2) would require a G sharp in this cadence:

and F natural in this:

a cadence being a way of giving a sense of finality to a phrase and thereby confirming the feeling of having arrived at a key.

The Melodic minor scale, being a linear concept rather than a vertical one, emphasizes the feeling of rise and fall in a melodic line by reaching up towards the peak of the scale and declining more noticably when descending.

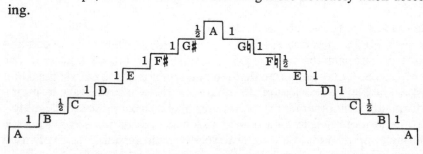

Since the CHROMATIC scale contains twelve semitones within the octave, the sum of the tones and semitones represented by the rungs on the ladder will always add up to twelve.

p. 53: Counterpoint
The term used to describe a musical texture in which two or more melodic lines pursue independent courses, each having a more or less equal claim to

242

our attention. Thus in a two-part invention, each 'part' will be of equal interest, our pleasure being derived from their interplay and interdependence.

p. 73: Canon
Literally 'rule', but in practice a technique whereby a line of music is made to follow itself at a distance. Simple examples are also known as Rounds or 'perpetual' canons, 'Three Blind Mice' or 'Frère Jacques' being perhaps the best-known. More sophisticated canons allow the 'shadow' version to move in notes of different duration (twice as slow or twice as quick are fairly standard) or starting on a different degree of the scale: thus a canon *at* the 4th means that the second line will copy the first at an interval a 4th away from it. A supreme instance of the technical ingenuity with which canons can be handled is Bach's *The Musical Offering* which has canons of every type.

p. 76: Suite
Although dance-music as a folk-art certainly dates back to periods before notation was even invented, it was only in the early seventeenth century that composers began to assemble groups of contrasting dances (originally in pairs and usually in the same key) so as to form a suite. Whether such dances were intended to be danced *to* is a moot point; as well ask whether the Slavonic Dances of Dvořák or the Brahms Waltzes are meant for dancing or listening. The general order of dances in eighteenth-century suites was *allemande* (medium pace) *courante* (Lit. 'running') *sarabande* (slow) and *gigue* (quick). Bach elaborated this to include French dances such as the *bourée, gavotte, menuet* or *passepied*.

p. 77: Scherzo
Literally a jest. The term had been used in the early seventeenth century to describe light-hearted vocal or instrumental music. Although it became almost obsolete between 1700 and 1750. Haydn, and more notably Beethoven, revived the term, Beethoven especially favouring it as a substitute for the minuet movement which had traditionally been used in symphonies, quartets and sonatas. A scherzo will nearly always be in 3/4 time, brisk in tempo, often brusque in manner. Like the minuet it often contains a contrasting central section called a Trio (not necessarily for three instruments!) after which the scherzo will be repeated.

p. 108: Sinfonia Concertante
A work that is neither symphony nor concerto, having aspects of both. Usually there are two or more soloists, normally members of the orchestra whose exceptional ability a composer would recognize by writing them harder parts than those of their colleagues.

p. 126: Two-part Invention

A composition, usually for keyboard, in which the composer confines himself to a single line in each hand, the two strands being of equal interest. The material will frequently change places from one hand to the other, a process called Invertible Counterpoint. This does *not* imply Inversion, i.e. turning a phrase upside down.

p. 143: Stave

The set of five lines on which music is written. A single line would give three notes, one on the line, one above and one below. Five lines therefore gives us the possibility of 11 notes not counting the extras introduced by the use of accidentals (sharps or flats). This is enough for the average voice; extra notes can always be provided by leger lines which may be regarded as temporary extensions of the stave.

The actual significance of the five lines is conveyed by a clef:

     = G

     = C

     = F

Thus the composer may select at will the stave most suited to his purpose. The piano, organ or harp, having a wide range of notes will use both 𝄞 and 𝄢 (also known as treble and bass clefs). The violin, flute, oboe or clarinet use only the 𝄞 while the bassoon or cello will mostly use the 𝄢, though for their upper notes they may move into 𝄡 (the tenor clef) or even, in the case of the cello, the 𝄞. The 𝄡 should really be thought of as the 'C' clef since it always represents 'middle' C; its position on the stave is a matter of convenience and depends on the pitch of notes most likely to be used by the instrument (or voice) concerned. Thus the viola plays primarily in the area covered by this stave:

⟵ Middle C

whereas the high notes of the bassoon can best be covered by a marginally different choice of lines.

⟵ Middle C

Early choral works employ C clefs in all parts except the bass, soprano parts being written thus:

More recently 𝄞 is used to indicate the actual pitch at which tenors sing or 𝄞 the pitch at which piccolos play.

244

Glossary of Musical Terms

Accelerando increasing in pace.
Accidental the term used to describe the signs for sharp, flat, natural, double sharp, double flat

Adagietto a 'little' *Adagio*, therefore not quite as slow.
Adagio lit. 'at ease', slowly. Often qualified as in *Molto Adagio*, very slow; *Adagio espressivo*, slow and expressive.
Affetuoso lit. 'affectionate' but also carrying implications of 'affected'; rather mannered.
Agitato agitated, usually in conjuction with a quick tempo.
Al fine 'to the end,' or to the word '*fine*' which may appear at some other point. Many arias finish with a reprise of the opening music; to save writing it out the composer will put *Da Capo al Fine*, 'From the beginning to the indication *Fine*'.
Allargando broadening; getting slower.
Allegretto a 'little' *Allegro*, therefore not quite as fast.
Allegro: brisk, going forward. Often qualified as in *Allegro Moderato*, moderately fast, or *Allegro con brio*, exhilaratingly fast.
Andante moving at a gentle pace, lit. a walking speed.
Andantino slightly quicker than *Andante*.
Animando growing in animation.
Animato animated.
Appassionato impassioned.
Appoggiatura a note stressed by timing rather than accentuation.
Arco with the bow (as opposed to plucked).
Arioso in the manner of an aria.
Arpeggio see Appendix.
Assai usually 'very' as in *Allegro assai*, very fast; but sometimes treated as 'quite' or 'fairly'.
A tempo in time, usually as a warning not to vary the tempo, or an instruction to restore it.

Attacca carry on with the shortest possible break.

Bagatelle a short piece unlikely to be too demanding intellectually; a trifle.
Ballett not a misprint for ballet but a vocal composition for several voices usually with a 'fa-la' refrain.
Baryton a string instrument akin to the bass viol but having 'sympathetic' strings. Haydn's patron Prince Nicholas Esterhazy played it, causing Haydn to write over 120 compositions for it.
Battery an early term for arpeggio; also the percussion section of the orchestra.
Bel canto a style of singing perfected in the nineteenth-century as used in Donizetti and Bellini operas.
Bémol French for flat (♭)
Bewegt German for 'moving'.
Bewegter Faster. *Mässig bewegt*, moderately fast.
Bis French for 'repeat'.
Blanche French, minim.
Bogen German for *arco*, with the bow.
Bourée French dance in 2/2 time. Also borry or boree, early English.
Bravura display of virtuosity.
Brio vigour

Cadence a way of concluding a phrase.
Cadenza traditionally an improvised display passage near the end of a movement; increasingly came to be composed as integral part.
Calando slowing down and dying away.
Camera lit. 'room'. The term chamber music is so derived; *sonata da camera* was used to describe secular instrumental music as opposed to *sonata da chiesa*, church music.
Cantabile in a singing style.
Cantata a composition to be sung rather than played, though usually with instrumental accompaniment.

Cantilena a sustained singing line.
Capella 'chapel.' *A capella* is used to describe choral music when it is unaccompanied.
Capriccio a composition involving elements of caprice.
Castrato adult male singer with boyhood voice retained by surgical means.
Chitarrone a large lute.
Clarino small trumpet for use in high register.
Col, coll', colla 'with the,' e.g. *col arco*, with the bow; *colla voce*, with the voice; *coll' ottava*, with the octave.
Comodo at a convenient or comfortable speed.
Con 'with', e.g. *con amore*, with love; *con brio*, with energy; *con dolore*, with sadness.
Corda 'string', e.g. *Una corda*, with one string. *Tre corde*, with three strings. These terms describe the contrast between 'soft pedal' on the piano when the hammer strikes only one string or normal when it strikes three.
Courante lit. 'running'. A nimble dance.
Crescendo growing louder.
Croche French for quaver (♪)
Crotales small tuned bells played with beaters.
Cuivré (Fr.), special 'brassy' effect in horn playing.

Da capo From the beginning.
Dal segno From the sign; an indication to make a repeat from a marked spot, usually shown as 𝄋 .
Decrescendo Decreasing; growing quieter.
Détaché (Fr.), detached, meaning a separate bow to each note in string playing.
Dièse (Fr.), sharp (♯)
Dolce sweetly, gently.
Dolente sadly.
Doloroso sorrowful.
Doppio double: *doppio movimento*, twice as fast.
Double croche (Fr.) semiquaver (♫)
Double stop two-note chord on string instrument.
Duplet two notes played in the time of three.
Dur (Ger.), 'major', *C dur*, C major.

Eilen (Ger.), 'hurry'. *Nicht eilen*, steady.
Einfach German for 'simply', (*semplice*).
Embouchure (Fr.), mouthpiece of wind instrument, but more often the shaping of the mouth to produce tone.
Empfindung (Ger.), 'feeling', (*espressivo*).
Entr'acte Music played between acts of a play, opera or ballet.
Espressivo expressively.
Etwas (Ger.), 'rather'.

f forte, loud.
Feierlich (Ger.), solemn, proud.
Fermata Pause.
Fine (It.) end.
Fioritura decoration, usually in vocal music.
Flautando playing with the bow near the fingerboard and almost skating across the string.
Flauto flute.
Forte loud (*f*).
Fortissimo very loud (*ff*).
Forzando strongly accented (*fz*).
Fugato in fugal style.
Fughetta a short fugue.
Fuoco 'fire'; thus *con fuoco*, fiery.

Gamme (Fr.), scale.
Getragen (Ger.), 'dragging', i.e. slow, sustained.
Giocoso happily.
Gioioso joyously.
Giusto exact or measured: *tempo giusto*, a measured and regular speed.
Glissando sliding, i.e. drawing the finger across the keyboard, across harp-strings, or sliding it along a string on violin, etc. Also practicable on trombone and some wind instruments.
Grace an ornament.
Grave slow and serious.
Grazioso gracefully.

Haupt (Ger.), principal, e.g. *Hauptstimme*, principal part or leading voice.
Impromptu a piece designed to sound like an improvisation; free-form.
Innig (Ger.), deeply felt; intense.
Intrada First movement of a suite; overture in original sense; an 'entrance'.

Jota Spanish dance in 3/4 time.

Kammermusik (Ger.), chamber music.
Konzertstück (Ger.), concert piece, usually for soloist(s) and orchestra.
Kreuz (Ger.), sharp (♯)

Lacrimoso mournfully, lit. tearfully.
Langsam (Ger.), slowly.
Largamente broadly.
Larghetto A 'little' *Largo*, therefore slow but not so slow as *Largo*. cf. *Adagio*, *Adagietto*.
Largo very slow: in nineteenth-century slower than *Adagio*.
Lebhaft (Ger.), lively.
Legato very smoothly.
Leggiero with a light touch.
Legno lit. 'wood': *col legno*, with the wooden part of the bow.
Leise (Ger.), soft. (*dolce*).
Lent (Fr.), slow.

Lento slowly.

Licenza 'licence' in the sense of freedom of tempo.

L'istesso tempo At the same speed (as before).

Loco As written, i.e. restoring normal notation after 8ᵛᵃ sign.

Lusingando tenderly.

Lustig (Ger.), jolly, cheerfully.

Maestoso majestically.

Maggiore in the major key.

Marcato marked with emphasis.

Marcia march: *alla marcia*, in the style of a march.

Martellato: (martelé) using a forceful stroke of the bow or alternate hands 'hammering' at the keyboard.

Marziale in a martial manner.

Mässig (Ger.), moderately; moderate.

Meno less, e.g. *meno mosso*, less quickly.

Mezzo lit. 'half', e.g. *mezzo forte* (*mf*), medium loud; *mezzo piano* (*mp*), medium soft.

Misterioso mysteriously.

Moll (Ger.), minor. *A moll*, A minor.

Molto very much. *Allegro molto*, very fast.

Mordent an ornament much used in early music.

Morendo dying away.

Mosso moving, i.e. lively. *Più mosso*, quicker, *meno mosso*, slower.

Moto movement; *con moto*, with movement.

Niente 'nothing', e.g. *al niente*, dying away to nothing.

Nobilmente nobly, in the grand manner.

Noire (Fr.), crotchet (♩)

Obbligato usually a decorative additional part, e.g. the clarinet in Schubert's 'Shepherd on the Rock' or the oboe in *Jesu Joy of Man's Desiring*.

Ohne (Ger.), without.

Opus lit. 'work', a term used to describe a composition, usually with a number, as op. 110.; supposedly chronological but very unreliable.

Ossia as an alternative.

Ostinato a repeated pattern.

Ottava octave, often shown as 8ᵛᵃ, indicating that music should be played an octave higher (or lower) than shown (see *loco*).

p piano, 'soft'.

pp very soft.

Parlando in the style of speech.

Pausa a silence or rest (*not* a pause which is *fermata*).

Perdendosi the same as *morendo*, dying away.

Piacevole in a pleasant manner.

Piangendo plaintively.

Più more, e.g., *più adagio*, slower still.

Pizzicato plucking the string.

Poco a little, e.g. *poco piu lento*, a little slower.

Poi then, in the sense of subsequently.

Ponticello the bridge of a stringed instrument. *Sul ponticello*, playing on the bridge.

Portamento 'carrying' across a gap in a melodic line by a subtle transition in pitch.

Presto very fast.

Prestissimo as fast as possible.

Prima first or formerly. *Come prima*, as at first; *prima volta*, the first time round.

Quartettsatz (Ger.), a movement for quartet.

Quasi as if.

Rallentando becoming slower (*rall.*)

Ripieno a term equivalent to *tutti*, meaning all players, but used in baroque concerted music to distinguish between the full band and a smaller group of solo calibre, the *concertino*.

Risoluto with resolution.

Ritardando same as rallentando, getting slower, commonly abbreviated to *Rit.*

Ritenuto holding back the tempo; not quite the same as *ritardando* since it implies a momentary change of tempo rather than a progressive one.

Ritornello lit. 'return'; either a recurring section, or a passage for orchestra in a concerto during which the soloist is silent.

Ronde (Fr.), semibreve (○) Also a Round Dance.

Roulade (Fr.), extended decorative passage for solo voice.

Rubato subtle variation of the tempo used for expressive purposes.

Saltando lit. 'leaping'; a technique of bouncing the bow off the string.

Sanft (Ger.), softly.

Scena a dramatic scene in opera or an operatic-style concert-piece.

Scherzando in a playful manner.

Schleppen (Ger.), dragging. '*Nicht schleppen!*'—do not drag.

Schnell (Ger.), fast (*allegro*).

Sciolto relaxed, loose.

Scorrevole smooth running.

Segno a sign, usually 𝄋 , a landmark to return to or make for.

Segue as follows; continuing.

Sehr (Ger.), very.

Semplice simply; unaffected.

Sempre always; e.g. *sempre forte*, staying loud.

Senza without; e.g. *senza pedale*, without pedal.
Sforzando strongly accented. (*sfz* or *sf*).
Sforzato
Simile continuing in a like manner.
Sinfonietta a light-weight symphony.
Smorzando dying away.
Soave smoothly.
Solenne solemnly.
Sopra above, as when the pianist's left hand crosses over the right.
Sostenuto sustained.
Sotto underneath. (cf. *sopra*).
Sotto voce 'beneath the voice', i.e. without tone.
Sourdine (Fr.), mute. (It. *Sordino*.)
Sordino a mute; also the dampers on the piano are *sordini*.
Spiccato a light *staccato* played from the wrist in the middle of the bow on a stringed instrument.
Sprechgesang (Ger.), pitched speech; stylized speaking following indicated rhythms and changes of pitch without the exact intonation of song.
Staccato detached: shown by a dot over the note-head, ♪ ♪ ♪ a more marked *staccato* is indicated with a dash.
Subito suddenly.
Suivez French equivalent to *attacca* or *segue*.

Tam-tam a large gong, very shallow with a flat centre; rich in resonance.
Tasto fingerboard of a stringed instrument.

Sul tasto, on the fingerboard; cf. *sul ponticello*.
Teneramente tenderly.
Tenuto held beyond the written length even if only slightly; sometimes a simple contradiction of *staccato*.
Terzetto normally a vocal trio, occasionally instrumental, light in character.
Tessitura the natural range of a voice or instrument; compass.
Timpani kettle-drums.
Toccata a composition for keyboard of a brilliant or improvisational kind.
Tranquillo calmly.
Trauermarsch (Ger.), funeral march.
Tremolando derived from a literal shaking of the hand; a rapid alternation of notes, or with stringed instruments a very swift alternation of the bow.
Troppo too much: *Allegro non troppo*, *allegro* but not too much so.
Tutti with everybody playing; also the orchestral exposition of a concerto.

Ubung (Ger.), exercise, study.
Umore humour.

Vibrato a slight deliberate trembling of the left hand in string playing which imparts a 'vibrant' quality to the tone.
Vif (Fr.), 'lively' (*allegro vivace*).
Vivace lively.

Zart (Ger.), tender.
Zärtlich (Ger.), tenderly (*teneramente*).
Zeitmass (Ger.), tempo.

Acknowledgements

The author is particularly indebted to the books listed below.

BAINES, ANTHONY (ed.), *Musical Instruments through the Ages*. Harmondsworth, 1961.

DAVISON, A. T. & APEL, W., *Historical Anthology of Music*. Harvard and Oxford, vol. I, 1949; vol. II, 1950.

DENT, E. J., *Opera*. Harmondsworth, 1940.

MARLIAVE, JOSEPH DE, *Beethoven's Quartets*. New York 1928.

MASON, D. G., *The Quartets of Beethoven*. New York, 1947.

ORREY, LESLIE, *A Concise History of Opera*. London, 1972.

ROGNONI, LUIGI, *The Second Vienna School*. London, 1977.

ROSEN, CHARLES, *The Classical Style*. London 1971.

TOVEY, DONALD, *Essays in Musical Analysis*. Oxford 1935–44.

VLAD, ROMAN, *Stravinsky*. Oxford, 1971.

WHITE, ERIC WALTER, *Stravinsky*. London 1966.

WOOD, ALEXANDER, *The Physics of Music*. London, 1975.

REFERENCE BOOKS

The Bodley Head History of Western Music (ed. Christopher Headington). London, 1974.

Collins Encyclopedia of Music (eds Westrup and Harrison). London and Glasgow, 1976.

Grove's Dictionary of Music and Musicians (ed. Eric Blom). London, 1954.

The Larousse Encyclopedia of Music (ed. Hindley). London, 1971.

A Short History of World Music, Curt Sachs. London, 1956.

Index

Index

Index